GEMCRAFT

How to Cut and Polish Gemstones

GEMCRAFT

How to Cut and Polish Gemstones

Second Edition

Lelande Quick and Hugh Leiper, F.G.A.
Revised by Pansy D. Kraus, G.G., F.G.A.

Chilton Book Company
Radnor, Pennsylvania

Copyright © 1959, 1977 by Lelande Quick and Hugh Leiper
Second Edition   All Rights Reserved
Published in Radnor, PA, by Chilton Book Company
and simultaneously in Don Mills, Ontario, Canada,
by Thomas Nelson & Sons, Ltd.
Manufactured in the United States of America
Drawings by Dara E. Yost

Library of Congress Cataloging in Publication Data

Quick, Lelande.
  Gemcraft.
  (Chilton's creative crafts series)
  Bibliography: p. 180
  Includes indexes.
  1. Gem cutting. 2. Gem carving. I. Leiper,
Hugh N., joint author. II. Kraus, Pansy D. III. Title.
TS752.Q5 1977   736'.2'028   77-4578
ISBN 0-8019-6242-0
ISBN 0-8019-6243-9 pbk.

Preface to the Second Edition

Since the original book *Gemcraft: How to Cut and Polish Gemstones* by the late Lelande Quick and the late Hugh Leiper, F.G.A., was published in 1959, the lapidary hobby has continued to grow and expand. The April 1959 issue of the *Lapidary Journal* listed 558 gem and mineral clubs. Seventeen years later, the April 1976 issue of the *Lapidary Journal* lists 1,187 clubs worldwide, of which 981 are in North America. The files of the *Lapidary Journal* now list over 6,500 dealers who supply those persons interested in one or more phases of the lapidary hobby, compared to the more than 2,000 dealers referred to in the first edition of this publication. There are many more clubs and dealers who do not send in listings for the *Buyers Guide* issue.

The principles of gem cutting are still basically the same; however, some persons become interested in specific areas and perfect their skills in these areas, developing a certain proficiency. This results in the broadening and specialization of specific areas. In recent years technological advances have resulted in new methods and products for the lapidary hobby, as well as for other aspects of our daily lives. This second edition of *Gemcraft* will include discussions of some of the various new methods and equipment and information concerning the use of diamond products specifically manufactured for the lapidary hobbyist.

In recent years the carving of gem materials has become so popular that it has become a specialty phase of the hobby, and several publications specifically about carving are currently available. Therefore, this second edition of GEMCRAFT will contain only a brief introduction to carving. Those persons who are especially interested in carving gem materials may wish to secure *Gemstone Carving*, a companion book published by Chilton Book Company.

PANSY D. KRAUS, G.G., F.G.A.

Preface to the First Edition

In presenting the following book on gemcraft the authors have endeavored to stay as far away as possible from gemology, the science of gems; mineralogy, the science of minerals; geology and paleontology, allied to the study of rocks. Out of our experience of the past 12 years in publishing a magazine for amateur lapidaries we have tried to pool the best information available in our extensive files and library, and from personal experience besides, so that we could present a readable and easily understood book about the principles of conquering the hardness of gem materials and turning them into gems for setting in jewelry, or into useful objects, or into just plain polished stones of beauty.

There is very little information in this book on how to build your own equipment, for the novice of today is a fortunate person in that many reputable and experienced manufacturers are producing machines and devices of all kinds that have been time-tested. We do discuss much of the equipment that is presently available and urge the beginner to send to all manufacturers for their literature and to make a personal study of it to adapt their hobby space and available funds to the equipment offered. In this connection, manufacturers have been making splendid progress in building smaller units adaptable to use in the smaller confines of city homes, apartments, or trailers.

For several years now the gemcutting hobby has been the fastest growing of the craft hobbies, and it is estimated that the number of persons following some phase of the rock hobby in America is about three million persons. Of these, probably a million are not particularly interested in cutting stones, for many are mineral specimen collectors who do not care to cut stones but rather prefer to collect and admire the natural specimens in the mineral family. Others are interested only in fossils, and of course countless others casually collect pretty stones and rocks for flower arrangements or rock gardens. From this large group the figure of two million actually interested in gemcutting appears to be supported by several factors. We have in our *Lapidary Journal* files the indexed names of about 200,000 persons who have been subscribers to our magazine, purchasers of our books, inquirers after information, members at one time of the 700 gem and mineral clubs, personal correspondents, visitors to our office and museum, etc. We are not optimistic enough to believe that we are lucky enough or sufficiently efficient to acquire the names of more than 10 percent of all persons in North America who are interested in cutting gemstones. This would therefore indicate a figure of two million potential gemcutters. However, we recognize that many of these interested persons are wishful thinkers; they are interested but they may never actually cut a rock.

Another factor on which we base our premise is that we also have in our files the names of more than 2,000 dealers who are catering to the needs of these interested people by selling them rocks, machines, supplies, books, and other needs. Probably as few as 10 percent of these dealers are garnering as much as 90 percent of the business, but even so it would take a potential market of close to two million people to support such a widespread business as the supplying of the hobby has become.

About 1 percent of all people interested in rocks now belong to a club study group usually operating under the name of a gem and mineral society. These groups are organized into regional Federations, each of which holds an annual convention in conjunction with a gem and mineral show put on by their members. These shows very often draw as many as 35,000 visitors over a weekend, and the reader is advised to visit one of them and observe all the facets of the hobby gathered under one roof. Schedules of these events are published regularly in the lapidary magazines. The only reason that more thousands do not belong to the clubs is that American society is so highly organized and so diversified in interests that time allotment for meetings and study has to be spread rather thin. If you become interested in gemcutting we urge you to attend a club meeting in your area. Five hundred fifty-eight of these clubs were listed in the April 1959 issue of the *Lapidary Journal,* with the time and place of meeting. This list is revised and published every April.

The reasons for the increasing popularity of the gemcraft hobby are many. First of all, it is a family hobby—an activity that can be shared by every member of the family. It is a hobby that can be followed in some phase every day of the year. It is not a seasonal hobby like hunting, fishing, boating, or sports. It requires no expensive gear used only a few days a year, no licenses or taxes. It provides an esthetic quality to a man's life, a satisfaction that comes from creating something, particularly something of beauty. But one of the most important reasons is that it supplies a man with the great blessing of doing something with his hands. When we say "man" we also mean women, of course, for there are almost as many women cutting gems as men—and they are good at it, too. Both men and women have been freed through modern inventions from so much of the drudgery experienced by older generations that they are searching for things to do, and they most enjoy doing things with their hands.

The authors hope that they have produced in this book the answer to the person seeking knowledge on how to cut gems. We have tried to discuss every phase of gem cutting except the tumbling process, for we do not consider that the tumbling of gemstones requires lapidary skill since it is a purely mechanical process. Nor have we discussed the making of jewelry, for there are many books available on this subject. We have provided an ample list of the available books on subjects allied to gemcraft, including good books on the tumbling process.

Our hope is that the reader, if he is not already a gemcutter, will be led through these pages to a new way of life and happiness and go down and explore the many byways in the study of the stones of the earth.

LELANDE QUICK and HUGH LEIPER

Acknowledgments

This Revised Edition of GEMCRAFT: HOW TO CUT AND POLISH GEMSTONES by the late Lelande Quick and the late Hugh Leiper, F.G.A., would not have been possible without the encouragement and cooperation of the many persons and business firms who so generously provided the latest information and photographs of the many new machines and products now available to the beginning lapidaries and hobbyists.

I wish to express my sincere appreciation to Dara E. Yost, illustrator, for her close association and cooperation in supplying the finished line illustrations for the Revised Edition of GEMCRAFT. I also wish to thank John Washalaski, photographer, Solana Beach, California, for his untiring efforts to supply me with the majority of the color photographs, as well as numerous black-and-white photographs which have been incorporated into the text of GEMCRAFT.

For the information and photographs concerning the faceted novelties, I wish to thank the artist-craftsman Jerry J. Muchna who designed and faceted them; Robert W. Jones for his expertise in recording and relaying to me the specifics of how the work was accomplished; and Jeffrey Kurtzeman, photographer, who supplied the color photograph of the faceted rose and the black-and-white photograph of "The Rickshaw."

The following manufacturers and suppliers were most courteous and generous in supplying photographs of and information about the newest equipment and supplies from each of their firms: Allen Lapidary Equipment Manufacturing Company; American Standard Corporation; Arrow Profile Company; Dorothy Blake; Brad's Rock Shop, Division of Lapidary Hobbycrafts; Covington Engineering Corporation; Crown Manufacturing Company; Crystalite Corporation (formerly Pacific Test Specialties); Diamond Pacific Tool Corporation; Earth Treasures; Fac-Ette Manufacturing Company; Gem-Tec Diamond Tool Company; Henry B. Graves Company; Great Western Equipment Company; Gryphon Corporation; Highland Park Manufacturing, Division of Musto Industries; Lee Lapidaries; A. D. McBurney; MDR Manufacturing Company; Prismatic Instruments; Ran-Co. Lapidary Products, Division of Standard Abrasives; Raytech Industries; Rose Enterprises; Jack V. Schuller; Terra Products; and Ultra Tec.

I also wish to express my appreciation to my secretary, Virginia Englebright, for her untiring efforts and assistance in typing the final work and in proofreading and to the following San Diego lapidaries and instructors for contributing information and cut stones for photographing: Larry Washalaski, Earl and Ann Manor, and Lester Stephens.

Contents

Preface to the Second Edition   v

Preface to the First Edition   vi

Acknowledgments   viii

Chapter 1
What Is a Gemstone?   1

Chapter 2
**Where and How to Collect
    Gemstones**   5

Chapter 3
**The Diamond Saw and Its
    Operation**   10

Chapter 4
How to Use the Slabbing Saw   13
    Description of the Saw   14
    Cutting the Slabs   16
    Thickness of Blade and
        Thickness of Cut   16
    Dishing of the Saw and Its
        Correction   18

Chapter 5
How to Use the Trim Saw   20
    Care of the Trim Saw   24

Chapter 6
Cutting and Polishing Cabochons   25
    Marking the Slabs   26
    Dopping the Stone   29
    Types of Grinders   31
    Grinding the Gem   35
    Sanding the Gem   35

Polishing the Gem   38
Removing the Gem from the
    Dop   38

Chapter 7
**How to Cut Star and Cat's-Eye
    Gems**   40
    Orienting a Sapphire Cat's-
        Eye   43
    Asterism in Other Stones   43
    How to Cut and Polish Star
        Sapphire   44
    Use of the Diamond-impreg-
        nated Wood Wheel   45
    Cutting Cat's-Eyes   47
    Filling the Pores   47
    How to Put the "Eye" in
        Tigereye   48

Chapter 8
**Special Cabochon Polishing
    Techniques**   49
    Azurite   49
    Black Coral   50
    Burnite   51
    Chrysocolla (Quartz)   51
    Dumortierite (Quartz)   52
    Fire Agate   52
    Garnet   53
    Goldstone   53
    Iolite   53
    Jade   53
    Lapis Lazuli   55
    Obsidian   55

Onyx 56
Opal 59
Petoskey Stones 61
Rhodonite 61
Turquoise 62
Unakite 63

Chapter 9
The Use of Diamond Products by the Lapidary 64
Advantages of Diamond Products 65
Types of Diamond Equipment and Products 65
Cutting and Polishing with Diamond 69
A Summary of General Information 73

Chapter 10
How to Facet Gems 75
Who Can Cut Faceted Stones? 78
The Value of the Hobby for Relaxation 78
Fundamentals of Facet Cutting 81
Vernier or "Cheater" Adjustment 86
Indexing 86
Necessary Cutting and Polishing Laps 88
Care and Cleaning of the Diamond Lap 88
The Polishing Laps 89
Scoring the Polishing Lap 90
Selecting the Gemstone Rough 91
Preparing the Preform 92
Grinding the Preform for a Round Brilliant 93
Making Preforms for Step-cut Gems 94
Proper Dopping Methods 95
Dopping the Brilliant Preform 95
Turning the Gem 98
Dopping the Step-cut or Rectangular Preform 98
Dopping Fancy-shaped Stones 99

Dopping Procedure for Heat-sensitive and Large Stones 99
Cold Dopping 99
Cutting the Girdle 100
Cutting the Girdle on a Step-cut Stone 100
Adjusting Angles at which Facets Are Cut 101
Planning the Correct Proportions for the Gem 102
Steps in Cutting a Brilliant 103
Cutting the Crown Facets 107
Cutting the Crown Girdle Facets 108
Cutting the "Star" Facets 110
Polishing the Crown Facets 110
Polishing Out the "Tail" on the Crown Mains 111
Cutting the Step-cut Gem 111
Polishing the Pavilion Facets 113
Cutting the Crown of a Step-cut Stone 113
Cutting the Double-Mirror Brilliant 113
Polishing Faceted Stones 116
The Lucite Lap 118
The Pure Tin Lap 119
The Tin–Type Metal Combination Lap 119
The Hardwood Maple Lap 119
The Muslin-faced Wax Lap 119
The Linoleum Lap 120
Flat Lapping on a Steel Plate 120
Ceramic Laps 120
Faceter's Trim Saws 121
Summary 122

Chapter 11
Collecting the Rare, the Unusual, and the Beautiful in Faceting Materials 125

Chapter 12
The Lapping Process 130
Equipment Needed 130
Size and Kind of Grits to Be Used 131
The Lapping Operation 131
Alternate Methods 133
Sanding and Polishing on Drums 134
Filling Pits in Flats 135

Chapter 13
How to Carve and Engrave Gems 136
    The First Seals 136
    How the Amateur May Do
      Carving 137
    Equipment Needed for Carv-
      ing 139
    Tools Needed 140
    Sawing Out the Blank 141
    Rough Grinding to General
      Shape 141
    How to Hollow Out a Piece 143
    Internal Grinding 144
    The Gem Carvings of Mrs.
      Olive M. Colhour 144
    How to Carve a Continuous-
      Chain Link Necklace 145
    Carvings and Sculptures in
      Gem Materials 150

Chapter 14
**The Making of Gemstone
  Novelties** 162
    Making Bookends 162
    Spheres 164

Chapter 15
**An Introduction to Mosaic and
  Intarsia in Gems** 173

Appendix
Useful Tables and Bibliography 180
    Other Books about
      Gemcutting 180
    Books on Minerals 181
    Books on Gemology and the
      Properties of Gems 181
    Books on Where to Go for
      Rocks 182
    Miscellaneous Books about
      Rocks 182
    Books on Jewelry Making 183
    Conversion Tables 183
    Clark Standard Sizes for
      Rocks 183
    Abbreviations 183
    Suggested Diamond Saw
      Speeds 184
    Conversion to the
      Metric System 184
    Diamond Abrasive Chart 185
    Table of Faceting Angles 186
    RPM Speed Tables 187
    Gemological Measures 188
    Birthstones through the Ages 189

Subject Index 190

Equipment Index 194

1 · What Is a Gemstone?

As the late George F. Kunz, great authority on gems, once wrote, "The love of precious stones is deeply implanted in the human heart." Indeed, man has developed an instinct and an awareness for any kind of stone, for until comparatively recent times, his very existence depended on what he did with stones. Stones first freed man from living in the trees and existing on a diet of insects, nuts, and fruits. He climbed down, and stayed down, when he found that he could conquer other animals by felling them with stones. He ate the meat and clothed his body for the first time in hides. At first he threw the stones, but as his reason developed he found that by tying a stone to a stick with leather thongs taken from the animals he had killed he could throw the stones farther.

Later man discovered that one stone was harder than another—that one stone could therefore be used to shape another—and thus the spearhead was born, and later the arrow (fig. 1–1). By the time man had advanced to the bow-and-arrow stage, he had gained dominance over all the other animals. He could now bring down his quarries from a safe distance since the arrow traveled far greater distances than a man could throw a rock and was propelled with much greater force. Thus was born the

Fig. 1–1 An ancient Chinese axe of nephrite jade and a piece of worked jade, reported to be more than 2,500 years old. (*Courtesy, Gordon R. Thomas*)

deadliest weapon that man has ever invented. People have survived attacks with some of the deadliest contrivances man has ever devised—mustard gas, gunshots, atom bombs—but relatively few men pierced with an arrow ever survived, for if death was not immediate, it soon occurred from loss of blood or from later infection of the wound.

The making of spear and arrowheads was man's first experience with the lapidary art. It is possible, because of this experience with pounding one rock against another, that he discovered how to make fire when the sparks from the striking rocks ignited the grass around him. Having discovered how to make fire, it was now his problem to control it. Therefore, when he built a fire he surrounded it with rocks to keep it from spreading, much as the hunter and the Boy Scout do today. He must have been greatly amazed indeed, when one day he saw a substance exuding from a hot rock. When the substance had cooled, it hardened—and man found that it was malleable, that it could be shaped much easier than rocks. At that point man became selective in his rock hunting. He had learned to distinguish between hard and soft rocks; now he had to search for rocks with mineral content, perhaps brown rocks for iron, green rocks for copper—no one really knows, for there was no recorded history at the time. But we do know that the Stone Age ended at that point and the Bronze Age and the beginnings of civilization started. However, it did not start all over the world at one time. It never did get started in some parts of the world. It had not started in much of America when Columbus came here in 1492. It has not started among the primitive tribes of New Guinea to this day.

It seems inevitable, as man achieved security and settled down to live in communities instead of following the nomadic life, that he started to gather possessions and that his first possessions were rocks. These were rocks he treasured above others because of their beauty, and thus he began to develop a taste for beauty which later developed in the lives of his descendants into the arts of today. The very oldest graves of early man sometimes contain the pretty rocks he gathered in his lifetime.

Through long, patient labor, man finally learned to drill these rocks and string them on thongs for the adorn-

ment of his body. And thus the world of gemstones came into being—a world that has not been with us very long compared with the ages of time.

And so we come to today, when the world still remains more than 90 percent rock on the dry land surfaces and where gemstones are a very small fraction of 1 percent of all that rock. Until comparatively recent times the owning of gems was confined to the very rich or to heads of state. Today, however, it is a rare man or woman indeed who does not have at least one or two gemstone items of some kind. Yet people know less about their gems than about any of their other possessions. There is nothing for which people spend more money and about which they know less than gems.

It is still the custom today in some uninformed quarters to class gems as "precious" and "semiprecious," but it is now becoming the custom to call all stones of intrinsic value "gemstones." No gem can really be "half-precious." In 1959 when the first edition of GEMCRAFT was published, the dictionaries had not yet caught up with this idea. However, *The Random House Dictionary of the English Language,* The Unabridged Edition, copyright 1967, does now include the word *gemstone,* as well as the terms *precious* and *semiprecious* with reference to gems. The *Webster's New Twentieth Century Dictionary,* Unabridged Second Edition, copyright 1970, does not give the term *gemstone.*

Because of their hardness, beauty, and rarity, the following stones used to be regarded in the trade as precious: diamond, sapphire, ruby, and emerald. Sometimes opal was included in this category, and some authorities even included the pearl, which is not a stone at all. All other varieties were regarded as semiprecious. These terms have been discontinued, for it is now recognized that any stone valuable enough, because of beauty and durability, to be cut and polished is really precious; consequently, all are classed as gemstones. There are probably no more than 100 varieties of gemstones in the whole world, and these varieties include stones used for ornamental purposes only, such as marble and alabaster. In the gem trade itself, however, jewelers now class gemstones into two classes—diamonds and colored stones.

The man who cuts and polishes these stones is called a *lapidary,* and the place where he performs his cutting is also called his lapidary. The term *gemcutter* seems to be replacing the word lapidary as it appears to be more readily identifiable as a definition in today's world.

In order to be classed as a gemstone, a stone must have certain qualities, although few gemstones possess them all. The stones must be durable or pretty or rare. The diamond is durable and pretty but not rare, while the emerald is durable, pretty, *and* rare, thus possessing all three qualities. Indeed, the emerald is the most valuable stone in the world of gems being rated with the ruby as above the diamond in monetary value.

A short definition of a gemstone is: *a mineral hard enough to take a high degree of polish and durable enough to retain it.* Nearly all gemstones are minerals. (Exceptions are jet and amber, which have been produced from living organisms—vegetation and tree sap, respectively. Pearls and coral are produced by animal organisms.)

A mineral is a naturally occurring inorganic material of definite composition, usually possessing an orderly arrangement of its atoms in a crystalline structure. When two or more minerals have grown together, the substance is called a rock, and occasionally a gemstone is a rock rather than a mineral. Lapis lazuli (blue stone) is a good example of this, as it is a mixture of lazurite, pyrite, and calcite.

It is not the purpose of the authors in this book on gemcraft to give a short course in gemology, however, and confuse the gemcutter before he even gets started. This is a craft book—a "how-to-do-it" book—and it makes no pretense of being a scientific tome. The authors maintain that the reader interested in learning how to cut gems, either for profit or for fun, can become an accomplished gemcutter without ever knowing that amethyst is only purple quartz or that citrine is yellow quartz. No doubt it will follow that, in his evolution, he will eventually come to the study of the things he is working with and will want to know the why and the wherefore of his beautiful gems. That is when other new worlds will open to him through his study of geology, mineralogy, gem identification, history, crystallography, etc. A list of good current books on these subjects will be found in the Appendix

Most of the gems with which the amateur gemcutter works belong to the quartz family. You will soon find that most of the varieties you will cut into cabochons will be agate, petrified wood, jasper, chalcedony, chert, and flint, besides many others—all of them in the quartz family of minerals: beautiful and hard, but never rare. They are the most plentiful varieties of gemstones on the earth and the most versatile in their ornamental possibilities and uses in jewelry.

The one common property that all gemstones possess is hardness, and herein our purpose is to show people how they can conquer it, for only by conquering this hardness can they convert a rough rock into a wonderful gem of deathless beauty. The whole gemcutting process is nothing more than a progressive series of abrasive experiences, so that a stage of coarse abrading is followed by stages that are finer and still finer, until no bumps or scratches are left to abrade.

For purposes of convenience, a German named Mohs (rhymes with *hose*) divided hardness into an arbitrary table of 10 degrees, placing diamond, the hardest known mineral, at the top of the list with a grade of 10. Talc, the softest mineral, was placed at the bottom of the list with a grade of 1. All other mineral substances fall between these two in degrees of hardness. Minerals below the grade of 5 are seldom ever cut as gems because they are too soft to be durable. Few amateur gemcutters ever achieve the experience of cutting a diamond. Therefore, most of the gems the reader is likely to cut will come between grades 5 and 9 on the Mohs scale. It should not be considered that grade 5 is half as hard as grade 10 just because it happens to be the half of 10. The diamond (grade 10) is, in fact, many thousands of times harder than any gemstone graded 5 in hardness. The full Mohs scale is given herewith:

Mohs Scale of Hardness

1—Talc
2—Gypsum
3—Calcite
4—Fluorite
5—Apatite
6—Feldspar (orthoclase)
7—Quartz (amethyst, agate, citrine)
8—Topaz
9—Corundum (ruby, sapphire)
10—Diamond

An easy way to remember the sequence is to take the initials of each graded mineral to form the sentence **T**hat **G**em **C**ontains **F**eathers **A**nd **F**laws; **Q**uiz **T**he **C**utting **D**epartment.

The one characteristic that influences the amateur lapidary or gemcutter more than anything else is beauty, and most of the beauty in any gemstone is latent until the lapidary begins his abrasive processes to bring out the hidden beauty. That is the fascination of the hobby, for it is the factor that makes the gemcutter feel that he is creating something—that he is an artist.

There are several factors that make a gemstone beautiful. The most important of these is color—the red of the ruby, the blue of the sapphire, the green of the emerald, or the marvelous beauty of all these colors combined in that most beautiful of all gems, the opal. The action of light on the gem colors enhances their beauty still further. If the stone is opaque, like jasper, it can be very beautiful with reflected light, called luster or sheen. When it is translucent and you can see *into* it, like an agate, it is still more beautiful. When it is transparent and you can see *through* it, as in the crystal gems like topaz and amethyst, you then have materials that should be cut with polished faces so that light can enter one face and be reflected from another. These faces are called *facets* in the gemcutter's terminology, and the process of placing the facets on the gemstone is called *faceting*. The refraction and the reflection of light create sparkle. The problems of bringing out these qualities in gemstone materials are described in the following chapters.

2 · Where and How to Collect Gemstones

Someone has said that 40 percent of the fun in the gemcutting hobby is gathering the stones personally, another 40 percent of the fun is obtained from giving the stones to others, and the remaining 20 percent comes from cutting and polishing them. This may be an exaggeration, but it is certainly the experience of those fortunate enough to collect their own materials that much of the fun comes from hunting the rocks and a great deal of pleasure is obtained in sharing one's finds with others.

Just as hunting dogs are usually hounds, rock hunters have come to be known as *rockhounds*. This term is now fixed firmly in the public consciousness from constant use in the press and in the various magazine articles that have appeared in nearly every important periodical of general interest published in the United States. Several years ago the word was regarded as opprobrious, but it is now widely accepted and will no doubt appear in new editions of the various dictionaries.

Rockhounding is found to a greater extent in the western states than in the eastern only because interesting and valuable rocks are more readily available there. The East has just as many rocks and mountains, but there is little public domain that is open to rock hunters; moreover, the verdure is so great that the rocks are not exposed for examination. The best collecting areas are the western mountains and deserts, where the evidence of rock formations easily can be studied and explored. Remember that rocks are everywhere—they compose more than 90 percent of all dry land. Even in flat, wet areas like Florida and Louisiana, through their persistent searching rockhounds have discovered many varieties of petrified wood, agate, and agatized coral that can be cut into beautiful gems. No matter where you live, there is a possibility that you can find beautiful rocks; and if they possess the qualities of a gem—hardness, beauty, durability—they may afford you a great deal of pleasure.

Always be observant for any activity that disturbs the earth's surface, for all such activities usually expose rocks that have not become weathered and discolored. In these days of intense highway-building activity everywhere and the custom of "using the hill to make the fill," rocks are being exposed everywhere in the cuts. Be on the lookout for interesting rocks at these locations. In the old days, when railroads and highways encountered a hill or a mountain, they went around it—now they cut right

5

through it. Practically no new railroads are now being built, but road-building activity is intense.

As stated before, the most prolific source of present-day rock supplies is in the western deserts, where little or no vegetation exists and the rocks are right out on top of the earth to be observed and gathered. While these pickings are not what they were 20 years ago, there are still many areas, practically unexplored, where the venturesome rockhound can discover the new varieties of agate, petrified wood, and sometimes valuable gemstones like jade.

Jade was unknown in the United States until rockhounds discovered it in Wyoming in about 1940. Since then, rockhounds have found jade deposits at several spots in California, Idaho, Oregon, and Wisconsin. Precious serpentine, very like jade and more beautiful in many instances because of its greater translucency, has been found in many states.

Other prolific sources of gem materials are the rivers and creeks of the United States, for they transport exposed stones from one place to another. We have in our museum a vial of gravel from the bottom of the Mississippi River that contains about 15 varieties of gem material in a single ounce, all transported from the streams that fed it from all over the country.

The best time to examine streams is in the summer months, when they are less filled with water. Examine the rocks along the shore and by wading. Particularly examine every sand bar, for this is where the stream runs quietly and the rolling rocks are dropped. The best place to look is at the head of the bars, for the heavier rocks drop here while the smaller, lighter rocks are carried to the lower end of the bar. If you are lucky enough to find an old *dry* stream bed, look under the boulders and between them and dig into the gravel. Some very valuable gems have been

found in such locations. A good example of this is the beautiful blue topaz found in dry creek beds in Mason County, Texas.

There are not many gemstone rocks reported from the eastern beaches, but the beaches along the Pacific coast are prolific in agate materials—particularly the Oregon beaches, where some of the most colorful agates in the world are found. Many California beaches also have fine agates and jade. The beaches of the Great Lakes have produced two beautiful varieties of gem material, particularly along the shores of Lake Superior, where thomsonites and agates are found. The Petoskey stones of Lake Michigan are very interesting. Summer is the best collecting time along the Great Lake shores, as they are snow-covered in winter.

Winter is the best time to collect along the Pacific shores, for then the ocean storms uncover the stones buried by the gentler summer tides in the beach sands. The turbulent waves wash up countless tons of new materials. It may be uncomfortable, but the best time to collect is during a winter storm. Otherwise the best time to collect is at low tide with the sun at your back. As you walk up the beach the sun will glint on the wet agates and you can see them better than when you walk into the sun. All rocks are more easily observable when they are wet, for then you see them in the approximate colors that will be theirs when they have been polished.

A rich source of mineral specimens is any area surrounding a mine, whether active or inactive, and quarries and gravel pits are mines. Material from the mines and quarries contains many valuable specimens, although they are seldom of gem quality unless they come from a gem mine, such as the tourmaline mines in San Diego County, California. Usually permission must be obtained to examine the dumps of these mines. The dumps of the old zinc mines at Franklin Furnace, New Jersey, reportedly have yielded a greater variety of mineral specimens than any other one spot on earth. The Crestmore quarry near Riverside, California, is reported to have produced the second greatest variety of materials of any spot in the world. However, practically none of the specimens gathered at either spot is of particular interest to the gemcutter, and permission to examine the dumps is not easy to procure at this time. Seek out the quarries and the mining dumps in your area and explore them first for experience.

There are now more than 900 gem and mineral clubs in North America, nearly all of which conduct field trips. If you happen to live in an area where a club exists, you will be welcome to go along, for the clubs are enthusiastic helpers of the novice rockhound. If you should acquire an interest in rocks, you should join and support your local group. The cost for dues usually runs between $3 and $10 a year. You will meet people in the clubs from every station in life, for an interest in rocks is a great leveler of people. These people will gladly show you how to cut and polish rocks, and you can gain untold knowledge by attending a few meetings and spending a few hours in someone's lapidary shop. Many of these clubs put on annual shows of their work to which the public is invited. Or they join with other federated clubs in huge gem and mineral shows, taking in the clubs in an entire region (like California or the Midwest, for example). The magazines catering to the hobby will tell you when these shows occur, and as soon as one is held near your home you should attend it. These shows often draw as many as 40,000 people and exhibit many thousands of examples of the lapidary art.

A list of the gem and mineral clubs, with their time and place of meeting, is published every April in the *Rockhound Buyers Guide* issue of the *Lapidary Journal,* selling for $2.50. This *Buyers Guide* issue contains gem-hunting stories for the traveling rockhound and lists most of the dealers who have anything to sell him. It is an annual encyclopedia of information that is a *must* in any rockhound's library, for it contains more than 1,900 advertisements of gems, cutting materials, machines, tools, and supplies from firms all over the world. Other issues of the *Lapidary Journal* (a monthly which sells for $8.95 a year in the U.S. and its possessions) regularly report news of gem finds, new gadgets and machines, methods of gem cutting, new ideas for utilizing gem materials, methods of silvercraft, news of the gem shows all over the country, and so on. A sample of the *Lapidary Journal* is obtainable for only 50¢ from the publisher's offices at 3564 Kettner Boulevard, P.O. Box 80937, San Diego, California 92138.

There are other magazines about the rock hobby that the gemcutter will find useful, although they do not emphasize gemcutting methods as thoroughly because they also cover several other fields of interest. Here they are, listed alphabetically:

Earth Science:
Bimonthly, six copies per year. $4 a year. Sample 40¢. Earth Science Publishing Co., Box 1815, Colorado Springs, Colorado 80901.

Gems and Minerals:
Monthly. $6.50 a year. Sample 50¢ U.S. and possessions. Gems and Minerals, Gemac Corp., Box 687, Mentone, California 92359.

Rock & Gem:
Monthly. $8 a year. Sample 75¢ U.S. and possessions. Rock & Gem, Behn-Miller Publishers, 16001 Ventura Boulevard, Encino, California 91316.

Rocks and Minerals:
Monthly. $5.50 a year. Sample $1 U.S. and possessions. Rocks and Minerals, Helen Dwight Reid Educational Foundation (Heldref Publications), Suite 302, 4000 Albemarle Street, Washington, D.C.20016, or Box 29, Peekskill, New York 10566.

All the foregoing magazines have accounts from time to time of where to go for rocks, and all of them have information now and then on gemcutting techniques and ideas. The *Lapidary Journal,* however, is the only magazine published exclusively for the gemcutter and jewelry maker.

Very important as a source of information are the "trail" books describing actual gemstone locations in various sections of the country. A list of these books will be found in the Bibliography in the Appendix.

Many good gem locations are private, and one can collect there for a fee. On such a basis diamonds can be sought in Arkansas; sapphires in Montana; rubies in North Carolina; agate-filled thundereggs in Oregon; moss agate in California, and so on. Several thousand gem-collecting localities have been described in books and magazine articles, but many of them are now depleted.

Twenty-five and more years ago, anyone could travel the roads of the West and gather surface gem materials almost without leaving the road. Surface pickings are scarce now, and rockhounds must dig at known spots in order to get worthwhile materials or else discover new spots far from the beaten tracks. There are still many prolific sources in undiscovered areas, particularly in Arizona, Nevada, Utah, Wyoming, Montana, and the Dakotas.

When gemstones were plentiful, thousands of rockhounds gathered and took home literally tons of materials. It is safe to say that, of the tens of thousands of tons of good agate and petrified wood materials taken into the back yards of America, probably every pound still exists somewhere in the rough or finished form. No one ever destroys a gem rock—indeed, they are practically indestructible.

If you are new to the hobby, scout your own area and become acquainted not only with living rockhounds but also with the families of those who have passed on, for the richest hunting in America is in the back yards and the garages of such people. If they charge you for the rocks you are still way ahead of the game, for it costs considerable money to travel great distances today for rocks. However, nothing can match the great thrill of finding material yourself. Once you have picked a likely-looking rock from the ground, given it a lick with your tongue to see what color it really is, nicked it with your hammer to see the inside, placed it in your back pocket as the special find of the day, taken it to the grinder's after your trip, and produced a real gem that you mount in a ring for yourself, you will find that you have acquired what rockhounds call the "rock pox"—and this is an incurable disease!

If and when you do indulge in gemcollecting travels, watch for some of the rock shops along the way, for there are about 2,000 of them along the country's highways. In these shops you will find a selection of the rocks of the proprietors' areas, and you will gain a great deal of useful information besides. The local dealer usually has better specimens of the rocks of his own locale than you are likely to find. Just to be safe, you should buy some rocks from him if only to see what you are looking for and to prevent coming home from your fishing trip with no fish. When you do go on a rock trip, always bring home more than your own requirements so that you have "swapping" rocks and some to sell to the unfortunates unable to make the trip who nevertheless are quite willing to help defray the expenses you incur in hauling the rocks to their door.

Some advice should be offered about how to dress for rock-collecting trips. The best advice is contained in this one word: "comfortably." Forget the glamour—you don't need it on a rock trip. You will be stooping a lot, bending over while hunting, squatting, digging in the ground and sitting on it. You should therefore wear clothes that are comfortable for these activities and clothes that you do not have to worry about. But above all, *wear stout shoes!* The shoes should cover the ankles; the shoes should fit you; the shoes must stand the scuffings of rocky terrain. Nothing can spoil a trip so much as a turned ankle caused by low shoes or a big water blister caused by an ill-fitting shoe. Hiking boots are ideal. Men can secure good army boots and shoes at the surplus stores.

You will need a rock pick and a sack for carrying specimens. A number of cardboard cartons should be carried in the car for hauling the rocks. Always carry a first-aid kit, and a snakebite kit besides, if you are going to a place where snakes abound—somehow rocks and snakes seem to go together. Your car kit should also include insect repellent and a remedy for sunburn. Do not enter desert trails off the main roads without plenty of water and some extra fuel. Always carry a shovel. The summer temperatures in the Mojave and the Colorado Deserts in California are often officially 120°F (49°C), but the ground temperatures are much higher. Should you become stranded or have a car mishap, you could die in a few hours without water. If you do encounter trouble, never start out alone for help and leave someone else alone while you go. The best advice one can give is to stay out of the deserts in the hot seasons unless you have company in one or more cars besides your own party.

If you are so situated that you cannot go to a club meeting or make field trips or travel at all, then you are dependent on the rockhound dealer for your rocks.

If you buy a large saw, you should then buy rough rocks by the pound and have the fun of sawing them. But the average rockhound does not need a large saw, so if you have none then you will have to buy slabs of materials by the square inch. There are about 4,000 dealers selling rocks in the United States and Canada. Most of them are selling the rocks of their localities as a side-pocket venture to supplement their income. Their overhead is little or nothing, and they usually sell good slabs of gem-grade materials for very little, especially considering the fact that their prices include recompense for their time and the expense of sawing the rocks. The great majority of those selling slabs sell them on a money-back guarantee, so that you are taking no chances except for a few cents' postage. These dealers get most of their business through classified and display advertisements in the various rock journals, and that is a good reason for subscribing to *all* of them just to read the ads of *all* the dealers. For only $25 a year, about $2 a month, you can keep up with new discoveries and ideas and keep refreshing and increasing your knowledge through the advertising columns.

If you are the average friendly American type, you will accumulate a list of correspondents with whom you can trade information and materials, and you will find that you will have opened up a whole new world of living. A rock trip especially is one phase of the hobby that the whole family, including the family dog, can indulge in, and they are usually delighted to do so. It is an important and satisfying facet of the gem-cutting hobby—and *it can be done in any season without a license.*

3. The Diamond Saw and Its Operation

Up to the 1930s, the amateur lapidary was really in difficulty when it came to sectioning large specimens. The only thing available to him was the mud saw, one of the dirtiest and noisiest machines ever devised by man. It usually consisted of a bin or box that was filled with a "mud" made of water and silicon carbide grits. Disks of steel, sometimes in a series, were mounted on a spindle, and they revolved through the mud. By clamping a rock in a vise and having weights pull the rock against the periphery of the revolving blades, the rock was sawed through, in time, because of the friction of the grit picked up by the revolving disks. It was a long, slow, discouraging, dirty, and noisy process.

In 1934, Wilfred C. Eyles was employed by the California State Division of Mines, and the problem of sawing specimens for the Bureau was presented to him. Eyles conducted a number of experiments and finally devised an 8″ (20.3 cm) diameter steel blade charged with small pieces of diamond set into notches made in the rim of the blade. Mr. Eyles was one of the founders of the Northern California Mineral Society in San Francisco, organized about that time, and the diamond saw came in for considerable experimentation among that early amateur group. It was widely predicted at the

time that the diamond saw would never come into general use because of the expense, but 20 years later it was practically impossible to find a dirty and slow mud saw anywhere. The diamond saws of today are much improved over Eyles'.

In the early days of the amateur gem-cutting movement in the late 1930s, almost the first tool the beginner bought was a diamond saw. A good cutting machine could be bought in those days for about $40, but most amateurs built their own rigs. Today we have many good saws available, and because of the prevalence of sawed slabs in the dealers' stores, very few amateurs start out with a slabbing saw; indeed, most gemcutters never acquire one at all because they find that the smaller trim saw is sufficient for their purpose.

Presented herewith are illustrations of some of the larger modern slabbing saws (figs. 3–1 and 3–2). Saws are much more expensive today because of the greatly increased cost of the diamond bort used in their making. However, the saw blades themselves are a far cry from those first blades, and because of perfection in manufacture, the life of a saw blade today is so much longer that the cost of operating a diamond saw over a period of time is much less than it was 20 years ago.

The first saw blades gave a lot of

Fig. 3–1 This 16″ (40.6-cm) Highland Park slab saw will accommodate any geode, nodule, or rough piece up to 5³/₄″ (14.6 cm) in diameter in its narrowest dimension. (*Courtesy, Highland Park Manufacturing Co.*)

trouble, and many gemcutters never did get started because they would buy a saw and it would not work. The trouble was not with the saws, however, but rather with the sawyers. They had purchased a complicated tool and did not know how to use it. They were like the small seven-year-old with his first watch—not prepared to handle such a valuable machine.

Diamond blades are called upon to cut a great diversity of materials varying in hardness, and the operator should not expect to cut all materials with the same speed. Metals used in diamond saws were either bronze or soft cold-rolled stretcher-leveled steel, steel that has been rolled level at the mill to take

out the wavy motion. It is entirely different from the steel used in ordinary wood saws, which are made of carbon steel. A diamond saw made from carbon steel would give no performance at all. The steel has to be ductile and malleable in order to take the diamond bort charge.

Today many of the standard notched blades are made with select GE "Man-Made" industrial diamonds that are blocky in shape with maximum friability for lapidary use. The diamond bort is usually evenly mixed into a nickel alloy, which is fused into the notches of select steel cores and then heat-treated to relieve most stresses; then the blades are usually tensioned by machine and by hand. They are a vast improvement over the older-type diamond blades. Today very little phosphor bronze is used for the thin, small trim saw blades. They are usually composed of either a steel core or a copper core.

Blades now come in two types. The *notched* blade has the diamond inserted into small notches around the rim. The *sintered* type has a rim that has been made of powdered metal and diamond powder. These powders are heated until they fuse, and the hoop is soldered to the rim of a steel disk. Both types perform well, but the sintered type will last longer because it contains more diamond and is more expensive than the notched type. Small blades for valuable crystal materials are sometimes as thin as a playing card and are made of phosphor bronze. The steel blades range in thickness from a few thousandths of an inch to ¹/₈″ (0.32 cm).

It is not the blade itself that cuts the rock, but rather the diamond in the blade that does the work—the conquering of one hardness by a substance that is harder than the thing being cut. Therefore, it is wise to "break in" a new saw blade by carefully exposing the diamond. Many methods have been suggested for doing this, but one of the best

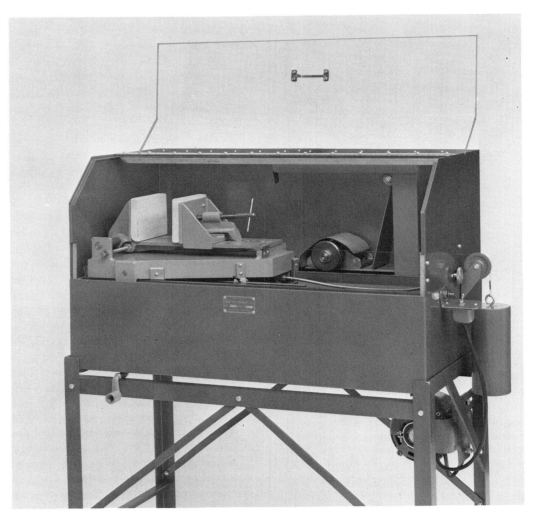

Fig. 3–2 A rugged Great Western hydraulic-feed slabbing saw, 20″ (50.8-cm) model. (*Courtesy, Great Western Equipment Co.*)

and most satisfactory is to first saw slowly through an ordinary paving brick.

The operator will discover many things about sawing that are baffling to him, and he will be inclined to think that there is something wrong with his saw. For instance, quartz crystal and agate are both quartz with a grade of 7 on the Mohs scale of hardness. The diamond saw usually saws through a quartz crystal with the ease of a cheese slicer cutting through a cheese. But when the agate is presented to the saw, the going

is much slower because its structure is cryptocrystalline and it does not break down as easily as the brittle quartz crystal. One would think that jade, being between 6 and 7 in hardness, would cut more easily than agate, but because of its toughness and compact nature it does not break down as readily as agate and usually takes twice as long to saw.

Further details of treatment of the saw blades themselves will be given in the next two chapters, in which slabbing and trim sawing are discussed separately.

4 · How to Use the Slabbing Saw

When the gemcutting hobby began getting its first impetus about 1940, most amateurs built their own slabbing saws, and some of them even made their own saw blades. The 1940s were wonderful years indeed, and the amateurs tied to their home bases during the war did more to develop the lapidary arts than had been accomplished from the beginning of time. The best ideas of the various homemade equipment were later incorporated in commercial machines, and most of the equipment now offered by dealers comes from thriving businesses started in the back yards of the amateurs of those days.

The slabbing saws offered today are splendid machines; with their new improved blades they give remarkable performance. However, the slabbing saw is not an absolutely necessary piece of equipment for the gemcutter as is the trim saw, used for sectioning the slabs that come from the slabbing saw. One needs room and privacy for a slab saw, for it is a fairly noisy operation, and in order to accomplish much, the saw must often run for many hours.

Because ready-cut slabs of materials were not so available in the early days, practically ever amateur had a slabbing saw of some kind; almost none of them had a trim saw. The situation is reversed today, for slabbed materials are readily available everywhere among the approximately 6,500 dealers serving the gemcutting fraternity. Not all amateurs have a slab saw, but practically every one of them has a trim saw. Most of the "one-man-band" types of lapidary outfits to be described later include a trim saw in their assembly.

But if you have the room for it, in a place where it will not disturb the family or the neighbors, the authors urge you to purchase a slabbing saw, for no piece of lapidary equipment offers so much fun. If you have never actually seen a rough rock slabbed into beautiful slices, it will be difficult for you to understand just how ugly and uninspiring some rocks can be on the outside and how marvelously interesting and beautiful they can be on the inside (fig. 4–1). The novice experiencing these things for the first time finds a new adventure in his life. When you have tramped the hills and desert valleys and found and brought home rocks that you hoped were good, there is hardly any greater anticipation in life than when you clamp a big rock into the saw and proceed to take slices from it—just like slicing a loaf of bread. When the whine of the saw announces that the first cut is about to drop off, the heart races faster, and

Fig. 4–1 Most petrified wood from Arizona is highly colored. This slab is yellow, light tan, reddish orange, and brown. (*Courtesy, Pansy D. Kraus,* Lapidary Journal)

when the parting comes, the average sawyer picks up the slab with avid interest. There are many hobbyists who enjoy slabbing so much that they concentrate on collecting unusual rocks and slabbing them only. Some persons have accumulated rather large collections of unusual and interesting slabs.

DESCRIPTION OF THE SAW

A rock slabbing saw (fig. 4–2) is little different from a woodworking saw in construction. However, in operation the saw blade must run through a coolant to eliminate the generated heat. The coolant is sometimes also referred to as a lubricant, because it does serve the purpose of cleaning off the bits of rock that

accumulate on the blade during the sawing process.

The saw must therefore be enclosed in a boxlike tank to hold the coolant, and the tank must be covered with a hood so that the coolant is not splashed over the operator or the vicinity of the saw. There are many coolants and just as many schools of opinion about them. They all seem to serve the purpose, but the ideal coolant is one that is odorless and fire resistant. Most of the coolants contain oil, and there is always some danger of fire. The best commercial product that the authors have used appears to be Corvus oil, a product of Texaco. It is a little difficult to obtain through regular Texaco service stations and must be secured in a five-gallon container from a Texaco wholesale depot. In some cases station operators will order it for a customer. This product has a low flash point so that it is practically fireproof because it is highly fire resistant.

The commonest form of coolant used in slabbing saws is a 50-50 mixture of kerosene and No. 20 grade engine oil. Nothing has been devised that is better than this combination, but it is objectionably smelly and does present a fire hazard. There are also a number of soluble oil products available from dealers, and there is even a preparation for making kerosene odorless.

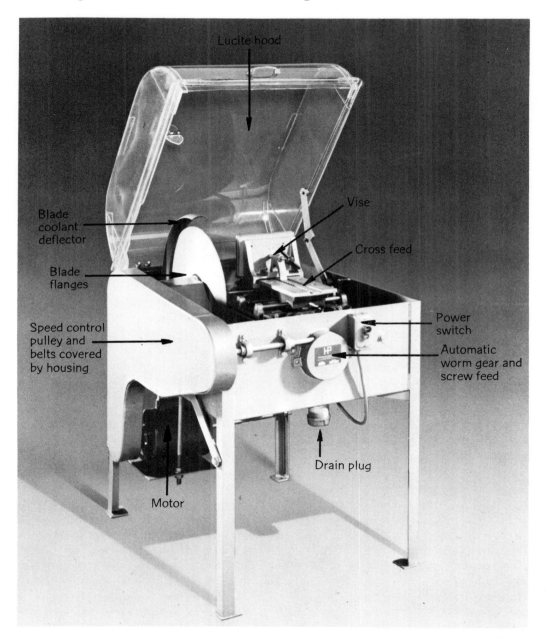

Fig. 4–2 Nomenclature of the slabbing saw. (*Courtesy, Highland Park Manufacturing Co.*)

The coolant should be removed and strained at frequent intervals, for dirty coolant is hard on blades and makes them wear much faster. Many sawyers make their own arrangements for pumping clean oil directly to the saw blade, and they also rig a filtering arrangement.

CUTTING THE SLABS

In the accompanying illustrations the reader will see the viselike arrangement for holding the rock and the cross feed apparatus for advancing the rock to a position for each subsequent slice after the first (fig. 4–3). The rock should be studied for the best possible result, for certain rocks with special properties, like tigereye and labradorite, should be cut so that the top of the finished stones, coming from the surface of the slabs, will show the chatoyancy of the stones. Jasper, wood, agate, and any rocks with special markings should be studied and sliced to get the best effect.

Be sure that the rock you are going to saw is good solid material, for if it should break while being sawed it could damage the expensive blade. Having clamped the rock securely in the carriage, advance the rock by hand until it almost touches the blade, engage the feed, then close the saw, and make the initial cut until it is approximately $1/2''$ (1.3 cm) deep. When the clean initial cut has been made, the blade should be backed out from the cut, the feed reengaged, and the saw restarted. A weight or screw feed arrangement will continue to feed the rock to the saw blade, but some saws come equipped with a hydraulic arrangement which feeds with a consistent pressure. A weight feed should be adjusted to the size of the rock being sawed: a light pressure feeds slowly, a heavy pressure feeds rapidly. The hardness and the toughness of the material being sawed will have a great deal to do with the na-

ture of the speed at which material can be sawed. For example, in sawing jade, the feed should be set at the slowest rate of advance, while for relatively soft materials it should be set at the fastest rate.

The greatest care should be exercised not to start a saw cut against a slanting surface, which will tend to cramp the edge of the saw sideways and at the same time serve to break out the diamond bits from one side of the saw blade. If necessary, before clamping the rock in the saw, either make a lateral saw cut across the surface to be sawed at right angles to the intended course of the multiple cuts or grind a flat area on which to start the saw. Attention to this detail will greatly lengthen saw life.

THICKNESS OF BLADE AND THICKNESS OF CUT

Manifestly, when you are sawing quite valuable materials, such as some agates and jades, which may cost all the way from several dollars to as much as $50 a pound, the width of the kerf or saw cut is an important factor. Many hobbyists have secured relatively thin copper or steel blades of $12''$ (30.5 cm) up to even $16''$ (40.6 cm) diameter for the special purpose of sawing such fine materials with a minimum of loss. In general, the larger the saw blade, the thicker will be the kerf which it takes, and the converse is also true; for more valuable materials, seek the smallest and thinnest blade available for the job.

Slabs are sawed from $3/16''$ (0.48 cm) to $1/4''$ (0.64 cm) thick for average material. It is poor economy to make the slabs too thin, for then there is not the proper amount of thickness out of which to cut the various forms of cabochons. Slabs $1/8''$ (0.32 cm) thick are to be frowned upon.

Unless you are a commercial operator cutting slabs for sale, speed is not essential, for too much speed and pressure wears out blades much faster. A promi-

Fig. 4–3a Check frequently for blade and carriage alignment and bearing wear. (*Courtesy, Highland Park Manufacturing Co.*)

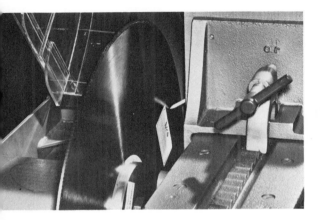

Fig. 4–3b With the pointer in the vise, check the same spot on the blade with the carriage first at the front edge, than at the rear. The blade is rotated so the pointer contacts the same spot. (*Courtesy, Highland Park Manufacturing Co.*)

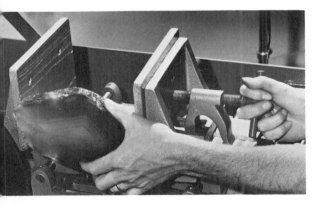

Fig. 4–3c Be sure the workpiece is held firmly in the vise and will not work loose during cutting. Start your cut by hand so that the blade is centered in the workpiece. The surface of the workpiece must not deflect the blade from the cutting plane; at all costs, avoid side pressure on the blade. Side pressure causes "dishing." (*Courtesy, Highland Park Manufacturing Co.*)

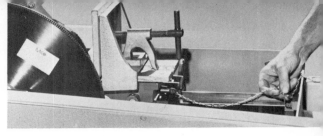

Fig. 4–3d Adjust the automatic cut-off trip chain for the length of cut (*Courtesy, Highland Park Manufacturing Co.*)

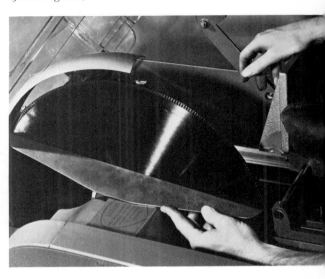

Fig. 4–3e Reverse your blade occasionally. "Sharpen" it when needed by cutting a piece of sandstone or 220-grit grinding wheel stub. Use a straightedge frequently to check blade straightness. Stop cutting if the blade becomes damaged. A bent, dished, or warped blade will wear out rapidly. Reverse your blade only if it is recommended by the manufacturer of the blade you are using. (*Courtesy, Highland Park Manufacturing Co.*)

Fig. 4–3f The crank-actuated cross feed vise has a very accurate adjustment for cutting successive slabs to the desired thickness. The carriage is locked in place with a thumb screw. (*Courtesy, Highland Park Manufacturing Co.*)

Fig. 4–4 Crown makes two sizes of slab-grabbers. The smaller one has straight jaws. The larger one has shallow V-shaped jaws for holding nub ends that are curved. (*Courtesy, Crown Manufacturing Co.*)

nent manufacturer of saw blades suggests that a 12″ blade should be run at 400 rpm to cut through an agate 1″ (2.5 cm) in size in eight minutes; the same saw will cut 1″ (2.5 cm) in four minutes at 800 rpm. A slow saw will turn out more slabs than the average gemcutter can possibly work into finished gems. The speeds can be varied by a three-stage pulley and V-belt. The standard ¼ or ⅓ H.P. motor used in saw operation has a standard 2″ pulley on the motor shaft and runs at a speed of 1,725 rpm. If the V-belt is attached to a 2″ (5 cm) pulley on the arbor, the speed remains the same. If the same belt is attached to a 6″ (15 cm) pulley on the arbor, the speed will be reduced to 505 rpm. By attaching a three- or four-stage pulley to the motor shaft, many combinations of belt positions may be made to give varied speeds. These speeds are given in the Appendix.

After a large rock has been sawed, the operator is left with the ends, or the "heels of the loaf." If the material is valuable it is suggested that the cutter use a "slab-grabber" which permits these nubbin ends to be held in the vise for further cutting (fig. 4–4).

DISHING OF THE SAW AND ITS CORRECTION

Care should always be taken to see that, at the finish of a slab, the material

is not allowed to slide past the saw. Many times the slab will break from the rock and leave a sliver on the rock just as the saw is completing the slice. This can be avoided to a large extent by hand feeding at the end of the slabbing process or by installing an automatic stop. A tap with a hammer will remove such a sliver.

If there is a sliver and it runs past the blade it will push the blade away from the vise. As the sliver is usually near the outer edge or bottom of the rock, it will slide past the blade from the outside toward the arbor hole and cause a metal spinning process in so doing. As it spins near the arbor hole the blade punches outward and becomes dished. With continued cutting this condition becomes exaggerated and increases the dishing of the saw, so that at each starting of the saw the cut is started at an angle instead of a flat face. The blade then becomes worn on the inside, or vise side, the diamond is loosened and lost, and the blade becomes useless, because it cannot cut when diamond settings are on only one side.

The saw blade should be taken from the arbor once in a while. Use a 1-foot (30 cm) steel ruler and place it on the blade across the arbor hole or axis. Do this in all directions and on both sides of the saw. If the saw shows a dish effect, it must be corrected. Place the blade on a flat iron surface and tap it lightly with a ball peen hammer from about 3″ (7.6 cm) in from the rim to the rim itself, turning the blade as you hammer toward the rim. *Never use the hammer near the arbor hole.* If this does not eliminate the dish, repeat the process on the *opposite* side of the blade and keep repeating until the blade is again absolutely flat.

There are many problems that will arise in sawing that cannot be discussed here for lack of space, but should you have problems that you cannot readily solve, it would be wise to contact the manufacturer of the blade you are using. Most saw blade manufacturers now maintain a blade repair department and will repair your blade for a modest fee or will recommend the proper solution to your problem. Some- times a blade cannot be repaired and must be replaced. If you anticipate sending a blade in for repair, always contact the manufacturer first, and they will tell you the proper procedure for returning the blade.

5· How to Use the Trim Saw

Using the trim saw is a far different experience than using the slabbing saw, for the sawing is done at high speed and the material is fed into the saw by hand. You can remove unwanted material far faster on a trim saw than you can on the grinders.

Mark the outline of the cabochon on the slab with an aluminum or bronze pencil by using a template, or draw your own design. Lead-pencil marks will wash off, so use the aluminum or bronze pencil (which you can make from a piece of stout wire).

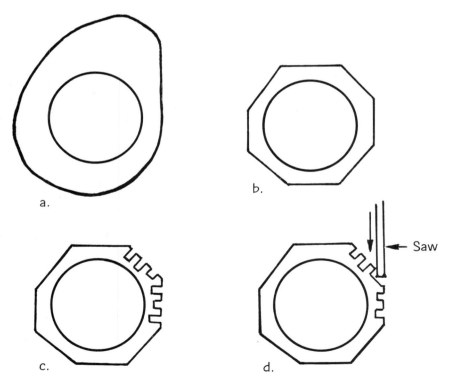

Fig. 5–1 Using the trim saw to saw out, notch, and trim cabochon blanks.

Fig. 5–2 A carving of a leaf-shaped dish hollowed out on a trim saw.

Saw off the unwanted material as indicated in figure 5–1b. Then proceed to saw notches as in figure 5–1c, and carefully trim off the "gear teeth" as in figure 5–1d. Do not saw too close to the outline of your cabochon. Many hobbyists no longer take the time to use notches but simply make successive straight cuts close to the scribed lines on the slab. If the hollowing out process is desired, then the notching system of using the trim saw would be applicable.

Saw blades on trim saws are smaller and thinner than on slabbing saws, and they can be run at far greater speeds. The problem of breaking them in is the same as with the larger slabbing blades. They should be run through a section of ordinary brick so that the excess metal on the periphery of the blade can wear down to the point where the embedded diamond is exposed, for the saw will not be effective until the diamond gets its chance to bite into the material. The coolant or lubricant is the same as that mentioned in chapter 4—a 50-50 mixture of kerosene and light engine oil, or the Corvus oil of Texaco.

The trim saw is a very versatile tool;

through experience the operator will find it useful in many lapidary problems. It can be used in many carving processes and in hollowing out techniques. Because of the roundness of the blade itself, a number of cuts can be made in a slab and then similar cuts made at right angles to them. This will leave a lot of "teeth" which can be taken out with pliers. The depression can then be ground to shape, sanded, and polished—and you have an ashtray (fig. 5–2)!

You will soon learn to plan your saw cuts by laying them out accurately on the slab with a metal pencil, allowing the width of a saw blade between each blank you wish to get out of the material. Remember to allow for the curvature of the saw itself. The underside of the cut will be farther advanced than what you can see on top.

When you are planning a matched set of pieces (as for a bracelet) out of one slab of material so that they will all match in color and pattern, careful planning and marking in advance are essential. When you start into a piece of jade that costs you $5 a square inch (80¢

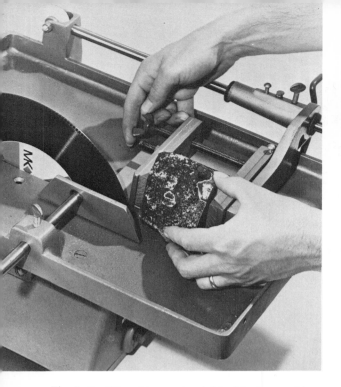

Fig. 5–3a The object to be slabbed is clamped in a vise. The cut is started by hand pressure. (*Courtesy, Highland Park Manufacturing Co.*)

Fig. 5–3b A bucket of sand is attached to the gravity feed cable to maintain even pressure throughout. The coolant deflector and canopy are put in place. (*Courtesy, Highland Park Manufacturing Co.*)

Fig. 5–3c The gravity feed is removed, and the cut is finished by gentle hand pressure. (*Courtesy, Highland Park Manufacturing Co.*)

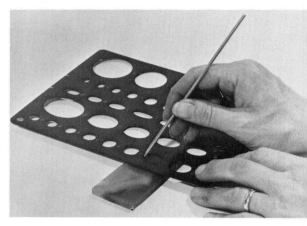

Fig. 5–3d A template is used to mark the shape desired on the slab. (*Courtesy, Highland Park Manufacturing Co.*)

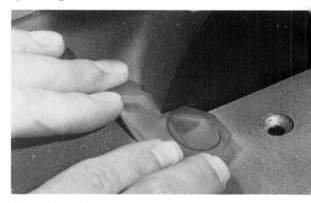

Fig. 5–3e The vise is removed and the slab held by hand to be trimmed to the scribed shape. All cuts must be made in a straight line. Be careful not to put side pressure on the blade. Successive straight cuts approximate curved lines that will be finished on a grinding wheel. Make all trim saw cuts outside the template mark. (*Courtesy, Highland Park Manufacturing Co.*)

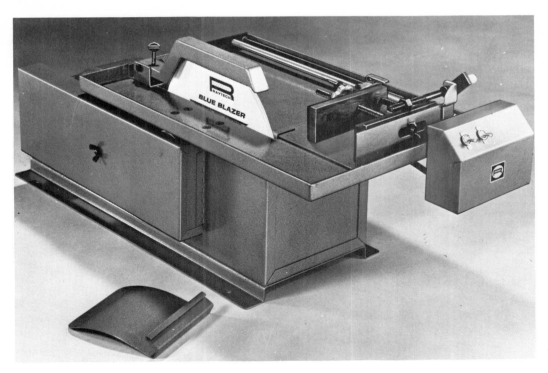

Fig. 5–4 The Raytech 10″ (25.4-cm) slab and trim saw has a cross feed screw and is a power feed. (*Courtesy, Raytech Industries, Inc.*)

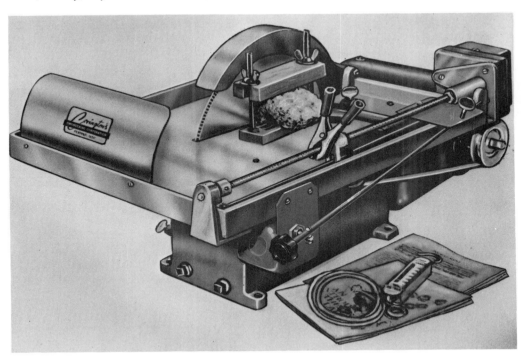

Fig. 5–5 The Covington 8″ to 10″ (20.3-cm to 25.4-cm) heavy duty trim saw has the motor mounted directly on the back of the saw. (*Courtesy, Covington Engineering Corp.*)

a square centimeter), you will want to know exactly where you are going. Because of the expense of some materials, many cutters have two trim saws: a large, husky saw, with a large, thick blade for rough work, and a small, high-speed slitter with a blade only 0.012″ (0.03-cm) thick—little more than the thickness of one of the pages in this book.

Many of the modern trim saws are designed so that they can also be used to slab small pieces of rough gem material which are too small to be slabbed in the larger saws. The usual method of using a trim saw is to make successive *straight* cuts until most of the excess material has been eliminated and the general shape of the cabochon is obtained. Do not at any time try to cut a curved line; standard trim saws are not designed to do so, and you will ruin your saw blade. The illustrations show the proper uses of the trim saw (Figs. 5–3a–e).

CARE OF THE TRIM SAW

By this we mean the care of the trim saw mechanism itself rather than the diamond saw blade. Before you start to use a new saw, see that it is properly lubricated. Some saws are fitted with "sealed for life" ball bearings. Do not lubricate these. Do not think that a squirt of light oil will help them do their job. This only dilutes the proper grease and may cause later trouble. Oilite-type self-lubricating bearings of a com-

Fig. 5–6 The Rock Rascal is a 6″ (15.2-cm) trim saw for trimming out cabochons by hand. (*Courtesy, A. D. McBurney*)

pressed bronze powder type can stand an occasional squirt of oil. If the bearings are fitted with a grease cup, see that it is kept full and changed when necessary. If there is a Zerk or an Alemite fitting, use a grease gun with the proper type lubricant for lightweight machine bearings. The shafts which carry saws need to be lubricated properly to keep them from wearing and getting sideplay, which can cause bad wear of the blade and crooked cuts. Remember to oil motor bearings with the proper light oil and keep belts tight, but not so tight as to cause bearing wear. Motors need ventilation, so do not cover them completely, and keep oil spray and water from them.

Several modern trim saws are illustrated and described in figures 5–4, 5–5, and 5–6.

6 · Cutting and Polishing Cabochons

Long experience in attending many gem shows in all parts of the country indicates that the cutting and polishing of cabochons is the form of lapidary activity most favored by the amateur gemcutter. It is usually the first form of gem cutting attempted, and it is the most rewarding in terms of the great variety of shapes, colors, and materials that can be used. Many of the materials used for cabochons can be gathered personally, and if they are purchased, they are far less costly than the crystal types of gems used in faceting. Cabochon cutting allows wide latitude for the artist to use imagination and selection.

The word *artist* is used at this point because a lapidary really is an artist more than a craftsman. Every man has within him a desire to be an artist; usually this is an unfulfilled desire in most lives because of the pressure of earning a living. While it is true that most of us cannot become great singers, musicians, painters, sculptors, composers, writers, and so forth because of a lack of some specific talent, it is within the ability of nearly every man or woman to become a competent lapidary and artist in stone within a very short time. For it will not be long before a beginner at the art of the lapidary can be producing gems that will amaze his

friends and bring him the recognition and admiration for which he yearns. This is one of the secrets of the wildfire growth of the gemcutting hobby during the last 35 years. The lapidary immediately ascends in the esteem of his friends and the community; he becomes important.

For an early try for success and achievement of immediate happiness, the making of a series of cabochons in different shapes is suggested. Indeed, the majority of amateur gemcutters never pass beyond this stage but continue to garner their gemcraft happiness from this one medium alone.

Cabochons are cut from slices of rock that have been produced by the sawing process described in chapter 4. These slices should be $3/16''$ (0.48 cm) to $1/4''$ (0.64 cm) thick for light stones and as large as $3/8''$ (0.97 cm) for heavier stones. Most ring stones should be cut from the light slices, and stones intended for pendants, brooches, bola mounts, and so forth should be cut from the heavier slabs. In purchasing slabs from dealers, one should buy the thicker slabs so that all manner of stones can be cut from them. When lighter stones are desired they will just require a little more grinding.

Slabs of material should be absolutely

25

flat, and all projections and rough edges should be ground away. It is not necessary to remove the saw marks from the flat surface, for this requires considerable wasted time. Saw marks on the individual blanks can be removed later.

MARKING THE SLABS

A close study of the slabbed material should be made before determining where the blank for the gem will be taken. After selecting the pattern, the color, and the design of the stone desired, a mark is then made with an aluminum pencil, using a template to outline the gem. The aluminum marks will not wash away while grinding (see fig. 6–6). Pencils can be purchased from dealers, but they can be made easily from a 6″ (15.2-cm) piece of aluminum wire or hack-sawed from a ¹/₈″ (0.32-cm) sheet, then ground to a fine point on the side of the grinding wheel (fig. 6–1). One pencil will last a long time. Lean it away from the template when marking.

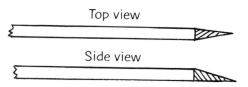

Fig. 6–1 Square marking pencil. Hack-saw square pencils out of a ¹/₈″ (0.32-cm) aluminum or bronze sheet. Keep them sharp by grinding them on the *side* of the wheel.

A piece of brass welding rod also makes a very good marking pencil since it is already round and can be cut to a length of 6″ (15.2 cm) or longer, if a longer pencil is desired (see fig. 6–2). The brass pencil, like the aluminum, will not wash off the slab.

Templates containing the various shapes and sizes used in standard mountings for jewelry can be purchased at dealers' shops for very little (fig. 6–2). The beginner is urged, however, to determine for himself the size of the stone he wants, according to the patterns he "sees" in his slab and according to the whim of the moment (figs. 6–3, 6–4, and

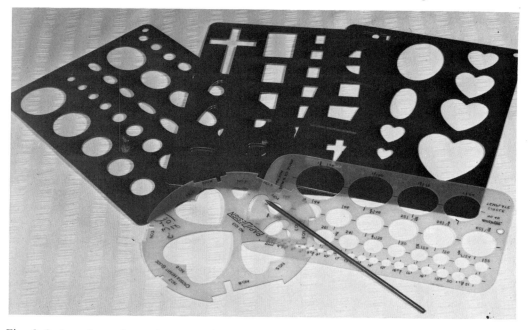

Fig. 6–2 A variety of templates may be purchased from your local rock shop. The marking pencil is a piece of brass welding rod with a point sharpened by grinding on the side of a wheel. (*Photo by John Washalaski*)

Fig. 6–3 Finished cabochons of agate, carnelian, and tourmaline. (*Photo by W. E. Davies*)

6–5). If the stone is to be mounted, then a template is suggested, but if the cutter merely desires to achieve a beautiful stone he should free-lance in his designing. This procedure offers more fun and satisfaction, and it develops latent artistic talent.

Templates come in various shapes of round, oval, and rectangular perforations, with the sizes indicated in millimeters (mm). Thus a 15 x 18 oval is 15 mm wide by 18 mm long, and the resulting gem will fit a commercial mounting of that size. The gemcutter should have available at all times several catalogs of the firms marketing mountings so that if he intends to mount his finished gem in a ring or a pin, he can make a selection of the piece desired and then cut the stone to the size indicated in the catalog illustration by using the template for accuracy. Many gemcutters later become silvercrafters and make their own

mountings. Cutting to standard millimeter sizes then becomes unimportant as the mounting is made to fit the stone rather than the stone cut to fit a particular mounting.

It is well to mark the slab with several blanks so that they can all be sawed out at one time for later use, or for sale or swapping (fig. 6–6). After the blanks are sawed they are further trimmed in the trim saw and notched and nibbled as indicated in figure 6–7. Nibbling with pliers (fig. 6–8) is dangerous, however, for it can hurt one's fingers and damage the stone unless one acquires skill—only too often gained at the expense of pain and costly material. While the process is usually suggested in gemcutting classes and articles on the subject, the authors long ago abandoned nibbling and now depend on the grinding wheel and skillful sawing to remove material.

Do not trim saw too close to the out-

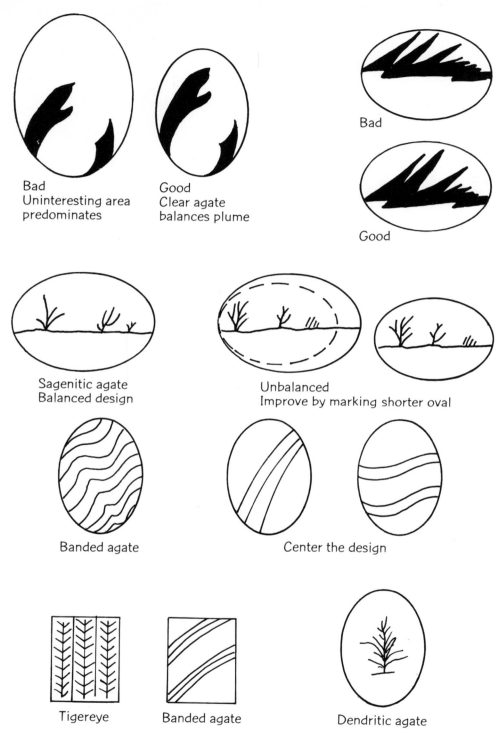

Bad
Uninteresting area
predominates

Good
Clear agate
balances plume

Bad

Good

Sagenitic agate
Balanced design

Unbalanced
Improve by marking shorter oval

Banded agate

Center the design

Tigereye

Banded agate

Dendritic agate

Fig. 6–4 Use balance in selecting the pattern in your cabochon.

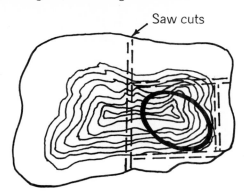

Fig. 6–5 Selecting the pattern.

Step 1: Blank sawed out

Step 2: Trimmed

Step 3: Notched

Step 4: Nibbled

Fig. 6–7 These are the four steps necessary to nibble a cabochon blank.

line. After the trim sawing operation is finished, the blank should be held in the fingers, applied with fair pressure to the 100-grit (coarse) grinding wheel, and shaped to within a pencil line of the aluminum marking. This slight excess can be removed later in the sanding operation.

DOPPING THE STONE

The stone is now ready for dopping. Many methods have been suggested for dopping, and the authors have never observed two individuals doing it exactly alike. There is really no one right way, as in faceting, or wrong way. The purpose of dopping is to place the stone on the end of a stick or other vehicle so that the lapidary will have greater facility in handling it. He also obtains greater safety and visibility. It is impor-

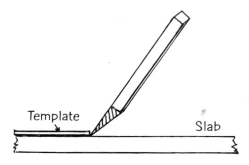

Fig. 6–6 Marking the slab.

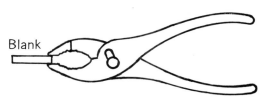

Fig. 6–8 A pair of ordinary extension pliers can be used for "nibbling" of blanks.

tant to have visibility, for if you cannot *see* what you are doing, you do not *know* what you are doing. In free cutting, without dopping, the fingers often hide the work.

The trick in dopping a stone is to get it on the dop and have it *stay* there. This is a problem that is often aggravating and discouraging to the beginner, for when the stone flies off the dop it is potentially dangerous, and many times the stone is destroyed in the process.

It is wise to dop several stones at a time, and when this is done, the wax should be placed in a small can on top of a self-made "stove," as illustrated in figure 6–9. Improved varieties of dopping wax can be secured from supply dealers. Buy at least two sticks—one to be broken into small pieces for the can, one to be kept in stick form for the dopping of single stones. Some persons like to dop a series of stones all at one time and prefer to use one of the several commercially made dopping pots similar to the one shown in figure 6–10.

Place an ordinary alcohol lamp under the "lid" of the stove. When the wax has melted to a creamy consistency, dip the dop stick into the wax and twirl it about until a large glob adheres to it. Meanwhile, place the stones to be dopped on the stove lid for warming, for a cold

Fig. 6–10 A commercially made dopping wax pot. (*Courtesy, A. D. McBurney*)

stone will not adhere to the wax since the coldness sets the wax.

Pick up the hot stone with the waxed dop stick and set it by shaping with moistened fingers until the stone is set as illustrated in figure 6–11. Do not touch the hot wax with unmoistened fingers. Taper the wax beneath the stone for maximum visibility and then set the dopped stone upright in a can of sand or in a board with holes that you have prepared for the purpose. After the stone is cool, it is ready for grinding.

When a single stone is being dopped instead of a series, time is saved by holding a stick of wax in one hand and the dop stick in the other. Thrust the end of

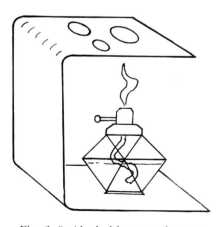

Fig. 6–9 Alcohol lamp and stove.

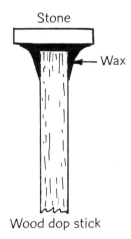

Fig. 6–11 Dopping.

the wax stick into the flame of the alcohol lamp and twirl it to keep it from dripping. Dig into the softened mass with the end of the dop stick until enough adheres for dopping purposes. Heat the stone by passing it over the flame a few times, using a pair of tweezers to hold it. The fingers can be spared possible burning by having a piece of steel around the shop. When the wax adheres to the end of the dop stick, the stick can be rolled on the steel, and the coldness of the steel will immediately set and shape the wax so that it can be manipulated more easily. Lacking a piece of steel, it is suggested that the cutter buy a wide-bladed putty knife or other bladed tool and use its surface for the rolling technique. Many lapidaries use a block of cold rock.

Many items are used for dop sticks, but experience in observing many lapidaries, as well as personal experience, indicates that the most satisfactory dop is a 6″ (15.2-cm) length of ordinary wood doweling. Buy several lengths in several diameters at your local lumberyard and cut them to the size that feels most comfortable to your hand. Dealers sell wood dops in bundles for very little. The best sizes are 1/4″ (0.64 cm) and 3/8″ (0.97 cm).

TYPES OF GRINDERS

Your cabochon blank is now ready for grinding and polishing, but before discussing these procedures, we would like to offer some advice on various types of grinders now on the market. In the accompanying illustrations are shown several of the leading types of vertical outfits of the "pot" type of grinder. Horizontal running saws, grinding wheels, sanding disks, and polishing wheels can be attached. These machines are the lowest in price and are ideal for the apartment or trailer dweller whose available space is at a premium. Some of these outfits contain a small diamond-charged saw blade and clamp-vise attachment so that one can cut up small, rough pieces of stones into small slabs. For the man with garage or hobby shop space, there are many types of vertical machines that are more costly but also more substantial and versatile. Several of these are described in figures 6–12 to 6–21. If you are mechanically inclined, you can build a satisfactory outfit of your own by buying an arbor and mounting it with the required wheels. A man with ingenuity and the tools to carry out his ideas, by studying commercial outfits, can devise many schemes for homemade equipment.

In response to the increasing demand for diamond products and equipment which can be used for *all* phases of gem cutting, whether your choice is cabochons, faceting, carving, or novelties, diamond products suited to your uses have been developed. For many years, diamond was considered a necessity only if you were faceting or cutting and polishing star rubies or sapphires. This is no longer true. Today many gemcutters, especially those specializing in cabochons or carving, are finding that by using diamond products and equipment they can more readily sand and polish some of the special materials which formerly presented a great many problems in achieving a fine polish.

Because of the wide range of uses and the wide variety of diamond products and equipment, as well as the combined and overlapping uses of diamond from one phase to another of the cutting and polishing of gem materials, a discussion of diamond products will be included in a later chapter.

Regardless of the type of machine used, some method must be devised by the cutter to bring water to the grinding wheels, for the gemstones must be ground wet so that they will keep cool, as the intense heat of the grinding operation will crack the stones. In the pot types, this can be achieved by

Fig. 6–12 This Gem Maker is designed so that the water attachment can be taken off and the unit laid on the back side with the dials on top; the slotted plate shown is then inserted in the cutout of the framework to form the table for converting to a saw. The water tank is mounted in the hole shown on the left of the photograph. (*Courtesy, Earth Treasures*)

Fig. 6–13 This Gemlap unit is furnished complete with the accessory kit shown in figure 6–14. Diamond grinding wheels designed for horizontal use may be employed. (*Photo by Jack M. Richards; courtesy, Brad's Rock Shop*)

Fig. 6–14 This accessory kit for the Gemlap unit can be obtained with either the 6″ (15.2-cm) or 8″ (20.3-cm) grinding wheels and sanding disks. (*Photo by Jack M. Richards; courtesy, Brad's Rock Shop*)

Fig. 6–15 The Rock Rascal model shown here is designed for two grinding wheels and no saw. (*Courtesy, A. D. McBurney*)

Fig. 6–16 A Crown arbor unit with an 8″ (20.3-cm) grinding wheel and a sanding drum combined for compactness. Arbors may be purchased separately. (*Courtesy, Crown Manufacturing Co.*)

Fig. 6–17 Basic Poly arbors can be purchased so that separate grinding and sanding units can be arranged for those who have ample space and wish separate units. (*Courtesy, Crown Manufacturing Co.*)

Fig. 6–18 The Cab-Mate shown here has the saw attachment mounted in place with the accessory units. There is also a preforming device which can be used for preforming cabochons or faceted stones. (*Courtesy, Henry B. Graves Co.*)

Fig. 6–19 Covington makes a belt sander which some prefer to the drum sanders. (*Courtesy, Covington Engineering Corp.*)

Fig. 6–20 This MDR bench model is a complete unit including a trim saw, two grinding wheels, and an end face plate for sanding disks and polishing disk. (*Courtesy, MDR Manufacturing Co.*)

Fig. 6–21 The Highland Park bench model has a sanding drum, two grinding wheels, a cotton flannel buff for polishing, and an end face plate which can be used for fine sanding or a leather polishing disk. (*Courtesy, Highland Park Manufacturing Co.*)

Fig. 6–22 Grinding a cabochon. The dop stick is held at an angle and applied just below center on the wheel. Always see that the wheel has plenty of water and use the entire surface to avoid wearing away only the center. (*Photo by Paul Samuelson*)

mounting a drip can over the wheel. In the vertical type, the problem can easily be solved by pouring water in the pan below the wheels but not touching them. Insert one of the new-type synthetic kitchen sponges under the wheels to carry the water to them. Care should be taken to see that idle wheels do not stand in the water, for then they become waterlogged on one side and may fly apart when the machine is started again. Always pull the sponge away from the wheel *before* turning off the power or proceeding to the sanders or polishers. The ingenious can rig up copper or rubber tubing, attached to a faucet, for controlled water drip.

Be sure that you allow the grinding wheels to spin several minutes so that the excess water which has been absorbed by the wheels can be thrown off. The wheels will retain a certain amount of water and if you just pull the sponge or shut off the water and immediately shut off the wheels without allowing them to spin for a short while, the water that is retained by the wheels will gradually seep to the bottom of the stationary wheels, causing them to be out of balance the next time you want to use them. This causes the wheels to be bumpy, and they have a tendency to whip when they are turned on again. Wheels that are out of balance create extra wear on both your arbor and the bearings.

GRINDING THE GEM

You are now ready to grind your gem. The initial grinding should be done on a coarse wheel of 100 grit and the finer grinding on a finer wheel of 220-grit bonded carborundum. Keep in mind that *the higher the number, the finer the grit*.

Hold the dopped stone at an angle between 25° and 30° and apply the stone with firm pressure just below the middle of the running wheel (fig. 6–22). Touch the wheel with a stroking rotating motion and keep moving it around and around and tilting it more and more until it is dome-shaped. This procedure is much like peeling an apple. Grind a flat bevel all around the stone but do not carry this entirely to the base at this stage (fig. 6–23). Now reverse the grinding procedure, from the bevel to the top, and when you get to the top of the cabochon ("bald head") be sure that you leave no flat spot to cause later difficulty in polishing. Use your eye and hold the stone at arm's length, slowly turning the stick in your hand so that you can see an even, sweeping arc. The stone should now have a permanent slight bevel at the bottom so that it can be set in jewelry mounts if that is later desired.

SANDING THE GEM

You will now have a roughed-out gemstone with many scratches on the surface. These must be sanded out with wet sanding cloth made with various sizes of carborundum grits. There are many types of sanders. The drum type is shown in figures 6–24 and 6–25. This machine is also supplied with the disk-type sander, to which disks of sanding cloth may easily be attached.

Much time was formerly spent in changing wheels as one progressed from a coarse grinding stage to a finer one. Today many machines come with disks of sanding cloth and a preparation

known as Peel 'Em Off cement. A thin coating of this cement is applied to the back surface of the disk, and the disk adheres securely to the fast-moving wooden or aluminum wheel, covered

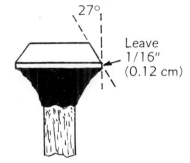

Step 1: Beveling

Step 2: Rounding the top

Step 3: Completing the arc

Step 4: Back Beveling

Fig. 6–23 Four steps in grinding and shaping a cabochon.

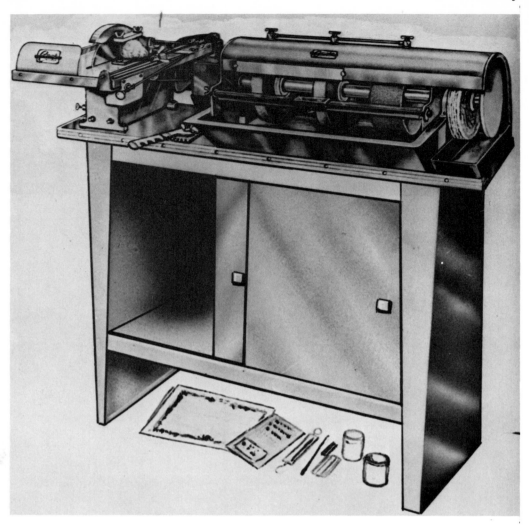

Fig. 6–24 A Covington complete "shop-in-one" unit includes stand and storage cabinet with two motors, one motor for the 10″ (25.4-cm) saw and the second motor for the grinding and polishing unit. (*Courtesy, Covington Engineering Corp.*)

with sponge rubber. When a change to another grit is required, the operator merely peels the cloth off the wheel and slaps on another grade of cloth. These cloths can be interchanged freely and cleanly, and much time and inconvenience are saved by not having to change wheels.

During recent years much has been written about wet sanding versus dry sanding. Twenty years ago wet sanding was practically unheard of, but more and more cutters are now using wet

sanding entirely. A sanding disk revolving at the usual motor speed of 1,750 rpm can generate a lot of heat fast, and the chance of burning or cracking a stone is very great. The dop wax gets hot, and the stone shifts on the dop or flies off altogether and breaks. These dangers are practically eliminated in the wet sanding method.

Wet sanding presents the problem of getting water to the wheels. They should be damp, but not dripping wet or so wet as to throw water all over the operator. This problem is easily solved with a modern spray bottle or an ordinary cheap paint brush. A spray bottle used for window washing is ideal. The beginner should experiment with both wet and dry methods and adopt the one he favors. Touch the stone to the cheek now and then, for the face is more sensitive to heat than are the hands. If the stone is hot to the touch it should be allowed to cool before proceeding. Pressure creates heat, and the pressure in

the sanding operation should be less than half the pressure used in the grinding operation.

It is at the sanders that the operator achieves the true shape of his stone. Here he removes obvious bumps and the scratches left from grinding. Care should be exercised at this point to avoid cracking the stone with too much heat, and any visible cracks should be completely sanded away. Stones should be sanded first on the 120-grit cloth and

Fig. 6–25 A Highland Park "one-man-band," a complete shop, includes a 10″ (25.4-cm) saw, 8″ (20.3-cm) grinding wheels, a sanding drum, a muslin polishing buff, a leather polishing face plate, and two motors. It is also available in a bench model. (*Courtesy, Highland Park Manufacturing Co.*)

then on the 220-grit. Many operators use 400 and 600-grit cloths in addition, but this is not necessary on all stones. If scratches persist, it may be necessary to return to the fine grinding wheel for a better grinding job, for the scratches may be deep-seated.

After the stone has been sanded satisfactorily, the operator should carefully wash both the stone and his hands, for if he proceeds to the polishers and carries one small grain of grit which becomes embedded in the soft polishing wheels, he will forever after have difficulty with his polishing because of the contamination.

POLISHING THE GEM

There are many types of polishers, but felt and leather buffs are preferred. These should be kept wet by applying water with a sponge, sufficient to keep the running buff wet at all times. Of the many types of polishing agents used through the years, the choice has now narrowed to two for all general purposes—cerium oxide or tin oxide. These products will satisfactorily polish most gem materials used for cabochons, but some gems (such as jade, rhodonite, turquoise, and malachite) present special problems that are covered in chapter 8. Cerium oxide appears to be the choice of an overwhelming majority of cabochon cutters.

Place about one tablespoon (14.78 cc) of cerium oxide in a shallow dish or vessel and cover with enough water to make a creamy paste. Add more water and the paste will remain at the bottom of the dish. Use a small paint brush to apply the polish to the running buff. Touch the brush to the center of the wheel and stroke it to the edge to distribute the powder evenly over the entire surface.

The dopped stone is now applied with very little pressure (much less than in the sanding operation) to the felt buff and rotated with a sweeping motion until it picks up a polish, and powder begins to cake on the stone. Wet the wheel again and dip the stone in the water in the dish. Do not let the polish get too thick, but keep it wet enough to run on the wheel and keep from caking. Now and then stir the mixture in the dish with the other end of the dop stick to get more powder into the water. The written word cannot convey to the reader the exact formula for the final polishing; only experience can help the operator until he comes to polish almost by instinct. It will not take long before the beauty of the gem comes up in the polished surface, and *that* is the moment of the great thrill for the gemcutter— the thing he has been working for and the fun he has been seeking.

At this stage the gem should be examined with a strong glass and any visual scratches polished out until the finish is mirrorlike. Hold the stone under a strong overhead incandescent light. When you can rotate the stone in your fingers and see a clear image of the light in the entire surface, you know you are finished. If there is a blurring or fuzziness, or scratches can still be seen, you will know you still have work to do. If you cannot correct the scratches or fuzziness with further polishing, then a return to the sander is indicated.

REMOVING THE GEM FROM THE DOP

When you are sure that your stone is finished, it can be removed from the dop by holding it over the alcohol flame until it is warm, but not hot. Do not hold it directly in the flame, but dowse it in and out until the wax is soft. Then lift it off with the fingers or pry it loose with a knife. Surplus wax can be removed from the stone with a swab of cloth, wet with a little acetone, procurable from your local druggist. Solox alcohol can also be used and is satisfactory. If you have several stones to be undopped and you have plenty of time, a wise, safe, and clean method is to place them in a pan of water and ice cubes. The stones will soon drop to the bottom of the pan. Or they can be left in the freezer compartment of the refrigerator for a short time.

Remember, there are no "pretty good" gems; an amateur should be satis-fied only with *perfect* gems, and a stone does not become a gem until it *is* perfect. It does take time to achieve perfection, but that is why the amateur is usually a better lapidary than a professional working for the market. To the professional time is of the essence, while to the amateur perfection and fun are of the essence. (See color insert.)

7 · How to Cut Star and Cat's-Eye Gems

The phenomena of asteriated or star stones and of cat's-eye gems which have a single moving ray of light across their surface have always been of great interest, but it is odd that the star material was tossed aside as worthless in the Far East until comparatively recent times. Only within the last hundred years have these beautiful gems come to be appreciated fully.

Asterism in any gemstone material is caused by regularly oriented inclusions which follow the natural crystalline formation of the type of material in which they are formed. For instance, in sapphire, the mineral corundum forms in a bipyramidal hexagonal form; that is, two pyramids of six sides each join together at the base to present tapering crystals, if they are of ideal shape. A great many are not, of course. However misshapen the exterior may be, the interior often presents the correct order of faces in hexagonal form which appear to have grown outward in six planes around a central starting point.

If the material formed naturally, and without any pressure or infusion of other foreign mineral matter, the resulting crystal might conceivably be sapphire of clear facet grade, or with a little change in the metallic pigmentation and crystal habit, the ruby. But, in nature, these ideal conditions are not always present, and the crystal grows under duress, in the presence of other minerals, particularly rutile (titanium dioxide), so that inclusions of these slim needles of a foreign mineral form parallel to the growth lines of the crystal. Some of the inclusions show as tubes which at one time may have contained such hairlike crystals, but are left after the rutile formed and was dissolved away.

The alchemy of nature is very diverse, and exactly how the process works is not always clear. It is enough that we can look at a thin slice of such material under the low-power magnification of a microscope and see that there are not simply flat bands of these inclusions running parallel to one of the six sides of the hexagon, but in fact there are masses of matted microscopic crystals of included rutile, all oriented to one or another of the six prism planes. It is therefore only natural, considering their arrangement, that they reflect light into three chatoyant lines, crossing at the center, onto a polished cabochon or, ideally speaking, a hemisphere. Moreover, there are to be observed 12-rayed stars, due to twinning, and these are not uncommon in the Australian material. On careful scrutiny it will be

40

seen that six rays are golden, while the intermediate six are bluish green. This might be due to the fact that sapphire can be twinned. Indeed, coloration can control crystal form; for example, (although basically the same mineral) the crystal habit of sapphire (used as the basis for fig. 7–1) is different from the crystal habit of ruby. In addition, when one tends to combine with the other in producing a rich purple, the cut gem is found to have a very delicate balance in the property of color absorption and will react similarly to alexandrite under various types of light sources. Indeed, it may well be that stones of this sort have been reported erroneously as "star alexandrite."

If you have the internal formation of a sapphire crystal in mind, now glance at the diagram and note that a perfectly centered star sapphire can be cut from *any portion of a crystal,* so long as the base is truly parallel to a cut made at right angles across the "C" or long axis of the crystal. Everyday lapidary practice (as performed by the Ceylonese gemcutters, for instance) is to make a centered star from any part of the rough crystal—top, side, or bottom—provided, of course, that the material is infused with the microscopic inclusions that are the basic cause of asterism.

Correct procedure is, therefore, quite simple, and the only trick is to orient the saw cut for the base of the intended cabochon at an exact right angle to the vertical crystallographic or "C" axis, paralleling the girdle of the intended cabochon's dome to this saw cut. An off-center star is therefore really inexcusable and is produced only through the avarice of the original Oriental cutter or carelessness. Many of the Ceylon star sapphires after importation must be recut here, to properly center the star, before they can be used. There is only one merit to this precutting by the Ceylonese: it does at least locate and guarantee a star of sorts in the material,

though stones treated in this manner of cutting are generally of rather poor quality and color. A really good and important piece of rough will not be so treated, even by the most poorly informed Oriental cutter.

It is to be observed that the characteristic inclusions are quite pronounced in some stones, while apparently being absent in others. These particular inclusions, commonly called *banding,* are also called *growth lines* or *phantoms.* They may sometimes be distinct at one end of a crystal and diminish in intensity toward the other. They may also be interrupted or distorted, primarily due to distortion in the growth of the crystal itself, and stones cut from these deformed parts will pass on the distortion; i.e., an arm of a star may be missing or might not be a normal straight line. Since these types of imperfections cannot be corrected, it is well to be able to recognize them early and not waste time and material on them.

Further, deeply colored stones tend to show a weak asterism due to the absorption of the reflected light by the dense pigmentation, whether blue, red, or brown. In addition, beware of any golden-yellow star sapphires that may be offered for sale. These probably have been cyclotron or radium-treated and turned that color from the original gray. Exposure to the sun or bright incandescent light will usually cause such stones to revert to their original color. Recently the process has been perfected to such an extent that many stones which have been treated in a cyclotron retain their color permanently.

To properly test a stone for a perfectly centered star seems a puzzling task, since of course the star moves over the surface when tilted or does not seem to be centered (to the uninitiated) even in direct sunlight. However, it is not at all difficult if you imagine a plane through the gem at the girdle, in both a north-south and an east-west direction.

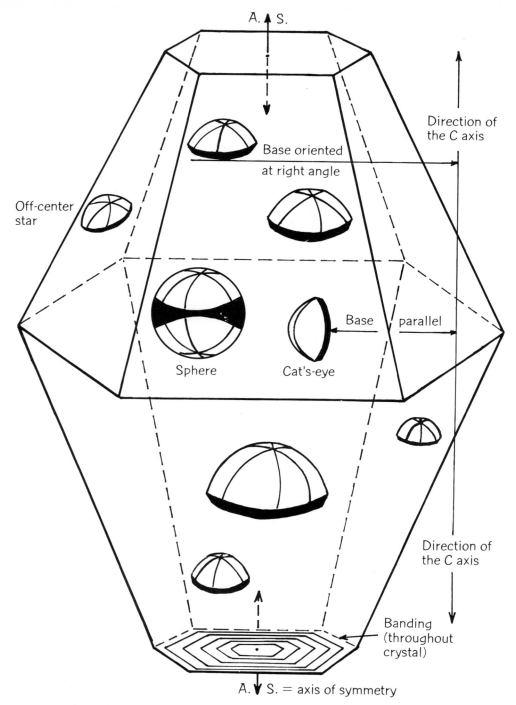

Fig. 7–1 The orienting of asteriated gems in a sapphire crystal. A star may be secured from any portion of a suitable crystal having the proper internal structure if the base is cut at right angles to the central axis of the crystal.

Now under a *single source* of unshaded incandescent light (unfrosted globes are best), imagine a line which is at right angles to both these planes (vertical) and bring the base of the stone into conformity with these two basal planes. If the star has been oriented correctly, it will be centered exactly where the imaginary vertical line should be. If the gem should be tested in the sunlight, tilt the gem so that the base is at right angles to a direct line to the sun and note whether the star is centered on this point. Not infrequently a stone is so filled with needles that a star will be observed from each separate bright source of light in a room.

ORIENTING A SAPPHIRE CAT'S-EYE

It has been incorrectly assumed by some that if a cabochon sapphire's banding is all in one direction, a cat's-eye will result. Not so, of course. A cat's-eye can be cut, but only if the base of the stone is *parallel* to the vertical or "C" axis of the crystal. There will then also be a star at each end of such a stone, but they will be pinched, and only half a star may be visible. If a sphere should be cut, there will be a star at each "pole" of the "C" axis.

ASTERISM IN OTHER STONES

Asterism is also known in many gemstones other than sapphire and ruby, the most common of these being quartz. This material is used extensively to provide the public with an inexpensive substitute, in a natural stone, for the star sapphire. The effect has been accomplished in most cases by applying a blue mirror material to the base of a cabochon made from asteriated quartz. While quartz exhibits sharp asterism, it has a glassy appearance and lacks the characteristic richness of the sapphire.

Natural unbacked rose quartz often may be cut to show a distinct star, simply by cutting a rounded shape and sanding it with water, after which it is oiled and the star apex located with a single source of pinpoint light in a dark room. A small light in a tin can, in the cover of which a single very small hole has been punched, will serve well. By locating the two points, the "poles" of the "C" axis, and marking with a small India ink cross, two stars can then be cut from the piece by sawing it in two at right angles to this axis. The cabochon can then be shaped either oval or round to conform to an attractive spacing of the arms of the star.

Garnet also provides asteriated material, but by no means in great quantity, and the asterism observed shows four-rayed, rarely six-rayed, stars. Moreover, four-rayed stars with good asterism are rather scarce, the rays usually being comparatively weak but well defined if present, due to the absorption of light by the deeply colored material. The four-rayed stars are the result of the inclusions being oriented at right angles to the axes of symmetry in the rhombic dodecahedron form of garnet, while six-rayed stars are created by the dodecahedron modified by the cube. Theo-

Fig. 7–2 Natural star sapphires showing six rays. In the synthetic material, the star is somewhat sharper but is not considered as valuable. (*Courtesy,* Lapidary Journal)

Fig. 7–3 *Top,* Orienting the rays of a star sapphire. Note that one ray is directly across the shortest dimension of the stone. *Center,* Orienting a star beryl (aquamarine). Note that one ray is placed parallel to the *longest* dimension of the stone. *Bottom,* Side view of the rough-ground and sanded star beryl cut to a slight dome. This is a preliminary step in locating a single long ray parallel to the longest diameter of the stone. The surface of the stone is oiled and observed under a single ray of light.

retically, 8, 12, or 16-rayed stars are possible. The best material comes from Idaho.

Asterism is also known, but more rarely, in beryl, diopside, labradorite, spinel, and tourmaline. The recently discovered star beryl and star aquamarine from Brazil provide very attractive gems with quite sharp stars, due to plates of ilmenite which have formed hexagonal branching inclusions, from the microscopic arms of which the rays are reflected to form the always six-

rayed star. Such material requires rather different orientation and will be discussed under the proper heading of cutting procedure. (See figs. 7–2 and 7–3.)

HOW TO CUT AND POLISH STAR SAPPHIRE

Since corundum has a hardness of 9, it is rather rough on silicon carbide or carborundum grinding wheels. Except for roughing out to general shape on a coarse grit grinding wheel, most of the cutting of the cabochon to shape should be done on the rougher side of the diamond lap, the stone being handled by cementing it to a wood dop stick. The blanks are of course first prepared by sawing segments of the proper size at right angles to the "C" axis of the crystal. The back is left flat in modern practice, though the imported stones all have a good deal of "belly" underneath to add weight. These have customarily been left ground but not polished. After flatting the back on the lap, touch the edges to the diamond lap all around to grind a reversed bezel of about 1/32" (0.08 cm) all around to prevent chipping.

Dome the top of the piece of rough and locate the arms of the star by sanding and oiling the stone. For sapphire, orient one ray across what will be the *shorter* width of the gem; the others will then take care of themselves as to position, if the gem is to be made into an oval cabochon. For star beryl, orient one ray the *long* way of the gem (fig. 7–4).

Proceed to grind the oval shape true to outline and as near a standard size as possible for ease in setting later. A set of templates will assist in arriving at a good shape that fits the rough without undue waste of material. Now stroke the stone around and around on the diamond lap, following a course of contact from outer bezel edge toward the center of the dome, as if peeling an apple. When

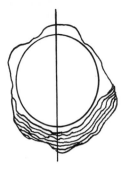

Fig. 7–4 Mark a long axis on the front, back, and edges of the blank. Next mark the rough outline on the *back* of the stone, aligning as shown here.

you have arrived at an acceptable and uniform shape of rather high-domed cabochon (figs. 7–5 and 7–6), turn the diamond lap over and proceed to fine-grind the surface all over, around and around. This will leave a very smooth surface, ready to take to the wood polishing wheel.

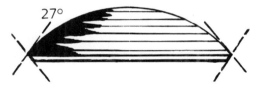

27°

Fig. 7–5 Cross section—side of stone.

An alternate method, after preliminary grinding, cuts the gem down by the use of rubber bonded abrasive wheels in which the grit is silicon carbide. These are used wet and will allow cutting-by-sanding to be done with successively finer wheels until the stone has been sanded to a very smooth finish, at which time the water is turned off and a finish sanding is done dry on the fine grit wheel.

Fig. 7–6 Cross section—end of stone. Note that the shape is an arc rather than a curve.

With the recent and continuing improvements in the manufacturing of synthetic gem materials, it is now possible for the hobbyist to purchase synthetic star ruby and star sapphire boule sections which are already oriented so that they will produce star stones when cut as a cabochon. Most of the star boule sections available to the hobbyist are the Linde Star stones. It is becoming increasingly difficult to purchase good star stones in the rough material, so many of the hobbyists who wish to cut a nice star ruby or sapphire are purchasing the star boule sections.

The boule section is usually somewhat larger than the stone you are expected to be able to obtain, but is generally listed and priced according to the finished stone the boule section is expected to produce. If you purchase a 6-mm (.24 in) by 8-mm (.30 in) boule section and you try to get a 7-mm by 9-mm stone from it, you will not have a real sharp star; the bands of the star will be broad and hazy. So if you are going to try cutting a synthetic star stone, be sure you cut the size which it is supposed to produce. When you try to cut a larger millimeter size than was stated, you automatically reduce the height of the crown and in so doing you reduce the sharpness of the star.

USE OF THE DIAMOND-IMPREGNATED WOOD WHEEL

Two-grooved wood wheels are used in polishing star sapphire or star ruby. These are of two types: those with the grooves laid out on the flat side of the wheel and those which have the grooves in the rim. The first type can be used readily on the spindle of a small horizontal pot-type grinder or on the faceting table, while the other vertical-type wheel can be mounted on the shaft of any horizontal spindle machine for vertical service. These can be purchased at a moderate cost ready-made with the

Fig. 7–7 The Blake polisher shows multiple wheels that can be charged with diamond compounds of varying grit sizes for grinding and sanding and polishing star stones and cat's-eyes. This type of unit is very popular. (*Courtesy, Dorothy Blake*)

proper diamond compound for their use (fig. 7–7), or they can be made from hard maple, poplar, gumwood, cherry, or other compact wood which has no prominent annular rings or resinous content. Such wheels, if made, should have the grain lying flat to the larger surface (fig. 7–8) and cut from the wood as in figures 7–9 and 7–10. They should be dipped in paraffin to seal the pores of the wood.

The first wheel is impregnated with diamond in the groove only, using 1,200 grit. This can be diamond compound, such as Elgin DYMO, which comes in a tube with an applicator, or diamond powder mixed with lipstick in a small ointment jar. The wax in lipstick has an excellent staying ability in holding the

Fig. 7–8 The preferred "run" of grain in a wood lap.

diamond to the lap. Only a small amount the size of a pea is used, into which the diamond powder is mixed. Both man-made and natural diamond powders are now available to the amateur lapidary at the moderate cost of about $3.50 to $4.50 per carat in all grit sizes desired.

The second wheel is impregnated with 8,000 mesh diamond, though 6,400 will do also. This is used for final polishing.

The actual polishing is done by stroking the gem on all sides on the 1,200-grit wheel until all evidences of dull

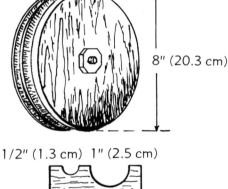

8" (20.3 cm)

1/2" (1.3 cm) 1" (2.5 cm)

2" (5.1 cm)

Fig. 7–9 Vertical wood lap, with grooved edge.

spots are gone and it begins to take on a shine. Test the orientation of the star at this stage by oiling the stone and viewing under a single ray of light from an incandescent lamp. If the position of the star is correct, wipe the stone completely clean and proceed to the final polishing with the finer wheel. Continue until you feel sure that the polish cannot be improved by additional work.

During the last several years, many new diamond products and diamond compounds have become available to

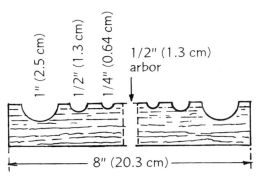

Fig. 7–10 Horizontal wood lap, with grooved side.

the hobbyist. These new products have been specifically manufactured for the lapidary hobby and are a great help in cutting and polishing some of the stones which need special handling and special techniques. These products will be discussed more fully in chapter 9.

CUTTING CAT'S-EYES

Some of the most attractive and valuable gemstones are those which are cut from materials having tubes or fibers lying in one direction, so that if a cabochon is cut in either a round or an oval shape with its long dimension across the fibers at right angles, a stone with a luminous single ray of light will result.

There are a considerable number of gem materials which possess this property in some of their forms, and the collecting and cutting of such stones has become a specialized part of the lapidary hobby among some fanciers.

The materials which have been known to produce gems of this sort are: chrysoberyl of the type called cymophane; scapolite; tourmaline; aquamarine, morganite, and green beryl among the beryl varieties; nephrite jade; williamsite (serpentine); dumortierite; kunzite and spodumene; apatite; spar; crocidolite (tigereye in all its colors); quartz; sillimanite (fibrolite); iolite; enstatite; sapphire; and a few others

that are too soft to be of any consequence.

FILLING THE PORES

Most inclusions that cause cat's-eyes are quite fine, and no special precautions are necessary in order to keep the channels or tubes clean where these are present. However, in some varieties the tubes are quite porous and open, so that the material must be treated in order to prevent sawing oil and polishing powder from getting into these pores and causing ugly "blackheads" on the surface of the finished stone. Any such material can be "filled" by dipping the rough successively in water-glass sodium silicate solution to which a few drops of a liquid detergent have been added to break surface tension and promote capillary action by the tubes in absorbing the water-glass solution. This should be warm and the jar set away for a time. Then remove and let the gem material dry, after which it should be immersed again. Repeat the process until the pores have become filled and are dry. The rough should be sawed in water only, else the cutting oil will get into the pores before you can protect them from the dirt the oil contains. Sometimes it may be necessary to grind a portion of a crystal off rather than sawing it, using the corner of the wheel to grind the rough into two parts or more. This need not be wasteful if the base of the stone is first ground on one side and the material ground off with a wide V-notch which will more or less match the curve of the finished cabochon.

After a stone is ground and sanded, redip in the solution before final polishing, to replace the water-glass that has soaked away from the ends of the pores. Let dry and proceed to polish. When the stone has been completed, soak it in clean warm water for several days to dissolve any remaining water-glass. This method will enable material to be cut which otherwise would not be attractive when finished. Many tourmalines are prone to have such open pores.

HOW TO PUT THE "EYE" IN TIGEREYE

The cutting of a tigereye cabochon with a floating eye has, for many amateurs, been a case of hope, luck, and try again. Many have never been successful in obtaining a floating eye, although of course the fixed eye is easy to obtain from the margin.

There is, however, a way to predetermine the hoped-for result. Take a slice of tigereye that has been properly cut, parallel to the grain of the fibers. A difference of 2° or 3° will make the difference between proper and improper cutting. Look across the slice at an angle of about 60°. You should see the half of the slice toward you either dark or light, and see the far half the opposite in color. Mark lightly with a pencil the dividing line between dark and light, and then hold the slice in the same plane. Rotate it end for end, and if the light side was toward you before, it should be toward you now even though you have rotated the slice.

Again mark the dividing line of light and dark and hope that your pencil marks are in the same place. Now turn the slice over so that the bottom becomes the top and you should have a reverse lighting effect. If the light side was toward you before, you should now have the dark side toward you, and that will remain true if you again rotate the slab in the same plane.

When you look down at the slice at 60° and see the dark side toward you, you are looking at what should be the *top* of the finished stone. So, place your marking template on the side where the *light half* is toward you, as this will be the

bottom of the stone. If you then cut a stone oriented in this manner, when you are through polishing you should have a stone with a floating eye of light. (This method of cutting tigereye was worked out by Walter H. Jayne, of Milwaukee, Wisconsin.)

Whether you use the system given here or one of your own, there are several things to remember. The straighter the fibers in your slab of tigereye, the better eye you will be able to produce. If the fibers are wavy, you will have only a chatoyant stone, not a well-defined eye. So select a slab with the straightest fibers that you can. Be sure that the slab is thick enough to cut a nice high crown. A low crown stone will not produce a good sharp eye. It will be a broad hazy band of light (fig. 7–11).

 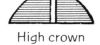

Low crown   High crown

Fig. 7–11 A low crown will produce a broad hazy eye (*left*) while a high crown (*right*) which has an arc will produce a fine sharp eye, providing the fiber structure is correct.

When you are grinding and sanding the stone, keep it cool so the fibers will not open up and cause a rough surface that will not polish well. Since the fibers are shorter at the crown of the stone, it is well to start your sanding strokes at the top and work from the top of the stone to the girdle edge so that you smooth the fibers down rather than opening them up. Do not waste the rest of the slab; it can still be cut into attractive cabochons even though it does not have a cat's-eye effect. Recently, there have been restrictions placed on the importing of rough tigereye, and the shortage of supply is already being noticed throughout the hobby. (See color insert.)

8 · Special Cabochon Polishing Techniques

In chapter 6 we discussed the cutting and polishing of cabochons, and the directions given there cover the great majority of the cabochons that the gemcutter will attempt, usually in the quartz family containing agates of all types, petrified wood, jasper, chert, and flint. There are many other interesting materials softer than 7, however, but usually the cutter is presented with problems, for the softer the material he is working, the more difficult it is to achieve a satisfactory finish on a cabochon.

Some of these problems are given in the following pages, in which the names of the gems are arranged alphabetically. (Hardness on the Mohs scale, specific gravity [S.G.], and refractive index [R.I.] are given for each.) Most of these methods have been tested by the authors, but all of them have come out of the long experience of nationally known gemcutters, and they have been published and are widely followed. These methods are not necessarily the only ones, or even the best ones, perhaps, but they happen to be the best procedures known to the authors at this time.

AZURITE

Hardness, 3½–4 S.G., 3.8–3.9 R.I., 1.73–1.83

Because of its softness, this material is very difficult to polish and is not prac-
tical for jewelry. However, it has such an intensely blue color that many gemcutters are attracted to it. Several methods have been given for polishing it, but the best results the authors have seen were devised by the "Pegboarders," an experimental group of advanced gemcutters within the Sacramento Mineral Society.

Microscopic examination reveals that a dull luster is caused by softer parts of the stone flowing completely over some of the polished areas. Heavy pressure accentuates this flow and causes undercutting. In order to overcome this, a thick coating of a chrome oxide paste is applied to a leather disk. The stone is worked against the disk with moderate pressure until the chrome oxide paste is quite dry. This technique forms a film over the surface which retards the flow, and as the film wears away under the friction of the drying surface, the various surface areas remain in place and the polish is generated evenly over the entire surface. The quick flow generated by the moist paste is suddenly halted by the drying film, and as the film is worn away by friction, the polish is improved only up to the point where the film is entirely removed. Repetitions of the process will improve the surface. Contacting as much area of the stone with the polishing disk as possible while removing the film will create an uninterrupted luster. Good preparatory work is essential, and while the stone may be polished after dry sanding, a final preparation on No. 600 wet sanding cloth will reduce undersurface imperfections to a minimum.

This method of polishing was also reported to be of great value in the polishing of rhodonite, lapis lazuli, and soft turquoise.

BLACK CORAL

Hardness, 3 *S.G.,* 1.35 *R.I.,* 1.56–1.57

Most of the black coral available to the hobbyist is Hawaiian black coral, which is usually in the form of small branches or cutoff pieces or sections. It normally grows in a treelike formation, and the larger tree and trunklike portions are generally used for carvings and decorative objects. The smaller sections and pieces are used for jewelry. When the branchlike pieces are cut or sliced into cross sections, they show growth rings. If the branches are cut diagonally, the rings appear to be elongated, and an elliptical oval cabochon can be cut and polished.

It is very soft and will grind away rapidly if you are not careful. Your grinding wheels should be smooth, because a bumpy wheel may loosen the growth rings. It can be cut with a hacksaw, but it is better to use a thin blade on your trim saw. If you have a faceter's trim saw, it is even better, and you will not lose as much material when cutting it. Black coral is very heat-sensitive; it can be dopped with the standard green dop wax, but do not put the cabochon blank on the dopping stove. It should be warmed very slightly by just holding it in your tweezers and passing it through the flame of the alcohol lamp until it is warm enough for the dop wax to adhere to the cabochon. If you prefer, you may cold-dop the cabochon (refer to Dopping Opal in this chapter).

Since black coral is so soft, do not use your coarse wheel for shaping and pre-

forming the cabochon. It is advisable to do all your grinding and shaping on a 220 or 320-grit wheel. Be sure to use an ample flow of water on your grinding wheel and during your sanding. Work carefully until you can determine the direction of the "grain" of the material, then work with the "grain," not against it. The material will cut rapidly, so be cautious or you will grind away more than you want to.

Wet sanding is essential, and you should use either 320 or 400-grit sanding cloth since your grinding was done on the fine grinding wheel. Finish your wet sanding on a 600-grit sanding cloth. You may use either a sanding drum or a face plate, whichever you prefer. The sanding should continue until all wheel marks and scratches have been removed and a semigloss finish obtained. Be sure to wash your hands and the stone on the dop stick before proceeding to the polishing buff.

When you start to polish your black coral, be careful not to allow any friction heat to occur. If you should let it get too warm, you will "burn" or "blister" the cabochon. The surface will appear to have reddish brown spots which detract from the appearance of the cabochon. If this happens, you will have to go back to your 400-grit sanding cloth and start the sanding process over again.

During the polishing stages, you will notice that the growth rings tend to collect and hold the polish, and it is difficult to remove the polish from them. However, the rings can provide attractive patterns in the finished cabochon. You can accentuate the pattern when you polish your cabochon by using a tin oxide and Linde A mixture (about eight parts tin oxide and two parts Linde A). Polishing should not be done on a hard felt wheel because too much friction is created. Polish on a soft leather disk mounted with a sanding disk cement on a face plate which has a sponge rubber padding. Apply the polish sparingly so that you do not load your polishing disk. You may repeat the process of adding polish as needed until you have obtained a mirror polish. It is not advisable to use several different types of polish on the same leather disk, so remove the leather disk and store it in a plastic bag for future use.

Another polishing technique can be used which is quite different from that ordinarily used. Two 4-inch (10-cm) cotton flannel buffs are purchased (the same type that is used for jewelry polishing). One of them is mounted on a tapered spindle, and on the buff a white diamond compound is applied sparingly, care being taken not to load the buff. Then, holding the dop stick firmly so that the buff does not pull it away from you, use an on-and-off stroke method; that is, touch it lightly to the buff and take it away, repeating your action while shifting the cabochon so that all areas of the cabochon are semipolished. Apply more white diamond compound as necessary. Using this on-and-off technique of polishing will help prevent too much friction heat from developing. This process should be continued until a satin finish is achieved.

Change to the second cotton flannel buff and use white jeweler's rouge on it. Use the same type of on-and-off technique, applying very light pressure and adding polish to the buff as needed until you have obtained a mirror polish. The white polish need not be removed from the growth rings since you have used it to accentuate the growth ring patterns.

BURNITE

(A rock-like mixture of azurite, malachite and cuprite, therefore no specifics can be given. See Azurite.)

Burnite is a variety of azurite discovered in 1952 at Battle Mountain, Nevada, by Frank Burnham, who gave it the name of burnite. It is a very beautiful blue material, very difficult to polish, but responding well to the methods given under azurite.

CHRYSOCOLLA (Quartz)

Hardness, 7   S.G., 2.68   R.I., 1.54–1.55

When a true rockhound sees a gem book refer to chrysocolla as a soft mineral of hardness 2 to 4 and dismiss it from the category of serviceable and beautiful gem materials (as some of the English books are prone to do), he simply makes a mental reservation that they do not know about the kind of gem chrysocolla which he has seen selling for somewhat fantastic prices for the very best grades. This copper silicate type of cryptocrystalline agate, colored with an infusion of the heavenly blue for which it is noted, is a gem material that can hold up its head in the best of company. It is both durable and beautiful and has become quite rare. Prices of $30 to $100 a pound ($60 to $200 per kilogram) are quoted for the best grades, and many who have some will not sell it at any price.

Chrysocolla of the above type can be ground the same as any agate, but it must be treated carefully when it is polished. A felt wheel kept quite wet with cerium oxide will suffice, but a final polishing on a loose muslin buff with tin oxide will improve the luster. Too much heat generated during the polishing state will ruin the cabochon by causing white spots to appear.

Chrysocolla is often associated with malachite, and many of the hobbyists like blue chrysocolla with dendritic patterns of the green malachite. This presents the cutter with the problem of polishing two materials of different hardness, since the softer malachite usually undercuts. With careful sanding and polishing, undercutting can be overcome. Some gemcutters prefer to use a firm, smooth leather polishing disk rather than a rough leather disk backed with foam rubber. A smooth leather disk does not have as much tendency to pull out on the softer materials. Again, many cutters, when working materials of varying hardness, are resorting to a final sanding and polishing with diamond to produce a finer polish (see chapter 9).

DUMORTIERITE (Quartz)

Hardness, 7, S.G., 3.36 R.I., 1.67–1.68

Certain materials are rather hard to polish and will not yield to the ordinary procedure. Dumortierite is one of them, on which the best finish apparently can be produced with a process of progressively finer sanding, ending by the use of a worn sanding cloth, used almost dry. Methods given herein for polishing rhodonite are reportedly successful with this material.

Dumortierite is a porous material. If you wish to cut a slab, be sure to soak it in plain water for several days. After it is saturated with water it can be slabbed without absorbing too much oil. Wash each slab immediately and thoroughly in mild detergent and water to remove the oil from the surface. When the water is dried out of the material, it should be almost its normal color. Here again, the use of diamond is now being applied. You can grind and sand in the usual manner on silicon carbide wheels and wet sand or dry sand as you prefer, but be sure to keep the stone cool. After you have finished on a worn-out 600-grit sanding cloth, switch to diamond for a fine sanding step and then polish with diamond. (See color insert.)

FIRE AGATE

Hardness, 7, S.G., 2.60–2.62, R.I., 1.53

This type of quartz is an entrancingly beautiful agate found in Imperial County, California, and at scattered locations in Arizona. Fire agate deposits which are producing some very fine stones have recently been found in Mexico. This agate has layers of iridescent limonite, or a type of iron oxide. These layers are between the layers of agate and are so thin that they are less in thickness than a breath upon a cold windowpane. If a lapidary is successful in cutting this material with the limonite layer near the surface, he has a unique cabochon that looks like a hot coal except that it has green as well as red fire. Leave a thin coating of agate over the fire layer.

The layers are built one upon another in a botryoidal or cauliflower-like form. No fire agate rough should be cut without close preliminary study. The cutter should abandon any idea of using conventional templates, because if he is lucky enough to find a good spot of fire, he should cut as the Orientals do—to get the largest stone possible from the available material and then make the mounting fit the finished stone rather than cutting the stone to fit a mounting.

Usually, the gemcutter is confronted with what appears to be a bubble of fire within his agate. His only recourse is to grind away the agate until he can see and study the limits of the bubble. This bubble effect is usually the simplest form to work with, and it has the best quality of fire. The best way to work this material is on the edge of the wheel, and it is much better to use a small wheel—one that you have been working on for a long time and which has been greatly reduced in size. By working several stones alternately you will find that some one of them will fit the changing periphery of the wheel, and this also tends to dress your wheel for you. The whole trick in working fire agate is to find the fire and then tease the stone until you have brought forth and saved as much of it as possible. It is entirely a grinding process, for sawing the small

Cabochons showing a variety of shapes: (*pink heart on left*) rhodochrosite; (*next three on top row, left to right*) nephrite jade; (*teardrop*) rhodochrosite; (*diamond on left*) malachite; (*rectangle*) nephrite jade; (*diamond on right*) brecciated jasper; (*green heart on left*) nephrite jade; (*square and cross*) nephrite jade; (*small teardrop*) jadeite; (*small teardrop*) nephrite jade; (*star*) tigereye; (*large teardrop*) chrysocolla; (*heart on right*) tricolored tigereye; (*hemisphere*) jadeite; (*bottom three*) jadeite. (*Photo by John Washalaski*)

Cabochons showing assorted gem materials: (*top, left to right*) desert picture stone, cherry opal, snowflake obsidian, chocolate opal, and turritella agate; (*row next to top, left to right*) petrified palm, petrified palm, datolite, cuprite, and cinnabar in agate; (*row next to bottom, left to right*) polka dot agate, Montana moss agate, idocrase, paisley agate, and pastelite; (*bottom, left to right*) malachite, thomsonite, moss agate, variscite, and sardonyx. (*Photo by John Washalaski*)

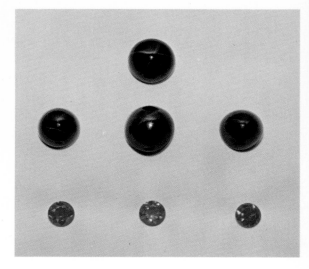

Star stones and cat's-eyes: (*left to right across top*) actinolite, apatite, tourmaline, and tigereye; (*centered below top two*) chrysoberyl; (*left to right, middle row*) tourmaline and star ruby; (*left to right, bottom row*) aquamarine, ring with two star rubies and six star sapphires, and scapolite. (*Photo by John Washalaski*)

Four star garnets and three faceted garnets. (*Photo by John Washalaski*)

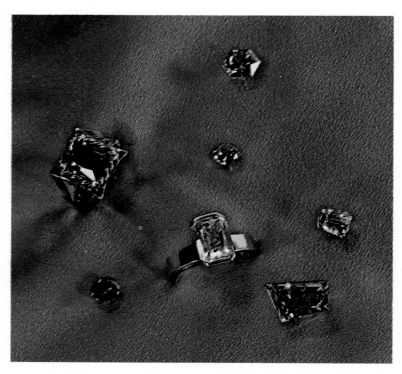

Faceted stones mounted in rings: (*top*) YAG; (*second row, left to right*) green YAG and tanzanite; (*third row, left to right*) garnet, aquamarine, and garnet; (*bottom*) golden beryl. (*Photo by John Washalaski*)

Special cabochon materials: (*top row, left to right*) azurite, fire agate, nephrite jade, and rhodonite; (*second row, left to right*) unakite, iolite, lapis lazuli, and goldstone; (*third row, left to right*) Australian fire opal, Mexican fire opal, and Australian fire opal; (*fourth row, left to right*) dumortierite, dumortierite, azurite, and turquoise; (*bottom row, left to right*) flower obsidian, jadeite, mahogany obsidian, and chrysocolla and malachite. (*Photo by John Washalaski*)

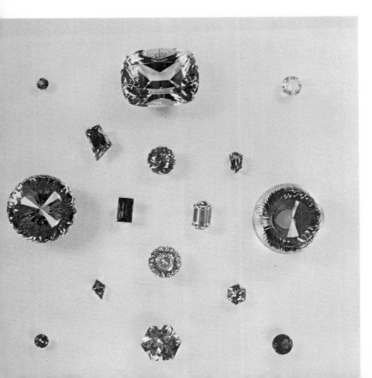

Faceted stones: (*top, left to right*) tourmaline, optical quartz, and sunstone (orthoclase); (*second row, left to right*) golden beryl, pink YAG, and tourmaline; (*third row, left to right*) laser glass, synthetic spinel, colorless YAG, and smoky quartz; (*triangle below third row, left to right*) topaz, titania (syn. rutile), and YAG; (*bottom, left to right*) tanzanite, lead glass, and amethyst. (*Photo by John Washalaski*)

Faceted rose of Brazilian quartz. Jerry Muchna spent 140 hours on this graceful flower. It is made of 18 pieces, all faceted, and has a total weight of 732 carats. (*Photo by Jeffrey J. Kurtzeman*)

Flats and spheres: (*top, left to right*) book ends, Brazilian geode, blue agate sphere, and rhodochrosite sphere; (*bottom*) three sets of quartz polyhedroids from Brazil; one set is crystal-lined, the other two agate-filled. (*Photo by John Washalaski*)

pieces that are available might destroy the possibilities of the gem, and once it is ground, the sanding and polishing are achieved by conventional processes previously discussed.

GARNET

	Hardness	S.G.	R.I.
Almandite variety	7–7$\frac{1}{2}$	3.83–4.23	1.79

(Most cabochon and star material is of this type)

Grossularite variety	6$\frac{1}{2}$–7	3.50–3.75	1.73
Green grossularite ("Transvaal jade")			

The only two varieties of garnet which are cut in cabochon forms are the almandite (carbuncles and star garnets) and the jadelike grossularite garnet from South Africa.

Almandite is rather brittle, and care must be taken in both grinding and sanding not to use too much pressure and to use very little heat, for it will crack readily. Ordinary sanding procedure will suffice, with successive stages of fine wet sanding on 200, 400, and 600-grit drum sanders. Following this, wash the stone and hands, and polish the stone on a felt buff with cerium oxide, using very little pressure. At this stage, too much pressure and heat will "pull out" the brittle garnet right from the surface. A final finish on a loose muslin buff with tin oxide will impart an extra brilliance. The ancient cutters used tripoli with good results.

The "Transvaal jade" type of grossular garnet is somewhat tougher and requires no special treatment except good, thorough sanding and polishing, but it should not be overheated in the process.

GOLDSTONE

This is not a gem but glass with inclusions of copper filings. It is attactive,

however, and desired by many cutters. Being glass, the polishing methods are the same as for obsidian, which are given later in this chapter.

IOLITE (Cordierite)

Hardness, 7–7$\frac{1}{2}$ *S.G.,* 2.63 *R.I.,* 1.54–1.55

This material cuts with a "ragged" appearance on the diamond lap and seems to be done best on a cast iron lap with fine grit (FF) in the case of a faceted stone. It polishes very easily on a tin lap with tin oxide, used in a very thin slurry. The lap has a considerable abrasive action, and allowance must be made for this in cutting the facets.

In making cabochons of this spectacular material, which shows so vividly the pleochroism of deep purple, blue, and yellowish gray, the cabochon preform should be made quite shallow to avoid the appearnce of "inky blue" which results when a stone is made too deep. Grind on a 100-grit wheel and follow on the 220-grit wheel. Thorough sanding with a *well-worn* 400-grit cloth, wet, is followed by a final buffing on leather. Either tin oxide or Linde A can be used for the polishing agent. Use sparingly and in a well-watered solution.

A spectacular exhibit piece can be made by orienting a cube to the three colors and facet-cutting the faces, or cutting on the flat lap and polishing by hand on the flat tin lap used for facet work.

JADE

	Hardness	S.G.	R.I.
Nephrite jade	6–6$\frac{1}{2}$	2.95	1.60–1.63
Jadeite	6$\frac{1}{2}$–7	3.30	1.66–1.68

There are two very definite forms of jade, and these are in fact two entirely different minerals: *nephrite* and *jadeite*. However, for all practical purposes, when it comes to polishing, they may be treated as one. Hence, in this section, when we use the word jade, it can mean either form of the mineral.

Once one of the authors stood behind a Chinese operating some of the ancient-type cutting and polishing wheels with which they turned out so many exquisitely carved and polished pieces. As weight was placed alternately on one treadle, then the other, causing the spindle to turn first this way, then that, back and forth, with no great speed generated, the thought came to the author that here, indeed, was possibly the reason why they did so well with jade. They use wet sanding and *much patience.*

Jade cutting is at best a slow conquering of the inherent *toughness* of the fibrous material. Jade is made up of myriad bundles of fibers, so intertwined that to break a block of jade with a steel hammer is virtually impossible. The hammer breaks or steel chips fly from the edge of the hammer face before the jade will part. Early attempts by amateur lapidaries to polish jade met with great trouble. Many were addicted to dry sanding, and their jade cabochons or pieces when dry-sanded showed some few bright areas, but for the most part only an ugly "orange peel" effect rewarded their efforts. Naturally, when they attempted to polish such a surface, the result was not good.

Jade yields readily to polishing, and a mirrorlike surface can be achieved if the material is good and not filled with inclusions of mica or chlorite, *and if the right methods are used on it.*

The first step is the sanding—*wet sanding at all times until a scratch-free surface is attained.* This starts with a 200-grit wet sanding cloth on a flat disk sander or a drum sander, backed with a thin, flexible backing of rubber or felt. When scratches have been reduced to the point where there are no large ones evident and the surface is even all over, proceed to a similar 400-grit fairly new sanding cloth, kept wet at all times, and sand still more until the surface begins

to assume a faint gloss. Continue until close examination shows no apparent uneven areas. Now sand on a rather well-worn 600-grit wet sanding cloth, kept wet, until no vestige of a scratch is evident. At no time allow the jade to become even a little warm; this is to prevent the premature start of a Beilby flow surface *before you are ready for it.* Inspect the stone quite carefully, looking for any places that need improvement, and return to the sander if there is need to do so. Your quality of later finish is won on the sander, nowhere else!

When you are certain that the stone has been sanded the best you possibly can, wash it, wash the dop stick it is on, and wash your hands. Get everything *thoroughly* clean. Now, take the stone on its dop stick back to the same worn 600-grit sanding cloth which you have been using wet, but have now allowed to spin until it is almost dry, and apply the stone to the sanding cloth *with as much pressure as you can muster,* letting the stone get hot for the first time. Stroke the gem from edge to edge in one direction on the sanding cloth, pressing evenly but hard as you do, with a swiping motion. In a very short time, if the earlier steps have been done as they should be, you will have what appears to be a fairly good polish. The stone may try to "ooze" on the dop stick, but if you keep pressing it back into place with the fingers you can keep it on. Examine the stone closely with a glass and note whether there are any dull spots at all. If there are, it will be necessary to return to wet sanding on the same worn 600-grit cloth. Then allow it to dry and continue as above for that portion of the stone needing attention.

For the actual final polishing, use an 8″ (20-cm) round wood disk, over which a piece of chrome tanned leather can be stretched and tacked. The padding consists of layers of felt built up to a low dome, over which the last $\frac{1}{4}$″ (0.64-cm-)

thick layer can be sponge rubber sheet. A flange of the right size to fit the end of your mandrel shaft is screwed to the back, where a set screw will fasten it to the shaft. The domed buff should be about 1½" (3.8 cm) thick at the center, with the leather coming out over the rim and tacked on the back side. Cutting the leather into 1" (2.5-cm) tabs will aid in stretching and tacking it, and it should be soaked and applied wet.

Another style of leather polishing disk can be made by using a one-quarter inch (0.64-cm-) thick piece of tooling calf leather with the tooling side, or smooth side, for the polishing surface. This disk can be cemented to a flat aluminum or wooden face plate with no sponge rubber padding behind the leather. This can be mounted on your combination unit in place of the sanding disk or on one side of one of your polishing arbors. This type of polishing disk is difficult to break in because of the very smooth surface, but it can be done with a little patience. Take a brush and a mixture of chrome oxide and water, start the disk spinning, and apply a very small amount of the polish; then, while the polish is still wet, use a well-sanded piece of agate and work the polish gradually into the leather. Before you start, be sure to put a shield around the disk, because the first few times most of the polish will spin off the disk, and you may look a little green yourself.

When you finally get the disk properly impregnated with polish, apply the polish and let the disk spin until it begins to dry slightly, then start polishing your jade cabochon. You will have to apply polish to the disk several times before you finish polishing the cabochon. This type of polishing disk can also be used for unakite, rhodonite, and lapis lazuli. (See color insert).

Make a polishing mixture of nine parts chromium oxide and one part Linde A polishing powder. Drop a tablespoonful of this in a glass half full of water and use a meat-basting fiber brush to apply it to the buff. Paint it all over the fresh buff and allow it to dry somewhat before it starts to spin, or there will be a nice emerald-green streak on the ceiling of your shop! Start the buff and allow it to spin until it is almost, but not quite, dry, then apply the jade on its dop stick with considerable pressure, using the swiping technique from edge to edge of the piece. It does not take long for this to bring up a truly polished surface that will stand a "light-globe test"—reading the numeral giving the wattage of a light bulb suspended with a white reflector over the working area, when reflected in the surface you have buffed. It takes a glass to see it, but if it is there then you can say you have a really fine polish on your jade. The jade should be allowed to get quite hot during this process.

LAPIS LAZULI

Hardness, 5½   S.G., 2.50–2.90

This beautiful blue material is really a rock consisting of lazurite, pyrite, and calcite, with lazurite predominating. Because of its three different hardnesses, this gemstone has always presented great polishing problems. However, the methods described under rhodonite herein are reportedly very effective with lapis lazuli.

OBSIDIAN

Hardness, 5   S.G., 2.3–2.5   R.I., 1.50

Obsidian is a glasslike material formed in lava flows that cooled rapidly. It comes in black, red, brown, and green colors, in addition to mixed shades. It is a very common material in the western states and is in plentiful supply. It is easily recognized in the field, for in addition to looking like glass, it breaks easily with a conchoidal or shell-like fracture.

Obsidian is a beautiful material to work with, especially for novelties like spheres, ashtrays, book ends, and so forth. It is not much used for jewelry because it is so fragile, and for this reason it has one great advantage over other gems—if you drop it you do not have to pick it up!

If you do not get an excellent sanding job on obsidian, you will get a disappointing polish, because each little hairlike scratch will show up in its mirrorlike surface.

The best polishing technique uses cerium oxide on a felt buff, the same method used by the optometrist in polishing lenses.

ONYX

Hardness, 3   S.G., 2.58–2.75   R.I., 1.45–1.65

The onyx that most lapidaries are confronted with is not onyx at all, but rather travertine. Popular varieties of this beautiful material come from Utah, near Death Valley in California, and Mexico. It is used for novelties such as book ends, spheres, dishes, clocks (fig. 8–1), and many other useful things. There are many methods of processing this soft material, but they all involve the use of oxalic acid. The late Oregon C. Barnes, whose dinnerware set (fig. 8–2) is famous, used the following methods:

Cut the onyx to the approximate size of the article you have in mind. After it is cut, chuck it in a four-jaw chuck, using leather strips between the jaws and the stone to keep the material from chipping. Center the rock and clamp it hard enough to keep it from slipping. Free tail stock (live center, ball bearing) is good for this purpose. The speed of the back gear should be only about 75 rpm. Have plenty of water running on the work at all times. Use soft tool steel (Rex or AAA), about 6 or 8 bits to start with, and keep lots of clearance. You will

need right and left and square cut bits and a cutoff tool 1″ (2.5 cm) x ⅛″ (0.32 cm).

Cut the bottom of any piece of work first, leaving a boss or shoulder to hold the piece when it is turned around. Cut each piece to the desired outer shape and smooth it as much as possible. Then turn the job around, but do not clamp the jaws too tight.

When you are ready to drill out the center, drill a ¾″ (1.9-cm) hole in the exact center of the job, cutting from the center to the outside. You may have to use a boring bar. When the piece is about as thin as you wish it (such as a cup or a tumbler), the cutting has to be done very slowly and with little pressure.

After this lathe work is complete, the polishing begins. Use a coarse rubbing stone to remove the tool marks. Keep changing to finer stones and always use plenty of water. Wet carborundum paper may also be used. After all the visible scratches have been removed, use some of the finest steel wool and 600-grit carborundum with water for the final rubbing. When the onyx shows a wavy effect, it is ready to polish.

A splendid polisher is a long nap carpet lap, turning at about 600 rpm. After the lap is thoroughly wet, pat on a generous amount of English putty powder and work it well down into the lap. Keep the onyx moving on the lap and use a lot of pressure, inspecting the work often. When the polish is high and glossy and free from all scratches, brush into the lap a small amount of oxalic acid solution, made of one part acid to nine parts water (about 3 ounces (85 g) of crystals to 1 quart (1 l, of water). A mixture of a half tablespoonful (60 cc) of crystals and about 4 tablespoonfuls (60 ml) of water in an old cup or fruit jar will last a long time. Polish vigorously and wipe the work dry with a soft cloth after wiping off all the acid.

The lap can be made from 1″ (2.5) x

Fig. 8–1 "The Fire Eating Clock," made of honey onyx by Richard Porter, Muscoy, California. (*Photo by Art Miller*)

Fig. 8–2 Dinnerware set made of Death Valley onyx by the late O. C. Barnes, whose methods are described in this chapter. It was owned by Walter Pilkington of Hesperia, California, who added many unique pieces, such as lamps. This is one of the finest lapidary accomplishments in the United States, representing many years of labor. The present ownership of the set is not known. (Photo by Clint Grant)

12″ (30.5 cm) cross-grain boards, laminated to prevent warping. It is turned to a saucer shape about 1½″ (3.8 cm) deep and filled with a strip of canvas, loose in the center and tacked at the edge. Over this goes the carpet, with a long soft wool nap. Carpet swatches can be had from almost any carpet store, where they are discarded every day. This lap is fine for cabochons, too, for great pressure can be used with little danger of burning the stones. Oxalic acid can be purchased in ounce cans from drugstores at high prices or at paint stores or lapidary supply houses by the pound at much lower prices. Since oxalic acid oxidizes, it should be prepared fresh before using. *It is a poison. Keep it away from children and pets.* These same methods can be used for many other soft materials, such as ricolite, travertine, and marble.

OPAL

Hardness, 5.5–6.5 *S.G.,* 1.9–2.3 *R.I.,* 1.43–1.47

Opal is essentially an amorphous material without any crystalline form, a hydrated silica which was apparently formed with extremely submicroscopic layers or films, although there is some recent scientific study which indicates there may be extremely small twinning present to account for the wonderfully beautiful coloring. Many regard opal as the most beautiful of all gemstones.

Opal contains a certain amount of moisture in its makeup. It is extremely brittle and will fly apart upon heating to a certain temperature. This temperature will vary considerably with different types, which may contain from as little as 2 percent to as much as 13 percent water. Rapid and uneven heating is particularly destructive to gem opal. It is impossible to dehydrate it without destroying it as a gem material. There are varying opinions about "curing" opal after it is taken from the ground. Some opal from Australia seems to need no special care and will apparently last almost indefinitely after being cut, with no change. On the other hand, certain types of Nevada opal, some of the most beautiful and colorful the world produces, defies cutting, having a form of tension which causes it to fly apart if any attempt at grinding or polishing it is made; or if very gentle treatment succeeds in getting a stone made, it will very often check with minute cracks. Various substances in which to immerse opal have been tried with the idea of maintaining its solidity and freedom from checking. Glycerine and water is a favorite of many, while plain water is used by others. Mineral oil has been, but should *not* be, used, for its nature is completely foreign to opal. Plain water is the best storage solution, for it never did opal any harm and may help maintain the moisture content. Wearing opals and handling them also aids in keeping them.

Cutting opal by grinding may sometimes be a somewhat tricky business; it all depends on the type of opal being cut. The best Australian and Mexican types and those from Honduras cut with the least trouble. Make sure that the grinding wheels are running completely true. If they are not and there is any slap at all, you are asking for trouble. True them up with a wheel dresser, either of the rotating star-wheel type or with a diamond dresser held against a steady rest. This is in order to avoid shock at any time.

Study the opal rough carefully and first strip away all "potch" (colorless areas) and sandstone backing by carefully grinding it on the edge of the wheel. View the opal carefully against a shaded light. The areas with greatest fire will be the most transparent when viewed edgewise. The fire often lies in parallel layers with gray "potch" between. Such an opal requires slitting with the thinnest blade you can muster on the trim saw. Most cutting oils cause no trouble while sawing.

Select the area of greatest fire and make this the center of the projected cabochon. If the opal is very closely layered rather than solid fire, sometimes the most effective use is to cut a rather high cabochon with the layers edgewise. Slitting parallel to the fire may also be done if the layers are thick enough, but this sometimes brings disappointing results. Such material may then be made into doublets, using a natural gray "potch" opal backing and a thin slice of fire opal cemented together by a method to be described later. There is, of course, no objection to making doublets of opal that cannot be used in any other manner, for no deception is intended. Opal sliced as thin as $1/32''$ (0.08 cm) has been so used in commercial stones made in Australia, and the finished pieces are remarkably beautiful. The backing is almost invariably "potch" with a black cement used between the layers.

Grinding Opal

After the opal cabochon has been visualized in the rough and the area selected, grind the black flat on a 220-grit wheel, resisting the temptation to use the side of the wheel in order to get it flat, for this is often lacking in water spray and tends to heat the opal. Mark out the oversize outline of the cabochon with a marking pencil and remove the excess by grinding with gentle pressure. Too much pressure will generate heat and cause chipping. Hold the opal in the fingers if it is large enough to grind without dopping; otherwise, grind the back and proceed to dop the blank before continuing.

Dopping Opal

The sheet aluminum "stove" and alcohol lamp are almost worthless in dopping opal; in fact, such brutal heating is almost a sure way to court disaster. Use a heat lamp and a pad of steel wool to bring the opal to dopping temperature. Ordinary dopping wax on a wood stick, brought to a temperature where it is almost flowing, will pick up the opal, and it can then be shaped with the moistened fingers, but one should avoid touching the surface of the hot opal with cool, wet fingers.

For more delicate opal, stick shellac will provide an excellent dopping material which melts at a lower temperature. For the most delicate opal, cold-dopping is indicated. To do this, mix a small amount of acetone cement with cornstarch to form a dough. Apply a thin layer of the full-strength cement to the end of the wood dop stick and another layer to the bottom of the opal. When it is almost dry, apply half the dough to the stick, the other half to the bottom of the opal, bring the parts together, and mold the dough to support the entire bottom of the blank. Lay it aside to allow the acetone to dry and the cement to harden, and proceed to grind. This cement may be removed by immersing stick and stone in a small jar of acetone. This method will dop any stone without heat.

Acetone is not a trade name; it refers to a type of cement. Any cement that has an acetone base is one that can be dissolved in acetone. If you have cement and cannot determine by the label whether or not it has an acetone base, put a drop or two on a piece of aluminum foil and let it harden. Then drop it into some acetone, and if it will dissolve completely, then it has an acetone base and can be used for preparing the dop material for your opals or any other very heat-sensitive gemstones.

When the preliminary grinding has been done, take the stone to the 220-grit wet sander and start removing all scratches, then sand with the 400-grit wet sander. At no time should opal be allowed to get hot. Then take it to the 600-grit sander for the final sanding.

Polishing Opal

Opal may be polished on the regular hard felt wheel with cerium oxide if it is kept wet at all times with a thick slurry of paste. Some purists claim, however, that this is too harsh, and they use a muslin buff with a rather loose face, applying tin oxide slurry wet and using very little pressure. This is the method of some of the older professional lapidaries. The material takes a very high polish, and if the sanding operation has been well done, there will be no difficulty in the polishing.

Making Doublets

If a doublet is to be made, grind a piece of gray "potch" for the back and flat it on a diamond lap or on a piece of flat steel with 400 loose grit. Do the same for the thin blank of precious opal, before either has been shaped, then clean both parts with acetone. Prepare a cement of (1) black chaser's pitch; (2) boiled Canada balsam heated to fluidity to which a little lampblack has been added (can be secured quickly by smoking the underside of a cool surface with a kerosene lamp); or (3) one of the new epoxy cements into which a little lampblack has been mixed. Warm the two parts of the doublet if the first two are to be used, after cleaning their surfaces with acetone. Apply a little of the cement with a watch-spring spatula and spread evenly on the base; then *slide* the opal wafer on, avoiding any air bubbles. Lay it aside until cool, and then grind and polish in the usual manner, making the edge of the precious opal the edge of the bevel of the cabochon and beveling and "pillowing" or flatting the bottom piece of "potch."

Dopping the Doublet

Since the temperature at which a doublet that has been put together with heat would also cause it to come apart or move if repeated in the dopping stage, use dopping compounds that have a lower melting temperature. A mixture of beeswax (one part) and rosin (two parts) gently melted together is one such dopping wax that can be made. Stick shellac is also excellent, especially if the stone and the dop stick are first given a preliminary coating of liquid shellac (a little shellac dissolved in alcohol will do). Or, the cold-dopping method previously described will do quite well. Alcohol will remove a stone dopped with shellac without affecting pitch, and polishing compound will not stick to the edge of the pitch where the two parts join. No unusual care is needed in grinding, sanding, or polishing except to avoid heating at any stage.

PETOSKEY STONES

This gemstone, of the same hardness as agate and sometimes called Petoskey agate, is valuable only as a curiosity, and it makes an interesting conversation piece for desk paperweights or bola mounts. The stone is Colony Coral (hexagonaria) and is a "native" of Michigan, named after the town of Petoskey in that state. It is difficult to polish, since the conventional felt buff-tin oxide method for agate produces only lackluster results. Use a $3/4''$ (1.9-cm-) thick plywood disk covered with foam rubber over which is stretched a piece of 10-ounce (280-g) canvas. Soak the buff with a saturated solution of oxalic acid and then apply tin oxide slurry. When the stone begins to "pull," apply more oxalic acid but very little more tin oxide. Sometimes the eyes in a particular stone will not polish at all, in which case it is best to abandon that stone.

RHODONITE

Hardness, $5^{1}/_{2}$–$6^{1}/_{2}$ *S.G.,* 3.5–3.68 *R.I.,* 1.71–1.75

Rhodonite is a massive gem mineral occurring in shades of pink, from very light to very dark, with black veinlets of manganese. It is very difficult to get a high luster, but the best pieces the authors have seen were polished on well-worn No. 220 sanding cloth at a speed of at least 2,500 rpm with no further polishing of any kind. The polishing methods given for azurite (see previous section) are reported to be very good. Because of its beauty and fair degree of hardness and its availability in large chunks at a reasonable price, rhodonite is much favored for novelties, such as ashtrays and book ends. Felt buffs do nothing for the material, but leather and cerium oxide seem to help.

TURQUOISE

Hardness, 6 *S.G.,* 2.76 *R.I.,* 1.60–1.62

Turquoise should be slit with water as the lubricant, for the cutting oil will color it a temporary deeper shade of blue, and this will often fade in a short time to an unlovely green color. Turquoise is rather soft, and care should be taken to make the cabochon preform a little larger than the desired finished stone, to allow for sanding. No difficulty will be experienced in grinding turquoise, for it has no apparent grain or texture to interfere with shaping it. Use the 220-grit wheel and go directly from this to the 220-grit sander, always wet. Follow this with 400 and 600 sanding, keeping the stone wet at all times. Back-bevel the lower edge.

Turquoise should be polished with tin oxide on a convex padded disk buffer run vertically at about 400 rpm. The face of this should be leather with the rough side out. The tin oxide is applied with a brush from a creamy slurry mixture kept in a covered container nearby, and polishing is started with the buff moist. As it proceeds, very short use can be made of the almost dry outer edge. Be careful not to overdo this, however, for turquoise cannot stand too much heat without showing white spots. Use a

swiping motion, starting the contact at one edge of the cabochon and completing the contact entirely across with each stroke. Do not hold the stone in contact with the buff and turn it, for this invites the buildup of heat. Such careful, heat-free buffing will soon result in a very high polish, although some grades which are not of the highest dense quality and deep color tend to yield a more velvety luster.

Never use ammonia, soap, or detergents on genuine turquoise—in fact, a good test of the genuine is to apply a spot of ammonia to the back of a suspected piece. If it is genuine, it will turn white, although Persian turquoise resists this test. Much synthetic "turquoise" today is made by combining copper phosphate powder with styrene and coloring matter to produce a product of excellent color and texture. This is being used in a great deal of the "Indian" jewelry made in Rhode Island for sale to gullible tourists. Genuine Indian jewelry will bear the mark of an Indian tribal council or a reputable maker, such as Maisel's of Albuquerque, whose artisans are Indian craftsmen.

"Coloring" turquoise that is pale by immersing it in warm colorless mineral oil or melted paraffin for 24 hours will give a temporary increase in the "blueness" of the stone, but this fades rather quickly and will exude the oil when warmed, later turning greenish. This practice is to be discouraged. The best grades of native turquoise come from Nevada, Arizona, New Mexico, and Colorado, with small amounts from California and a few other western states. The very best colored hard material comes from Iran (Persia) and can be obtained from gem importers. There are many fine turquoise pieces mounted with diamonds lying in family heirloom chests, for the gem was featured at one time by Tiffany's of New York, who operated the old mine at Los Cerrillos, New Mexico, for a time. The very extensive prehistoric mining there emphasizes that turquoise was one of the several gem materials called *chalchihuitl* (along with jade) and miscalled "emerald" by early Spanish translators (a fact that has led many authors, even some modern ones, astray when they attribute emerald to Mexico). Also consult the method for polishing azurite.

Recently turquoise has again become very popular, especially in Indian jewelry. Several new methods have been devised to stabilize and improve the color and the hardness of the turquoise. Those stones which have been impregnated with silicon or some of the newer resins are very stable and do not lose their color. It is also very difficult to determine that the turquoise has been treated when these newer processes have been employed. If you are using this type of material, it should still be handled with care and not allowed to get hot. The same methods should be used as with the natural untreated material.

UNAKITE

Hardness, 6–7   S.G., 3.25–3.50   R.I., 1.74–1.76

This is a form of green epidote often cut as a cabochon but principally cut into novelties, such as ashtrays. It contains pink and red inclusions like freckles, which are probably feldspar or mica, and is a great favorite with the German cutters at Idar-Oberstein. Very good deposits occur in Virginia. It is not an expensive material. Use cerium oxide on a felt buff after conventional cutting.

9. The Use of Diamond Products by the Lapidary

In the early development of the lapidary hobby, diamond abrasives were used only where it was considered a necessity, which was mainly for the faceting laps and diamond saw blades. This was primarily due to the expense of diamond products and the lack of knowledge concerning the uses of diamond products by the lapidary.

Most of the technological advances that were taking place were directed toward the industrial application of diamond products rather than their use by the lapidary.

The source of supply for diamond laps and powders was usually limited to the manufacturer of faceting machines or an occasional lapidary supply company which would stock diamond powders in vials containing 1 carat of diamond, usually in those grain sizes considered necessary for faceting laps, such as 100, 400, 600, and 6,400 grit for cutting and polishing laps. Many lapidary supply companies did not stock diamond powders but would be willing to send in special orders for those customers who needed them.

Diamond saw blades were easier to obtain, since most hobbyists have some type of trim saw or slab saw. Many faceters would obtain blank copper laps and charge their own laps, a subject which will be discussed in chapter 10. Most faceters who preferred to charge their own laps used copper laps, because they were easier to charge initially and could be recharged with the same grit-size diamond powder with considerable less expense than replacing them with new commercially impregnated diamond laps.

Continuing technological developments have resulted in new products and less expensive manufacturing processes for those new products. In turn, manufacturers and suppliers were looking for new markets for their products; as a result, some companies are now producing a much wider range of diamond products designed specifically for the lapidary. These include new and better saw blades in a wider variety of sizes and thicknesses, ranging from 36″ (91.4-cm) diameter saw blades to 4″ (10.2-cm) diameter saw blades. Other diamond products now available include a wide variety of laps, wheels, sanding disks and belts, core drills and carving tools, a variety of diamond compounds in syringes for use as abrasive and polishing compounds which can be applied to a variety of hard wood laps, and wheels and cups for grinding and polishing star stones and chatoyant gemstone materials (figs. 9–1 to 9–3).

Fig. 9–1 A diamond bar dresser for truing silicon carbide grinding wheels. (*Courtesy, Crystalite Corp.*)

There has been a sufficient number of diamond product manufacturers and suppliers to promote a healthy competitive market, thereby keeping the price of diamond products down within the price range that the lapidary hobbyist can afford to pay. New equipment specifically designed to accommodate the newer diamond products is shown in

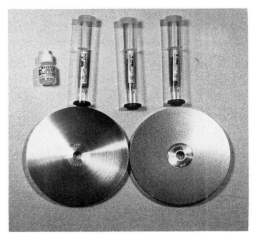

Fig. 9–2 Diamond disk and compounds. (*Courtesy, Crystalite Corp.*)

the accompanying photographs. Many lapidaries prefer to rough out their gemstones or cabochons on silicon abrasive wheels and then do the sanding and polishing of the cabochon with the diamond disks or pads, and some machines have been designed to incorporate such combinations.

ADVANTAGES OF DIAMOND PRODUCTS

It is true that diamond products are more expensive than standard silicon carbide supplies; however, they have several advantages which more than

Fig. 9–3 Crystalrings, peripheral diamond grinding wheels. (*Courtesy, Crystalite Corp.*)

compensate for the higher costs that are initially expended. Some of the major advantages are compactness, the low noise factor, the wide range of materials which can be cut and polished with diamond, and the cleanliness of operation, as well as the added length of the cutting qualities of diamond.

TYPES OF DIAMOND EQUIPMENT AND PRODUCTS

The cost of the basic machines used for cutting cabochons is comparable to that of those machines designed for silicon carbide wheels and sanding disks or belts. The extra cost involved is due to

Fig. 9–4 The Diamond Miser is is a small, compact unit designed for sanding and polishing which can be used in apartments, campers, or anywhere that has an AC power source. (*Courtesy, Ran-Co Lapidary Products*)

Fig. 9–5 This 45° Covington unit has a trim saw, grinding wheels, its own water system, and sanding and polishing disks. (*Courtesy, Covington Engineering Corp.*)

Fig. 9–6 The Gryphon Ten-In-One Lapidary Workshop unit is designed so that it can be set at any angle necessary. If vertical wheels are desired, it can be set at the proper angle; moreover, the unit can be tipped so that its working lap is parallel to the base of the machine to provide a basic master lap for a faceting head. (*Courtesy, Gryphon Corp.*)

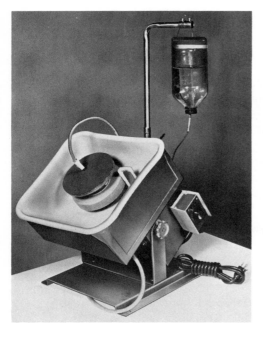

Fig. 9–7 The Ray-Tilt 6″ (15.2-cm) gem maker has a trunnion mounting which allows you to select any angle you wish. It is equipped with a silicon carbide grinding wheel, while above it the diamond sanding and polishing disks can be quickly changed. (*Courtesy, Raytech Industries*)

Fig. 9–8 The Professional Diamond Demon is equipped with Quick Disc changing for grinding, sanding, and polishing. It is compact and portable. (*Courtesy, Crystalite Corp.*)

Fig. 9–9 The Demon Combo includes a trim saw and a vertical running face plate for grinding, with interchangeable sanding disk and polishing pads. (*Courtesy, Terra Products*)

Fig. 9–10 The Genii has two grinding wheels and interchangeable spool drums for sanding and polishing. It is compact and quiet. (*Courtesy, Diamond Pacific Tool Corp.*)

Fig. 9–11 The Coronette has two grinding wheels with a recirculating lubricant system, four diamond sanding drums, and an end face plate for polishing pads. (*Courtesy, Gem-Tec Diamond Tool Co.*)

Fig. 9–12 The Crown diamond polishing unit is designed to sand and polish star stones, cat's-eyes, and cabochons. It has a cover which can be placed over it when it is not in use. (*Courtesy, Crown Manufacturing Co.*)

the diamond wheels and compounds, which are the expendable items. There are three basic types of machines for cabochon cutting (figs. 9–4 to 9–12). The first type generally incorporates two vertical grinding wheels and two or more wheels that can be charged with diamond compound for sanding, plus a disk for final polishing. The sanding wheels may be either wooden wheels or composition wheels. The second type provides for the grinding wheels, either one or two, and an end face plate on which sanding disks or polishing disks may be mounted. Remember, you should have a separately charged disk for each grain size of diamond. Each disk should be stored in a plastic bag or mailing envelope to prevent contamination when it is not being used. The third type incorporates the use of both a silicon carbide grinding wheel and a master lap mounted over the wheel, so

that one can change diamond disks for the various grain sizes or grits needed for sanding and polishing. All of these machines are compact, reasonably quiet, and much cleaner to operate.

Occasionally you will hear someone say, "I sure wish I could have some cabochon cutting equipment, but I can't because I live in an apartment," or they may say, "I live in a mobile home park and I cannot make that much noise." Diamond units are the answer to such statements, and the additional lasting qualities of the diamond products will offset the added initial cost (fig. 9–13). Most mobile home parks allow one or two storage facilities, and a small compact trim saw could be set up in one of the storage facilities. Apartment dwellers often have a garage or a service porch area where a trim saw could be used. If the saw and motor were mounted on a base plate or board, it

Fig. 9–13 The lady of the house has converted one corner of the second bedroom into a lapidary corner. She has her faceting unit in the corner, a compact gem drill to the right, and a diamond cabochon unit next. She also has a 10″ (25.4-cm) vibrating lap which does not show in the photograph. (*Photo by John Washalaski*)

could be portable and could be set into a lock cabinet when not in use. Or perhaps there is a dealer or club close to your area where you would be permitted to use a trim saw.

CUTTING AND POLISHING WITH DIAMOND

Now that diamond products are being widely adapted to the cutting of cabochons, as well as faceting and cabbing star rubies and sapphires, here are some suggestions which may be helpful to those who are considering diamond products for cutting and polishing cabochons. Whether you select the vertical running wheel type of equipment or the type of unit designed for using flat laps, you should have two grinding wheels or laps for the initial grinding and shaping of the cabochon, a rough grind and a fine grind, as well as several sanding and polishing stages (fig. 9–14). There are several combinations available. Some manufacturers recommend an 80-grit wheel for roughing out the stone and fine grinding with a 220-grit diamond wheel. Others recommend a 100-grit or 180-grit wheel for roughing out the stone and then a 600 or 1,200-grit wheel for fine grinding. Please do remember that, even though you are using diamond, a lubricant of some type is necessary. A lubricant serves two purposes: first, it keeps the grinding operation cool so that friction heat does not develop; second, it keeps the wheels or disks free of slug and waste which has been removed from the stone. When the rough grinding is finished, you will need several progressively finer grits for sanding and polishing. Some manufacturers recommend water on the two grinding wheels; others recommend a special lubricant. It is recommended that the beginner select whatever brand of diamond products he prefers and then follow the manufacturer's recommendations until he becomes proficient

Fig. 9–14 Galaxy diamond grinding wheels are available in both rough and fine grinds. (*Courtesy, Diamond Pacific Tool Corp.*)

in handling their products. Each manufacturer has designed his products to work in conjunction with his other products. When you have become proficient in using diamond products, then you may wish to experiment with different combinations and other products.

Be careful not to contaminate your sanding wheels or disks. You should use a different disk for each of the different grits used for sanding. Be sure to clean your hands and the stone between each of the sanding stages and before going to your final polishing process. Some manufacturers recommend a cleaning solution designed for that specific purpose or a mild detergent soap and slightly warm water.

Cutting a Jadeite Cabochon

The stone desired was a jadeite buff-top cabochon (fig. 9–15a). A buff-top cabochon is flat on the back and has a very low or shallow crown on the top, which is usually only about 25 percent of the total depth of the stone. It is difficult to cut this type of cabochon without having a flat spot in the center of the

Fig. 9–15a Burma jadeite buff-top cabochon (*left*) and three Wyoming nephrite cabochons with the corresponding rough (*Courtesy, Crystalite Corp.*)

Fig. 9–15d Doming the buff-top cabochon on a peripheral diamond wheel. (*Courtesy, Crystalite Corp.*)

Fig. 9–15b One drop of Eastman 910 on one of two flat surfaces for fast dopping. (*Courtesy, Crystalite Corp.*)

Fig. 9–15e Crystalpad, Flexo-Disc, and contact cement ready for bonding. (*Courtesy, Crystalite Corp.*)

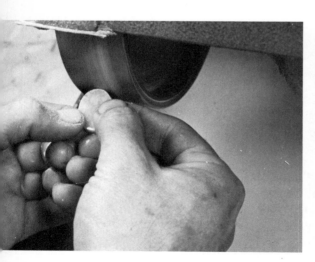

Fig. 9–15c Grinding a cabochon to the edge outline on a 100-grit peripheral diamond grinding wheel. (*Courtesy, Crystalite Corp.*)

Fig. 9–15f Mounting the Flexo-Disc and pad on the machine, which is threaded for fast spin on and off. (*Courtesy Crystalite Corp.*)

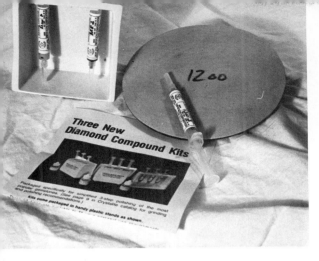

Fig. 9–15g The 325, 1,200, and 50,000 diamond compound used for three-step smoothing and polishing. (*Courtesy, Crystalite Corp.*)

Fig. 9–15i Polishing with diamond compound charged on to a pad. (*Courtesy, Crystalite Corp.*)

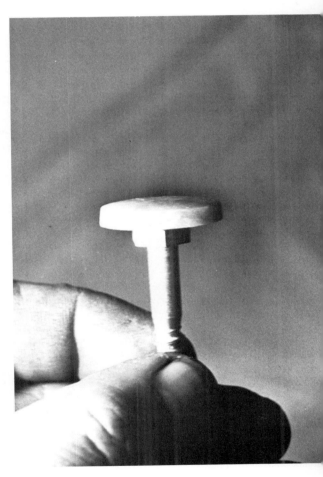

Fig. 9–15h Applying extender fluid after charging and spreading the diamond compound. (*Courtesy, Crystalite Corp.*)

Fig. 9–15j A shaped 18 x 25 mm (.71″ x .98″) buff-top cabochon. (*Courtesy, Crystalite Corp.*)

top of the cabochon. Jade cabochons, both jadeite and nephrite, have a tendency toward "orange peel" polish due to their internal structure (see chapter 8). The diamond unit used was one which had a 100 and a 600-grit grinding wheel with a recirculating pumped lubricant and an end arbor on which different flat laps and pads can be mounted for the sanding and polishing procedures.

The cabochon was marked with a template in the usual manner and then taken to the trim saw and trimmed from the slab with a series of straight cuts. Then the saw oil was washed from the cabochon blank with warm detergent soap and water. If you prefer, you can hand hold the cabochon blank and, on the 100-grit wheel, finish rounding the shape of the oval which was marked with the template and then dop the cabochon. If you do not like to hand hold cabochon blanks, then dop the stone before any grinding is started. Since the gemstone was jadeite and therefore tough and not especially heat-sensitive, it was dopped with a cyanoacrylate cement, such as Eastman 910, which will not allow the cabochon to shift should the heat during the final polishing be sufficient to allow the regular dop wax to soften (fig. 9–15b).

If you should use this type of cement, remember that it is a contact cement and must have a clean, flat surface to form a good bond. It is not a filler cement. You should have dop sticks which have a flat, smooth surface, such as a large, flat-headed aluminum roofing nail or flat-headed bolts that are free of marks or burrs. It will set initially in several seconds, but it should be allowed to cure for several hours for a better bond. Should you be working with heat-sensitive stones, be sure to follow your usual methods or those recommended for special materials (see chapter 8).

After the cabochon is dopped, continue to grind it to the proper shape on the 100-grit wheel (fig. 9–15c). Continue to grind and shape the cabochon until the desired shape is obtained. To shape a low crown or buff top, start at the outside edges of the stone and work to the center (fig. 9–15d), checking frequently to be sure you are not overcutting, as diamond cuts considerably faster than the silicon carbide wheels. When this step is completed, then move to the 600-grit wheel and repeat the same process but continue to grind until all of the 100-grit wheel marks have been completely removed. When this step is finished, the cabochon should have a matt finish which does not show any undercutting. Then you are ready to start the sanding process.

The sanding process was done with resin-treated pads which were charged with diamond compound, backed with a solid, semiflexible rubber disk. The resin-treated pad retains the diamond compound, and the solid rubber disk is flexible enough to allow a certain amount of pliability but will eliminate or, at least, minimize the problem of "orange peel" effect which so often develops during the sanding process.

The resin-treated pads used have a sticky film on the back which is protected by a paper covering. The solid, semiflexible rubber disk should be coated with a contact cement (fig. 9–15e); then the paper back is removed from the resin pad, and it is pressed onto the semiflexible rubber disk with the thumbs (fig. 9–15f). Do not use Peel 'Em Off cement. If any of the resin-treated disk protrudes over the edges of the semiflexible disk, trim it off with a sharp pair of scissors. When this is completed, charge the pad with the diamond compound you wish to use. The first sanding stage should be done with a 325-grit diamond compound (fig. 9–15g), since it is necessary to continue to remove the wheel marks and imperfections that were left by the 600-grit wheel. To charge the pad, the diamond compound is spotted around the pad in a circle and smeared into the pad evenly with the finger tip. To properly charge a 6″ (15.2-cm) pad requires about 0.5 g of diamond compound. A special lubricant extender is added before each stone is sanded (fig. 9–15h). The purpose of the lubricant extender is to loosen the charge and flush the cutting waste from the pad and to prevent excessive friction heat.

Even though the 325-grit wheel appears to be coarser than the 600-grit wheel, remember that it performed a cutting and grinding process and that it is necessary to use a coarser sanding process to remove the remainder of the wheel marks and imperfections. The diamond compound lays into the pad and, by using a very light pressure, you can get a smoother finish, since very slight cutting action is experienced.

The next sanding process, a semipolishing process, should be accomplished by the use of 1,200-grit compound. Be sure you wash your hands and the cabochon. Do not mix different diamond grits on the same pad. When you remove the 325-grit pad from the grinding unit, store it in a plastic wrapper or bag to prevent contamination and save it for later use with another cabochon. Pads should be recharged only as needed; they will smooth quite a few cabochons before they need to be recharged. The occasional reapplication of a drop or two of the special lubricant extender fluid to the pad while you are working will help control the friction heat which has a tendency to develop when pressure is applied in the sanding process.

The 1,200-grit sanding process is completed in the same manner as before except that you can use a little heavier pressure. The system described here has recommended a silicon oil fluid rather than water as a lubricant. The 1,200 grit will give a very good finish, usually equal to the polish obtained by standard methods. However, for a high porcelain finish on your cabochon, remove the 1,200 grit and again change to another pad which is charged with 50,000-grit diamond compound and apply more pressure as you work the cabochon (fig. 9–15i). When you are finished, you should have a very high shiny procelain finish (fig. 9–15j). Many cabochons can be finally polished on a 3,000-grit diamond, and the 50,000 grit is not necessary. When you are ready to remove the cabochon from the dop stick, place a sharp knife blade at the joint of the dop stick and the cabochon and give the knife blade a light sharp blow.

A SUMMARY OF GENERAL INFORMATION

Most diamond compounds are sold in syringes for easy use and storage (fig. 9–16). The syringes are usually marked in graduated fractions of 1 or 2g, whichever the capacity of the syringe may be, and you can determine how much has been used to charge a pad or disk. Most

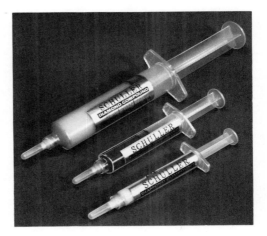

Fig. 9–16 Diamond compounds are often sold in syringes for easy use and convenience in handling and are available in most micron sizes. Usually they are color coded; however, there is some variation in the coding between different manufacturers (*Courtesy, Jack V. Schuller*)

manufacturers also color code the different grit sizes; however, the color codes tend to vary with the different manufacturers. In general, they are fairly similar, but they are not discussed here because of the variability. You should familiarize yourself with the particular product you are using. The amount of diamond concentration in the compound also varies to some extent with each manufacturer. While the grit size has been established according to the Bureau of Standards, the concentration is established by each manufacturer as a part of their manufacturing process and is considered a trade secret not given out to the general public or competitors.

From time to time, you will hear sales personnel and manufacturers of diamond products refer to the Bureau of Standards. The Bureau of Standards was formed for the purpose of establishing nationally recognized requirements for products being manufactured and also provides a basis of common understanding of the characteristics of the products. Even though the standards originated within a given industry, compliance with the standards is strictly voluntary, and the Bureau of Standards has no regulatory power to enforce the provisions established.

The standards were originally developed and published in September 1963. At that time, it was sometimes difficult for the user to get diamond powder graded to, or within, certain specifications. The standards have recently been revised. The National Bureau of Standards "Voluntary Product Standards" PS 62–74, issued by the American National Standards Institute on 16 October 1974, is now the accepted reference for governing the quality of micron diamond. The purpose is to establish nationally recognized standards for sizing diamond powder in micron (subsieve) sizes and also to provide a common basic understanding between the seller and the purchaser with reference to particle size and quality.

10 · How to Facet Gems

For a good many hundreds or perhaps even thousands of years after man had learned to make use of colorful and decorative gemstones for personal adornment, for seals and scarabs, fetishes or other articles used in religious ceremonies, he was content to grind and polish them into relatively simple forms. Beads and pendants were among the earliest forms, often pierced by laborious drilling.

There are no exact records to show the date when gems began to be faceted, which is the art of cutting and polishing flat planes or facets on a gemstone in such a manner as to enhance its inherent color and brilliance. At first, it seems probable that natural faces of crystals were simply rubbed on a flat abrasive stone, and then polished by rubbing on a finer surface of wood or leather.

India, apparently, must be credited with the first work of this type. Indeed, there are still in existence examples of diamonds cut and polished in this fashion, and some of these were first illustrated by copperplate engravings in the old English book dated 1678 which recounted the journeys of Jean Baptiste Tavernier (figs. 10–1 and 10–2). Much of the evidence is circumstantial. Tradition establishes that India was producing diamonds, gold, rubies, and "white iron" before 1000 B.C. The iron was a necessity for cutting diamonds. Bronze (which was, of course, known for a considerable period before the use of iron and steel) would not allow cutting of diamond—it was too soft.

Somewhere back in antiquity man discovered that diamond rubbed against diamond would abrade the crystal form in which it was found into a shape more to the liking of the wearer. Sometime, somewhere, it was also discovered that the diamond chips and dust from this operation, if applied to an iron plate, would eventually create a flat, polished area or facet if the crystal was rubbed long enough on one spot. Now diamond does not cut in just any place or direction desired; hence, these first facets were placed more or less haphazardly over the surface of the rough crystal. But they did something for the diamond, releasing from its interior brilliant reflections and fiery prismatic flashes of color such as to make the gem the most sought-after possession of monarchs.

We have no way of knowing who first applied the principle of the wheel to the cutting of facets on gemstones. We only know that two methods survive today among native cutters of India and Thailand (Siam), and since there is a ten-

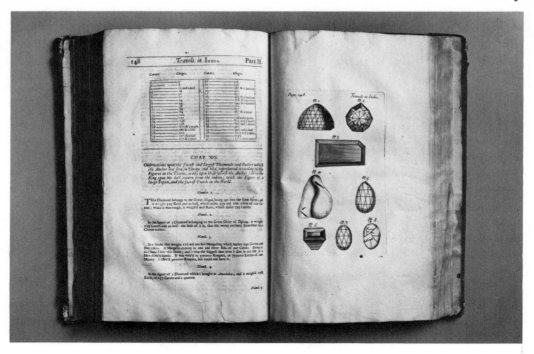

Fig. 10–1 A page from the past, showing copperplate engravings from an old book (1678). Shown at the upper left is a diagram of the Great Mogul diamond, which has since been completely lost. Right is a diagram of the Duke of Tuscany diamond, later called the Florentine diamond. The archaic form in which stones were first faceted is also shown. (*Photo by Paul Samuelson*)

dency for methods long used to remain unchanged to the present day, we may surmise that these are the identical methods used much earlier. Much of the early work on ruby and sapphire was done by holding the gemstone in the fingers after the fashion of the native cutters of Thailand today, who cut the stone by rubbing it in a swinging arc across a washboardlike piece of wood held in the lap as they squat on the floor. A small pile of corundum grit on a palm leaf at their side, plus a basin of water in which the lower end of the "washboard" is placed, supplies the lubrication. In India at the present time, much of the cutting is done on a very crude wheel whose axle is mounted horizontally, so that the iron wheel revolves vertically. A short, curved bow with a loose thong of leather for a bowstring is the means of causing the wheel to re-

volve back and forth as the bow is stroked with a short pulling action of the right hand. The gemstone is held in the fingers of the left hand, and the facets are applied entirely by eye. Crushed imperfect corundum crystals were first used as the cutting medium, but today the synthetic carborundum or silicon carbide has largely replaced it. The polishing was done in a similar manner, using a compound largely consisting of rice straw ashes, which contain silica.

Early writings disclose that Kautilya stated that "Southern India [including Ceylon, perhaps?] produces gold, diamonds, rubies and other gems." This was about 400 B.C. Note that the word *gems* is used. They were apparently cut, not rough, gemstones. Cyrus the Great conquered Babylon about 538 B.C. and caused his scribes to boast of the

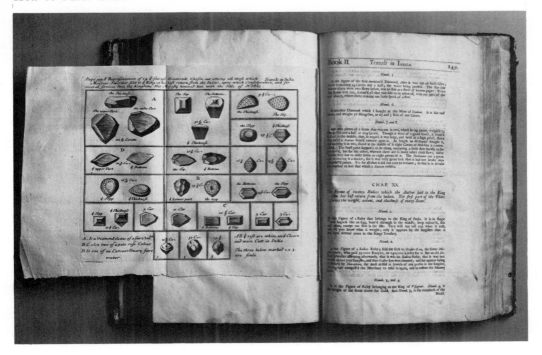

Fig. 10–2 A double-spread insert of a copperplate engraving from *The Travels of Jean Baptiste Tavernier,* an English book published in London in 1678. It shows the earliest forms of faceting done in India. In some instances it will be noted that only the natural faces were polished. Tavernier brought many famous diamonds back to Europe, among them the unique Tavernier Blue, out of which the Hope diamond was later cut. From the collection of the late Hugh Leiper, F.G.A. (*Courtesy, A. Muir Ramsay, Glasgow*)

number of talents worth of gold, silver, diamonds, and rubies which he had taken. Alexander the Great defeated Malavas and his allies in India in 326 B.C. and received, in settlement of his demands for indemnity, diamonds, pearls, and 100 talents of "white iron" (cast iron). At that time, man was just emerging from the Bronze Age, and iron had a value above the price of precious metals. Also, it took iron to cut diamonds.

While early cut gems are known, definitely faceted gems are not mentioned until after the founding of Venice. By A.D. 600 Venice had become a haven of learning and the arts, including jewel cutting. Mention is made of faceted gems for the first time, in the description of a gold cap for the Doge or Duke Tradonico (A.D. 836–861) containing a

diamond with eight facets and a large ruby cut "so it sparkled with red fire." Also, a great cross in the center of the cap was composed of 23 cut emeralds. *Someone, somewhere, faceted those gems.*

There are records that the Low Countries began to take a place in the cutting of gems by about A.D. 1200. In 1458, Louis de Berquem, of Bruges, Belgium, is credited with cutting the first brilliant-cut diamond. Apprentices who learned the art there later spread the cutting of diamonds to Paris, London, and Portugal. The sixteenth century saw Spain overrun Portugal, which had harbored many Jewish gemcutters who had been expelled for religious reasons. They settled in Holland and Belgium, and Amsterdam and Antwerp became the cutting centers for the diamond trade.

The Spanish conquest swelled the coffers of Europe with the riches of Mexico and Peru. The Portugese, the Dutch, and the English traveled to India by water. World trade in compact and readily carried goods, such as gems, spices, and silks, bloomed. Many people grew rich as a result, and rulers and their courts spent money lavishly on gems and furs. The commerce that resulted proved to be an elemental push that brought about the opening of the trade routes of the world. The galleons sailed to every part of the globe in search of gems, spices, and gold to feed the thirsty markets of luxury-loving nobles and kings and their "ladies," if the word can be used for the courtesans who figure so largely in the annals of the French and other courts.

It was at this time that Tavernier made his sixteen journeys to India—fifteen of them overland and only one by water. He was a trader *par excellence* and took out from Europe the baubles he found that the Indian rulers desired, in exchange for which he traded for or purchased some of the most famous diamonds, rubies, sapphires, and spinels of history, and served to introduce to Europe at the heyday of its greatest wealth and splendor up to that time the jewels they desired.

Because a gemstone does not deteriorate and neither time nor rust corrodes its brilliance and beauty of color, the cutter of a faceted gemstone should approach the task with a feeling that what he does to the "rough" shall be well done, for the results of his work will long outlast him. Every gem ever mined in the world is still somewhere—in a museum, in a private collection, or lost in the earth—unless it has been crushed or burned and thus destroyed.

WHO CAN CUT FACETED STONES?

Among the first comments heard around an exhibit of faceted gemstones are exclamations by people who *imagine:* (1) that it requires exceptional eyesight to be able to cut a faceted stone, (2) that exceptional skill or steadiness of hand is necessary, or (3) that faceting is something which only the advanced hobbyist or a professional cutter can do. This latter supposition has no doubt been fostered by the fact that the cutting of diamonds in particular has been for several hundred years rather tightly controlled by guilds who kept their methods secret, trained apprentices only in numbers that would insure high wages, and otherwise led the general public to believe that there was a lot of very hard and difficult training necessary. It is quite true that in order to learn to cut diamonds a considerable apprenticeship is necessary, but it is beyond the scope of this book to discuss such facts. We are concerned only with cutting gemstones ranging in hardness from that of sapphire and ruby (considered to be 9 on the Mohs scale) down to possibly 5, though stones with the latter hardness are delicate and do not always wear well.

All of these suppositions are wrong. A ten-year-old boy with no previous gemcutting experience has been taught to facet an acceptable stone within a few hours, simply by following directions. Some of the most capable faceters are women who learned the art from reading directions; indeed, many faceters of gems are self-taught (fig. 10–3). The author has seen visiting relatives who had never cut a stone of any sort (cabochon or otherwise) turn out a finished brilliant in five or six hours, unaided except for following directions. Those people were not especially skilled, adept of hand, or possessed of exceptional eyesight—*they just followed directions.* That is the way anything may be learned, including faceting!

THE VALUE OF THE HOBBY FOR RELAXATION

Many business and professional men, surgeons, dentists, attorneys, and others

Fig. 10–3 Faceting done by a self-taught amateur, Mrs. Betty Campbell, of Washington, D.C.

who do concentrated work and have a tendency to become very intense if they stick too closely to their jobs find in faceting the ideal hobby which can take their minds completely away from their everyday affairs. Faceting does require *concentration* on the job and nothing else while the hobbyist is working, and this is its greatest value in terms of relaxation, health, and pleasure—in addition to the beautiful gems created, of course.

The greatest assets a student of faceting can have are the desire to attain perfection and the willingness and patience to persevere in each step until perfection has been reached. The faceting of gems

Fig. 10–4 A Sapphire faceting unit mounted on a kneehole-type faceting table. Motor base and master lap spindle are integral, and the entire unit can be stowed away readily when not in use. It is only necessary to plug it in and supply a drip can and waste water container. (*Photo by John Washalaski*)

Fig. 10–5 Girdling position. (*Photo by Paul Samuelson*)

is not for the slapdash, impatient, "that's good enough" type of lapidary worker. Anyone who can see well enough, with or without glasses, to read these lines can cut acceptable faceted stones. Steadiness of hand is not involved, though a fine sense of touch does help. Surgeons and dentists often become exceptionally good cutters of faceted stones.

FUNDAMENTALS OF FACET CUTTING

In order to cut a piece of clear gemstone rough, to place upon it the accurately planned set of facets which are first ground, then polished to a predetermined size, it is necessary to have certain fundamental things:

1. A faceting bench or desk, the center of which is open, *on* top of which, or *in* the top of which, can be fitted the spindle bearing the master lap to which will be affixed the cutting and later the polishing laps used in the various operations. This should not be too high from the floor—about 29″ (74 cm) is best. It can be as little as 30″ (76 cm) in width and 26″ (66 cm) in depth, and the top preferably should be made of waterproof plywood or covered with Formica. One type of facet head is equipped with drain pan and motor and is designed to rest on top of the cutting bench (figs. 10–4 and 10–5). Another type mounts the master lap in a recess in the table and has the motor underneath, with a drain for excess water coming out the rear. Still another type of table is shown in fig. 10–6.

2. The facet head itself. In these modern times, we are not dealing with either the methods or the equipment of olden times. This is no ox-cart age we are living

Fig. 10–6 Another type of table that can be adapted to a faceting table; extra small accessories can be kept in the drawers. (*Photo by John Washalaski*)

Fig. 10–7 The Sapphire faceting unit is complete with motor, head, master lap, and bearing in one unit. It also has a dial speed control for the lap ranging from 0 to 600 rpm. The head assembly may be purchased separately. (*Courtesy, Arrow Profile Co. and M. D. Morang Co.*)

Fig. 10–8 The Lee faceting unit is complete with radial vernier and can be used at variable speeds. The base is all aluminum, and dops can be realigned without extra adaptors. The head assembly may be purchased separately. (*Courtesy, Lee Lapidaries*)

Fig. 10–9 The American Facetor is a new concept in design; it is compact with programmed gears to simplify cutting operations, has a variable lap speed, and can be supplied with a base or can be mounted in your own table or base. It is well counterbalanced. (*Courtesy, American Standard Corp.*)

Fig. 10–10 The MDR Master faceting unit is one of the most widely used units. It comes complete with mast, base, master lap, bearing, and pulley and has a variable speed control and a microadjustment on the head for raising or lowering the head. The head assembly may be purchased separately. (*Courtesy, MDR Manufacturing Co.*)

Fig. 10–11 The Graves Mark I unit is completely self-contained and has all the necessary accessories, as shown here. All you have to do is plug it in and you are ready to start faceting. (*Courtesy, Henry B. Graves Co.*)

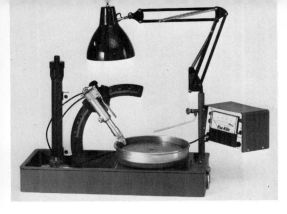

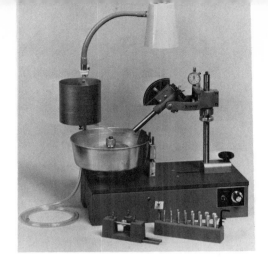

Fig. 10–12 The Fac-Ette faceting unit is complete and has a full 16″ (40.6-cm) protractor. It does not use a removable chuck, and the dop arm is balanced. The radial cheater has a 100 to 1 ratio with the top spindle. (*Courtesy, Fac-Ette Manufacturing Co.*)

Fig. 10–13 The Exacta Classic 200 unit comes complete. It has an electronic control which allows for variable speeds and a compound dial indicator which eliminates squinting to adjust the vernier; it also has a micro-height adjustment. It is available in right-handed or left-handed units. (*Courtesy, Crown Manufacturing Co.*)

Fig. 10–14 The Ultra Tec unit is also available in right-handed or left-handed units. It has all the modern features, including the variable speed control. All of the dials are designed for easy reading. It is compact and easy to use. (*Courtesy, Ultra Tec*)

Fig. 10–15 The Prismatic Accura-flex Model H–71 has the deluxe floating rackgear and the Selectra-Matic base. It also has the microvernier assembly. Several models are available. (*Courtesy, Prismatic Instruments*)

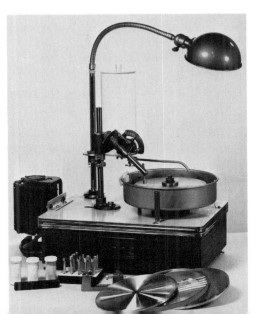

Fig. 10–17 The Allen faceting unit has a sturdy, well-made facet head with all essential features and includes the master lap and base. (*Courtesy, Allen Lapidary Equipment Manufacturing Co.*)

Fig. 10–16 The Raytech-Shaw faceter is a successor to the original Scott faceter. It has been redesigned, retaining the best of the Scott unit, and has a unique hand-held facet head, so that it can be held in any position necessary for directional polishing either with the grain or cross grain. (*Courtesy, Raytech Industries*)

in, nor do the authors see any need to worship the fetish of old-time ways, such as the jam-peg and cone methods used for several hundreds of years by the professionals in cutting gemstones other than diamond. We use and recommend a standard *faceting head,* of which there are a number now on the market (figs. 10–7 to 10–17). There is a very wide range in price, depending upon what features the individual faceter wishes to have incorporated into his own faceting unit. Some faceters prefer to purchase the facet head only and build the lap assembly into a special table or workbench. Others prefer to buy the complete unit, which can be set on a sturdy table or kneehole desk.

In this book we will discuss the Sapphire unit which is in the medium price range and has a motor but not the cutting and polishing laps. The Sapphire faceting unit, originally designed and manufactured by G. L. Higgins of San Diego, California, is now being manufactured by Arrow Profile Company, Hazel Park, Michigan.

Essentials of the facet head

Whatever facet head you select, it should have certain fundamental features, and these should include:

1. A free-running vertical spindle on which is attached firmly a horizontal running master lap plate, which has been lathe-turned after mounting to ensure that it runs very true. This spindle is supplied with bearings of several types in the different units. Some are of oilite porous bronze and are fitted with oiling cups. Other improved bearings are made with a taper to take up bearing wear and leave the spindle true-running through a long life, and this is an excellent feature. Still others are equipped with ball bearings and give long life and excellent service.

2. A ¼ H.P. continuous-duty type of motor, preferably rubber-mounted to lessen vibration. In one type of facet bench, the motor operates with the shaft

in a horizontal position. In the other type in which the motor is to be bolted to the end of the bench under the table, the motor is required to be operated with the shaft in a vertical position. A motor should be selected, therefore, which is equipped for such service, with proper thrust bearings.

3. If mounted under the work bench, a motor should be equipped with a 2″ (5.1-cm) V-groove pulley, while the spindle should have a 10″ (25.4-cm) pulley of similar V-groove design. Oval leather belting can be cut to the proper length and fastened together with flexible copper wire, the ends of which can be turned in and pounded into the leather to prevent annoying "clicking" against the pulley. It is rather hard to find the exact length of endless rubber belting to fit. This setup will provide a lap speed of 350 rpm. This speed can be increased, as you grow more proficient, by changing the size of the pulley on the spindle to 8″ (20.3 cm), 6″ (15.2 cm), or even 5″ (12.7 cm) if desired and shortening the belt. It is well to provide a separate belt and pulley for each speed desired, but this can be done later.

The facet head itself should have a stand rod or mast, preferably of Monel metal or stainless steel so that it will not rust from the water spray often present. This should be fixed to a base, which is machined to a true and accurate right angle. This stand rod base is most often slotted to receive a bolt which has a tinned wing nut, by which it is to be fastened to the table, which should have a series of bolt holes or slots to receive the hold-down bolt. The mast will need to be moved up close for certain operations and quite far back for others, such as the grinding of the circumference or girdle of the gemstone. The portion of the table on which the mast rests should be a part of the same board into which the master lap bearing is fitted, so that the two are parallel and the mast at a true right angle to the base, and the lap itself. If such a facet table is to be constructed, this subtable is a piece of waterproof plywood mounted 2³/₄″ (5.99 cm) below the top of the cutting table. Check to see that the stand rod is true in both directions when it is clamped in place by the bolt fastening it. This can be done with a carpenter's square.

In this type of facet bench, an aluminum drain pan is provided by cutting a circular hole in the table top 9¹/₂″ (24.13 cm) in diameter, which is centered over the spindle of the master lap bearing. A very good drain pan can be made from an aluminum ring mold of the type used for making gelatin desserts (fig. 10–18). This should be about 1¹/₂ quarts (1.5 l) capacity. With tin snips which are made to cut curved lines, the interior rim is then cut down to allow the master lap to be fitted on its shaft without rubbing the underside of the face plate. A drain tube is made of a piece of ³/₈″ (0.97-cm) copper tubing, split at the end and riveted to the bottom of the drain pan. Dopping wax around the joint will make it watertight, since the aluminum cannot be soldered. A rubber tube on the end of this drain will take away the small amount of drain water to a container or drain.

The portion of the facet unit which is attached to the mast by slipping it over the round shaft, or in some other types by dovetailing to the mast, is the *head* itself. It contains a swing arm which is

Fig. 10–18 A drain pan made from an aluminum ring mold can be used for the "well" in a faceting table. (*Photo by Paul Samuelson*)

pivoted on supports at the end of which is a chuck to hold the metal dop on which the gemstone to be cut is fastened. This pivoted arm is equipped at the rear with a gear or plate, either with teeth or with holes at regular intervals, into which a trigger can be set to hold the arm in position so that one face or facet at a time may be cut. A quadrant and pointer indicate the angle which the central axis of the swing arm bears to the face of the master lap. Thus, by raising the height of the swing arm fastening on the mast the angle will be *decreased,* while by lowering the height on the mast the angle will be *increased,* until eventually 90° is reached. The arm will then be in a horizontal position for cutting the girdle of a gemstone. The gear notches or teeth are engaged by a trigger, which can also be set so that the trigger does not engage, and therefore will allow the arm to be pivoted concentrically about its own center. Thus, a perfectly round preform can be ground by setting at 90° and rotating the gemstone on its dop—the first step in cutting a brilliant stone.

Since it is advisable to have the facets in the bottom portion (the *pavilion*) of a gemstone to be placed exactly opposite the same types of facets in the upper (*crown*) portion of the stone for maximum brilliance, some facet heads are provided with means to make this possible automatically. In one type of faceting unit, this is done by providing grooved dops, and the chuck is also provided with a spring-key which fits into this groove, so that a gem may be cut, removed from the chuck, and turned for cutting the other half while remaining in true alignment. Other makes of facet units provide for this by having the rear end of the metal dops beveled to fit a recess in the chuck, thus securing similar alignment of crown and pavilion facets. A simple means of accomplishing the same effect without such aligning devices will be described later and is pictured in figure 10–33.

The angle at which the swing arm is

held in relation to the master lap determines the angle at which a facet is being cut when it is in contact with a cutting lap fastened to the master lap. This is adjusted to the major height needed by moving the holder up or down the mast as needed, then locking it into position. Many facet heads also provide for a further microadjustment of height, which is of great benefit in accurate cutting of facet corners to meet exactly; especially during polishing, it helps greatly to find the exact "flat" at which the facet was cut. Look for this feature on any facet head you are considering.

VERNIER OR "CHEATER" ADJUSTMENT

All laps, after considerable use, will develop a slightly cupped surface. If there is no means of adjustment to compensate for this wear, it is naturally more difficult to do accurate cutting than it should be. Likewise, it is a fact that, with a revolving lap containing many fine particles of diamond as the abrasive, the outer circumference of the lap revolves at a faster speed than the inner portion of the same lap. This brings more abrasive into contact with a given area of the gemstone than a similar portion of the lap nearer the center. Even in the length of a facet being cut, especially in step-cut stones in which the facets may be rather long in proportion to their width, this effect results in a facet that is cut away faster on that portion which is nearer the outer edge of the diamond lap when being cut. Many facet heads of modern design provide for pivoting the facet arm to the left or the right as may be needed, by quite minute amounts, to compensate for this effect. In this manner, the edges of long facets can be kept truly parallel while being cut and polished. In the cutting of certain types of stones, when there is no gear tooth setting which will turn the swing arm in a manner which will allow a "skew cut," this can be attained easily by moving the swing arm to the left or the right with the vernier attachment which has a pointer. Right and left "skew cuts" can then be made by setting the vernier equally on each side in succession. In polishing, if the overcutting of a facet (because of circumferential grinding noted above) has taken place, a simple adjustment of the vernier will compensate and enable the mistake to be rectified while polishing proceeds.

INDEXING

It was noted earlier that the position in which the swing arm is held is governed by a trigger which fits in the teeth of a notched gear attached to and turning with the pivoted chuck. This index gear may have 32, 48, 64, or 96 gear notches or holes, evenly spaced, so long as it is divisible by 8, since most gemstones are cut with at least 8 principal sets of facets above and below the girdle. Five-sided stones may be cut on a gear which has 60 teeth, or other types may be used for special types of stones. A conversion table is shown in figure 10–19, by means of which a set of directions for one type of gear can readily be converted to whatever gear with which your own machine may come equipped. "Recipes" for cutting various shapes of gemstones use these numbers around a circle in order to allow the cutter to follow the settings and cut a symmetrical stone. These "recipes" give the order of cutting, the angle setting, and the number of each facet in each row (see figure 10–31).

Note that the above operation is simplicity itself. Suppose your "recipe" reads (for a brilliant): "FIRST, CUT FOUR FACETS AT 43° ON NUMBERS 32, 16, 12, AND 24."

The first step is to raise the holder on the mast and fasten it a *slight bit higher* than 43°, for the reason that you will be cutting away rough gemstone on a swinging arc to get down eventually to a finished (rough ground) facet which is at

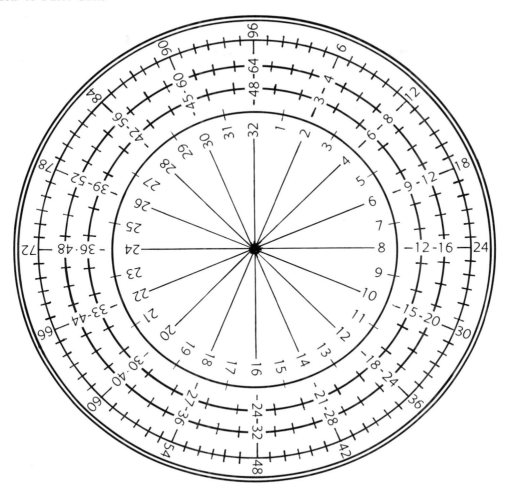

Fig. 10–19 Conversion table for faceting units equipped with indexing gears that do not coincide with printed directions. This allows a transposition to be worked out from any one gear to any "recipe."

an angle of 43° with the table. Therefore, the first setting should be at about 44.5°. Set the trigger in No. 32 and proceed to cut the facet down by gently touching it down to the diamond lap, on which water is allowed to drip. (How far to cut will be discussed shortly.) After the first facet has been cut, the index gear is rotated so that the opposite number, No. 16, is under the trigger pointer, and this facet is then cut. If the first angle setting you made was correct and the finish-cut reads 43° as it should, turn to No. 8 position and cut this facet. Then the opposite facet, No. 24, is cut to a depth only at

which it comes to an *exact point* with the other three facets. It should likewise be the same depth as the first three, if the stone has been mounted on the dop correctly. If these first four facets are cut the same size, you will now have a square in their center. To make an octagon of this (the *table* or top of your gemstone will always show an octagon or eight-sided shape), simply cut off the corners of the square equally—four of them. You do this by indexing No. 4, then the number opposite it, No. 20, then No. 12, followed by No. 28. The depth to which they are cut is watched by cutting them until they come to a point, at which time they should be the same depth at the girdle all around. These are the eight *pavilion mains*. (This example is given out of context in order to show you the use of the index gear.)

NECESSARY CUTTING AND POLISHING LAPS

While a very few fragile gemstones may require an iron lap and loose grits, these materials are for the more experienced cutter who has advanced through the standard gemstone materials. In general, all cutting of gemstones other than diamond itself, with which this text is not concerned, will be done on a double-faced solid copper lap which has been impregnated with 400-grit diamond on one side and 800-grit on the other. Another of similar type has a 600 and 1,200-grit combination; it simply cuts more slowly, but leaves a more finely grained surface on the facets, promoting easier polishing. One lap is sufficient at the start. These come already charged. This charge may be added to in time, according to instructions to be given later in this book. However, under normal usage, it will require a considerable amount of facet cutting before the laps will need any additional diamond powder.

CARE AND CLEANING OF THE DIAMOND LAP

The diamond lap should be stowed in a flat cardboard box with a lid, such as a typewriter carbon box, when not in use. It should never be allowed to fall edgewise to the floor, for to do so will dent the edge and render this area unusable. Neither should any object ever be allowed to fall on the lap and dent its surface, for this will create a low spot with a rim of higher surface around it over which it will be hard to work. When a diamond lap seems not to be cutting well, the reason is that a deposit of gem debris from

the cutting has formed around the points of broken diamond which are embedded into the copper lap. In order to free the lap of this debris, obtain a new *medium grit* carborundum *pocket hone* (fig. 10–20) and keep this in its little case, to be used only on the diamond lap. Use plenty of water as a lubricant, have the lap running, and place the hone down diagonally across the entire face of the lap, generally about 2¾″ (5.99 cm) wide on an 8″ (20.3-cm) lap. Then with gentle contact and a swinging motion from side to side, allow the whetstone to remove the debris. It will not harm the lap in any way, for it is far too soft to cut the diamond grits. Do not use it so long that the copper turns bright; that is not necessary. It will be found that after this treatment, the lap will again cut like new. This treatment is necessary every few hours when some of the softer materials are being cut. Other than for this care, the diamond lap requires no special treatment.

It may be recharged with diamond powder by spreading this evenly over the lap surface, which has been moistened with olive oil. Rock the diamond into the copper by pressing with a semicircular piece of agate. Persevere until all the diamond grains are embedded in the copper lap. Rinse with benzine over a porcelain plate. Allow the residue to evaporate and save any leftover diamond for later use.

With the increasing use of diamond products in all phases of gem cutting, one of the main problems for the beginner is contamination of the laps. It is especially difficult to prevent contamination of double-faced laps, since the side which is not in use is resting on the master lap. This can be solved by using laps which are charged only on one side. More recently, some of the companies who are specializing in diamond products are now manufacturing laps which are basically aluminum and which are charged on one side only. However, the

Fig. 10–20 The faceting lap can be kept sharp and cutting well with a carborundum hone. Apply completely across the wet lap face and switch back and forth while it is running. (*Photo by Paul Samuelson*)

double-sided copper laps are available and will probably continue to be readily obtainable. The faceter who prefers to charge his own laps will usually use copper laps. The newer diamond products are discussed more fully in chapter 9.

THE POLISHING LAPS

There are a number of polishing laps which are useful for special materials. One good rule is not to mix polishing materials on the same lap, either at one time or by reusing a lap on which one type of polish has been used. The laps the authors consider necessary for standard facet work are:

1. A Lucite lap, 8″ (20.3 cm), scored on both sides. Use one side for cerium oxide and *so mark it;* use the other side for Linde A and *mark it.*

2. A pure tin lap, possibly one cast so that the surface only is tin and the base another metal, in order to save the scarce and expensive metal. This should be used only with Linde A and *so marked.*

3. A tin-type metal combination lap, somewhat harder than pure tin. This is necessary with certain stones that do not polish readily on tin. This may be used with chrome oxide.

4. A hard-metal lap of special composition especially cast for the use of *diamond powder for polishing,* to be used only with 6,400 diamond powder or compound. Other finer diamond powders may be used on other laps, *or on parchment papers which are cemented to a flat disk of metal* with Peel'Em Off cement, a nondrying cement of great utility to the lapidary. Oil is the lubricant used with all diamond polishing laps. A special type obtainable from Elgin National Watch Company or from MDR Manu-

facturing Company is excellent. One bottle will last a very long time.

5. A hard maple wood lap, the surface of which has been sealed by dipping in melted paraffin.

6. A muslin-faced wax lap prepared with beeswax according to the method given in *Gem Cutting: A Lapidary's Manual,* by John Sinkankas (see appendix). This is used for very soft gemstone materials.

7. A very useful lap may be made of ordinary ¼″ (0.64-cm) thick battleship linoleum cemented to a piece of waterproof plywood, and it is used to polish the girdles of gems. Here various polishing materials may be used in succession if desirable.

Of these, the two essential ones for the beginning faceter are the first two, and with these a great many gemstone varieties can be handled. The others may be added one at a time as needed. It is very important to keep all laps from becoming contaminated with any foreign matter of any sort *at all times.* This means that they should be covered at night, even when on the workbench; they should be handled by the edge and center hole only, *not gripped with the fingers;* and they should be stored in record envelopes, each on a separate shelf in a small cabinet which has a door (fig. 10–21). There is a great deal of grit blowing around at all times, and this should be kept off of laps. If a lap does become contaminated with foreign matter and starts to scratch the finished gem, scrape the surface clean with a razor blade or a sharp knife while it is revolving on the master lap, then rescore the surface and recharge with polishing agent.

SCORING THE POLISHING LAP

A completely flat lap will not polish effectively or quickly. In most cases it is very difficult to secure a good polish if

Fig. 10–21 A lap storage unit or cabinet to prevent contamination of faceting and polishing laps by foreign matter, grit, and so forth. (*Photo by Paul Samuelson*)

the scoring has become worn down. This scoring can be done with the point of a knife (fig. 10–22) and a ruler, but a far better, easier, and quicker method is to use a small knurled steel wheel about 1″ (2.5 cm) in diameter, which has diagonal parallel scoring on it (fig. 10–23). This is fitted with an axle and handle. It is held at a tangent to the flat surface of the freely turning lap and pressed down to indent the surface, moving from the inner edge outward to the rim. Then turn so that the diagonal scoring will be at right angles to the first score marks and repeat the process. The result will be a multitude of tiny crosshatched score marks all over the surface. Now take a smooth piece of agate that has been polished, hold it against the surface as the lap revolves, using water as a lubricant, and press down the ridges left by the score marks. Apply fresh polishing powder *sparingly* to the wet surface in little dabs and work it all over the surface with the fingertip. The lap is then ready to be put back into service.

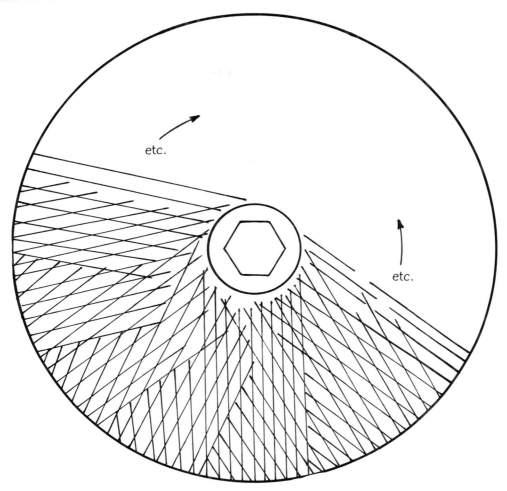

etc.

etc.

Fig. 10–22 Tangential scoring done with the point of a knife. (*Courtesy, John Sinkankas*)

SELECTING THE GEMSTONE ROUGH

The faceter who is just beginning the study of this fascinating hobby should confine himself to the cutting of quartz gems at first. This need not be just clear quartz, for there is ample citrine (yellow), smoky, or amethyst (purple or orchid-colored) quartz available which does not cost too much and affords excellent practice.

In the case of a sculptor, as one once remarked, "If you want to carve an elephant, you just get a block of stone and cut away everything that does not look like an elephant." In selecting material from which to facet gemstones, look first of all for *clarity* and *freedom from veils, feathers, or fractures,* then get the best *color* available. Visualize the size and the shape of a finished gem *within the rough.* Refuse to buy material so badly broken up that it will not afford good cutting room. In each instance, decide which surface will become the table and where the bottom of your stone will be. If there is cleavage to contend with, see that the table can be placed at least 5° to 15° off the cleavage, which cannot be polished. This will ensure that no other surface of a facet will

Fig. 10–23 A scoring wheel for keeping the surface of faceting laps in condition, consisting of a small, knurled wheel in a handle. (*Photo by Paul Samuelson*)

likewise be on a cleavage plane. This is especially necessary in topaz, for it has a perfect and easy basal cleavage. Gem dealers are equipped to give you a wide selection of materials and to cater to your needs as your skill advances. Do not be rash and attempt to facet rare or costly materials until you have fully mastered the fundamentals of faceting.

It is wise to store separate lots of gemstone rough in small "gem papers" or cabinets with plastic drawers and many dividers, and always to label each lot with the date acquired; from whom; the correct name of the gem material; also such interesting things as its refractive index (R.I.), specific gravity (S.G.), hardness (H.), and any unusual properties. Be sure to note the locality from which each material came, for this is often required information if the gem is to be entered as a competitive exhibit in a gem show. There are often several

world locations of each gem material, and it is interesting to collect examples of each known locality for comparison.

PREPARING THE PREFORM

Getting started right at faceting is relatively simple, but the rules must be observed and not skimped over or ignored. One of the first fundamentals is an accurate *preform,* as the ground and prepared blank of a gemstone is known. The ease with which the gem can be cut and polished depends to a considerable extent on the accuracy of the initial steps.

After having selected a suitable piece of gem rough, decide where the *table* should be. First, take the piece in the fingers and grind a flat area with the 220-grit wheel and copious water at the spot you have selected for the table. Now place the coarser side of the diamond lap *up* on the faceting table master lap, and fasten it there with the center nut. Apply a drip of water from a drip can to keep the surface of the lap wet at all times and flush away the cuttings. If the gem rough is of such size that it can be grasped between the thumb, index, and middle fingers (a triangle grip), then the easiest way to grind the table of the gem is to hold it by hand. Even very small pieces can be ground by pressing them to the lap with only the tip of one finger. When a good flat surface has been secured, turn the diamond lap over to its finer-grit side and repeat for a few seconds, grinding to a very fine surface. This takes only a moment.

Remove the diamond lap and substitute a polishing lap. In the case of quartz materials, this should be a Lucite lap. Turn up the side which has been prepared for cerium oxide polishing powder. Keep some of the powder near the work bench in a small, round-bottomed ointment jar which has a tight screw cover and apply a little as needed with the moistened fingertip. The authors do not favor sops, cloth dollies, sponges, or other means of applying polishing powder, for such agents only introduce their own debris and other contamination onto the polishing lap. It is well to add a little water to the powder so that it has the consistency of thick cream in the container. Keep this covered at all times except when in use.

Holding the stone only in the fingers, using the three-finger grip, apply it to the face of the polishing lap, on which a slow drip of water is applied from the drip can. In a very short time you will note that a polish is beginning. Persevere until there is no visible scratch left when the surface is examined with a 10-power hand glass or loupe. This will take only a few minutes. Further details of polishing will be given later in a separate section. If the stone is too small for the table to be polished by holding it in the fingers, apply the warmed stone to a metal dop (see Dopping the Brilliant Preform). Set the indicator of the facet head at 45°. Place the angle dop provided with each set flat on the surface of the cutting lap. Insert the end of the dop into the chuck of the handpiece and tighten it carefully to ensure that the bottom face of this angle dop is parallel to the lap in both directions. Now insert the dop stick with the stone attached into the angle dop and lock it in place. Again reset the pointer to 45°, apply water to the lap, turn on the motor, and gently set the face of the stone down on the lap. In only a few moments a flat will be ground. Now turn over to the finer side of the diamond lap and touch the surface of the stone to this briefly, taking care not to cut away any more gem material than absolutely necessary. Now replace the cutting lap with the Lucite polishing lap and reset the angle marker to 45°, for the two laps are different in thickness; hence, the angle reading is altered when the change is made. With the microadjustment screw, carefully adjust the height of the handpiece holder on the mast so that the table of the gem is truly parallel with the surface of the lap. When this is achieved, proceed with polishing the table. Always use polishing powder sparingly; too much balls up and will cause scratches to form.

After you become more experienced, you will find that you will need to use this latter method very little—the first is simpler and easier.

GRINDING THE PREFORM FOR A ROUND BRILLIANT

With a perfectly flat table ground and polished on the face of a piece of gem rough, take the stone back to the rough 220-grit grindstone and proceed to grind a circular blank, keeping the edges at exact right angles to the table. Use a template which has numerous round holes graduated in millimeter sizes, for the reason that all settings for faceted stones are made to conform to these millimeter dimensions. Try to secure the largest circular preform the piece of material will allow, to prevent waste of valuable gem material, and grind it as nearly a true circle as possible by hand. Keep in mind that the depth of the preform needs to be almost equal to the width; the finished depth will be approximately 70 percent of the finished width. Use a vernier caliper rule for taking these measurements. It is better to take care at this point that you are providing *enough cutting room,* than to learn later that you have too much width for the amount of depth. In a case such as this, the bottom facets of the pavilion or lower portion of the stone will not *"close";* they cannot be made to meet properly while still maintaining a correct cutting angle, which will reflect light back to the eye rather than letting it leak out of the bottom of the stone.

This is one of the greatest faults of the native gemcutter in many countries. He

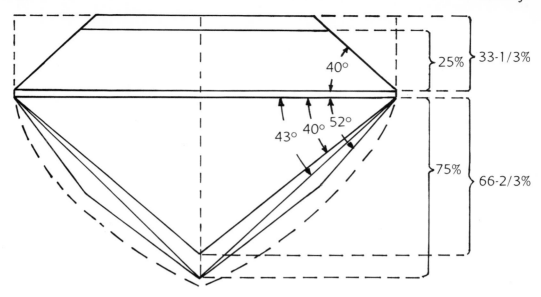

Fig. 10–24 Proportion starts with a well-shaped preform.

knows very little about the fact that all gems have a certain angle which varies with their refractive index, *below which light is not returned to the eye.* The ability of the gem to do this is a combination of refraction, reflection, and the particular luster of the polished surfaces. A stone which is improperly proportioned and too shallow in the proportion of its width to its depth will show an outer rim of brilliance, but the center will be dead and lifeless. This is often called a "fish-eye" stone.

Having ground the girdle edge at right angles with the table, turn the bottom of the piece of rough to the wheel and carefully grind away the excess

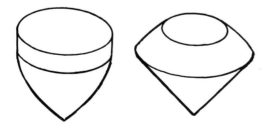

Fig. 10–25 A preform should look like the diagram on the left, not be cone-shaped like the one on the right.

until you have a turnip shape (*not a cone*), allowing the upper or girdle portion to be about one third of the height, and the lower or "turnip" portion about two thirds (figs. 10–24 and 10–25). Oval preforms are made in the same manner.

MAKING PREFORMS FOR STEP-CUT GEMS

In making preforms for rectangular or eight-sided stones which are to be step-cut in the so-called emerald cut, observe the proportions which yield the most attractive shapes (fig. 10–26). The laws governing these proportions go back to the famous Greek artisans and cannot be improved upon. A proportion of 1 to 3 yields a narrow stone, 2 to 3 a standard rectangle, while 3 to 5 is a better-looking proportion for the larger stones. The same rule of one third of the depth for the girdle and crown and two thirds for the pavilion prevails, except that in the case of quite pale material, when it is desired to enhance the color, this is sometimes made one fourth of the depth in the crown and three fourths in the pavilion. Pale amethyst,

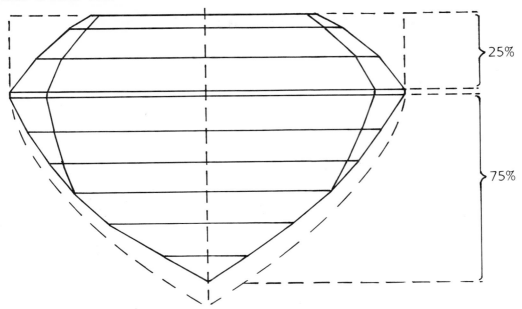

25%

75%

Fig. 10–26 Proportions for the step-cut gem. Three steps above, five or six below, are desirable for colored stones.

morganite, aquamarine, topaz, and kunzite are often deepened in color by this means. Note that the bottom of the preform is ground into a "Dutch barn" shape to allow ample room for the facets to be placed at proper angles in the pavilion (fig. 10–27). The corners are just barely touched, for they must be ground accurately to the same size on the facet head itself.

PROPER DOPPING METHODS

Equipment needed:

Fundamental
    An alcohol wick lamp
    An alcohol jet torch (Lenk)
    A metal "stove"
    3-way dopping block (Gemlap)
    Set of metal dops, all sizes, in duplicate pairs
    A dop holder block—a 1″ (2.5-cm) ferrule with a ¼″ (0.64-cm) hole in it
    1 pair long-nosed tweezers
    1 pair long-nosed pliers
    1 single-edged razor blade
    Solox alcohol for fuel and cleaning (procurable at paint stores)
    1 stick dopping wax

    1 stick shellac
    1 tube acetone base cement
    56 g (2 oz.) cornstarch
    A pocketknife
    Small can of shot for holding and cooling dops

More advanced (for heat-sensitive and larger stones)
    1 infrared heat bulb and reflector in gooseneck student lamp
    1 pad steel wool
    1 block sawed rock for base

DOPPING THE BRILLIANT PREFORM

Select two cone-shaped metal dops two thirds the diameter of the round

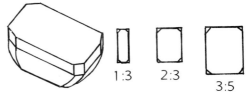

1:3   2:3   3:5

Fig. 10–27 *Left,* Shape the preform like a "Dutch barn." *Right,* Correct proportions should always be stated in millimeters.

preform. Clean both of any old wax, and rub the face of the outer edge of the cone on one dop until it is bright. Light the alcohol jet torch and warm the metal of the dop with the bright face in the flame to ensure that it is dry. Now apply a small amount of fresh dopping wax inside the cone of the dop—too much is useless. Do not allow the wax to burn, as this impairs its adhesive qualities, but warm it next to the flame, not in it, until it drips. Meanwhile, warm the preform, table down, on the metal stove with the alcohol wick lamp under it, having first wiped all surfaces of the preform with alcohol or acetone to ensure that there is no grease on it, even that of the human skin. Handle the stone only with the tweezers after it is clean. Hold the dop while being warmed in a holder made of a piece of hardwood dowel, into the end of which a $^1/_4''$ (0.64-cm) hole has been drilled. Hold this in the right hand and bring it down close to the jet of the torch, but not in it, so as to get the wax glistening and bubbly, and then, with both stone and wax hot, bring them together, pressing the dop down firmly against the *table* of the gemstone, which has previously been cut flat and polished.

Have the three-way dopping block ready and place the warm dop with the stone attached in the right-hand side V-way and clamp the holder tight. Now place one of the brass face plates that come with the V-block in the left-hand V-way (fig. 10–28a). Bring the jet flame of the torch against the *metal* of the dop stick, not the wax, and warm it until the wax glistens. Now press the free end of the face plate on the left against the point of the preform firmly, at the same time moving the edge of the preform so that it is as nearly centered on the dop as possible. This can be done best with the edge of the fingernail, which is less sensitive to heat than the skin of the fingertip.

In order to center the stone with accuracy, place the second brass face plate in the V-way which is at right angles to the other two. Bring this forward into contact with the edge of the preform. Slightly loosen the fastening clamp on the right-hand V-way and rotate the dopped stone against the brass face plate. If the stone is not centered and is eccentric, it will push the face plate away from one edge *by the amount of error in centering* (fig. 10–28b). When this error has been determined, rotate the preform on its dop 180° so that the gap becomes visible—a white card under the stone will aid in seeing this gap. Next, move the brass face plate inward toward the stone *one half* of the visible difference. Now, with the jet flame, rewarm the stem of the dop until the wax will allow the stone to be pushed over to the center position with the thumb nail. Next, turn the stone 90° and repeat the checking and moving of the stone in the same manner. When you have finished, the stone should be able to be rotated completely, touching all around or very nearly so in case the preform has not been ground truly round.

This process of fastening the preform to the dop on which it is to be cut, if not done accurately, can upset all other calculations, and a misshaped gem will result. The table is the one accurate face that exists at the start and from which all other angles on the gem must therefore be determined. If it is not fastened accurately with the dopping wax to the dop itself, it introduces an error of angle into every facet on the stone. What you should do now, before removing the dop from the V-block, is to repeat the heating and squeezing process first described, to make sure of *actual contact after centering*. Having done this, you now have a visual method of proving the job has been done. Remove the dop with the preform on it and lightly oil the bottom portion of the preform, rendering it transparent. By looking into this it can be seen that there is a

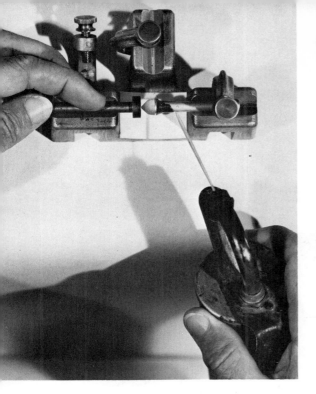

Fig. 10–28a Step 1: Leveling the stone on the dop. (*Photo by The Harper Leiper Co., Houston*)

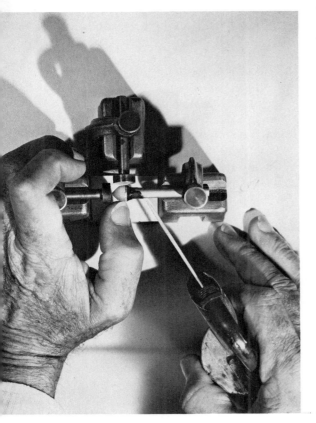

Fig. 10–28b Step 2: Centering the preform. (*Photo by The Harper Leiper Co., Houston*)

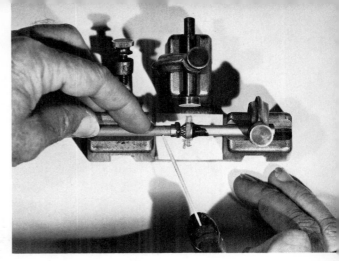

Fig. 10–28c Step 3: Preparing to turn the stone on the dop after the pavilion has been cut and polished. (*Photo by The Harper Leiper Co., Houston*)

Fig. 10–28d Step 4: The stone is now cemented to two dops. (*Photo by The Harper Leiper Co., Houston*)

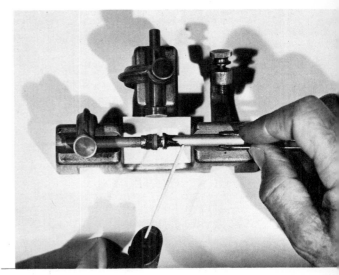

Fig. 10–28e Step 5: Separating the gem from the first dop. The stone has not been turned. (*Photo by The Harper Leiper Co., Houston*)

bright metallic ring of contact near the outer edge. If this circle is complete and equally bright, the job has been well done. If one side shows a darker shadow of dopping wax still between the face of the gemstone and the dop edge, then naturally the stone is not yet true on the dop. Place it back in the V-way and again reheat and press with the left-hand brass face plate on the point of the preform. Then visually test for accuracy again.

The above method presumes that *the pavilion of the gem will be cut first,* and this is the method used by a great many of the most skillful and accurate faceters in this country. At the same time, many faceters prefer to cut the crown of the gem first, in which case the bottom, or pavilion, of the stone is dopped into the cone and the table surface trued against the brass face plate. If the preform is inaccurate, it has a tendency to force the gem off center in trying to get it concentric and is *wasteful of valuable gem material,* for if it is not centered and concentric, you must grind away and lose much of the weight saved by the first process You will not always be cutting inexpensive material; hence, the authors believe the first method to be both more accurate and more economical. When fine gem rough approaches $8 to $20 a carat—$40 to $100 a gram, as it conceivably may do in some types—then such methods justify themselves.

At this place, in order to cover the dopping procedure entirely, we will presume that you have now cut the pavilion (or crown) of the gem and need to redop it in order to turn the gem so that the other portion may be cut.

TURNING THE GEM

To make this change, place the dopped stone in the right-hand V-way and clamp it in place. Take a second dop stick of the same size as the first one used, warm it, and apply fresh melted

wax inside the cone. Place the warmed dop in the left-hand V-way and press the wax against the finished portion of the gem. Now apply more heat with the jet flame to the *stem* of the dop, as shown in figure 10–28c, then again press until the gemstone has absorbed sufficient heat to obtain good adhesion. By close inspection, the eye can see that the wax has melted to true adhesion. Continue to warm the stem and to press against the end of the dop itself with a bit of wood until you are certain that this has been secured (figure 10–28d). Allow the dops and the gem to cool naturally; they are now fastened end to end. After they are completely firm and cool, the transfer can be completed by directing the jet flame at the *stem* of the first dop on the right-hand side, letting the metal carry the heat to the stone. When this bubbles and glistens, use the pliers and pull this dop *straight back* in the V-way, thus separating the dop from the gem. Now pick up the cool dop from the left-hand way, which now has the transferred gem on it, and clean off the excess wax with a single-edged razor blade, after which the surface can be cleaned with a small amount of alcohol on a piece of cloth. Be careful not to get the alcohol on the base of the gem and the new wax, as this will soften it.

You are now ready to insert the dop in the handpiece and proceed with the cutting of the other side of the gem. This process of separating the two dops is shown in figure 10–28e.

DOPPING THE STEP-CUT OR RECTANGULAR PREFORM

The essential procedures are the same as for the round brilliant, except that two centering operations must be performed. First, bring the long sides of the preform into a center alignment. Then turn at right angles and center the short sides, thus preventing the waste of material that would result if it had to be ground away in order to effect a correct centering of the preform on the dop.

DOPPING FANCY-SHAPED STONES

The dopping position is determined by the position of the culet, or point of the pavilion. For instance, it will be noted that in the pendeloque or pear-shaped gem, this culet is located under the center of the bottom or rounded portion of the teardrop; hence, the pre-form will need to be dopped with two thirds of the length (the pointed end) on one side of center, and one third (the rounded end) on the other side of center. Free-form shapes of modern stones cut without true symmetry of faces will often need to be dopped off-center. Oval stones or cushion-shaped stones (rounded corner rectangle) need to be dopped in a manner similar to the rectangular step-cut preform. With all of these shapes it is to be noted that the pavilion *must* be cut first.

DOPPING PROCEDURE FOR HEAT-SENSITIVE AND LARGE STONES

Since a metal stove method of heating is rather harsh treatment for some gem materials that are heat-sensitive at best and tend to crack or cleave (and especially with the larger preforms of standard gems, or when dopping a number of gems at one time), a better method of bringing gems gently to the necessary temperature to effect a good bond with the dopping wax has been devised. This is so easily variable as to temperature that it can readily be adapted to the most sensitive materials.

An infrared heat bulb is procured and inserted into a metal reflector on a gooseneck-type student lamp. A block of stone and a pad of steel wool complete the equipment (fig. 10–29).

Place the stones to be heated on the

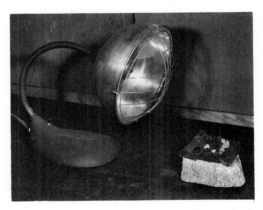

Fig. 10–29 Use a heat lamp and a pad of steel wool for dopping sensitive gems. (*Photo by Paul Samuelson*)

pad of steel wool and place this on the block of stone. Focus the rays of the heat lamp on the pad at a distance determined by the amount of heating desired. This will soon bring the preforms to an even temperature, which may be varied simply by moving the block and pad nearer or farther way. By this method, the stones may be felt with the tips of the fingers or a crumb of wax placed on the table of the preform as an indicator; when it melts, the stone is ready for dopping. By this method, a number of stones can be held at the correct temperature while dopping proceeds. Large preforms can be heated readily without subjecting them to "one-hot-side" heating, such as they would get on a "stove." This method greatly simplifies dopping a number of preforms at one time, which is often advisable.

COLD DOPPING

Some gem materials are so heat-sensitive that they cannot stand the amount of heat required to get a good bond with wax; hence, a cold-dopping process is helpful. A good cold-dopping compound can be made by mixing a small amount of acetone base cement with cornstarch. Make this into a rather wet dough. Apply a very thin coating of the pure cement to the dop and the table surface of the gemstone and *allow to dry*. Next, apply a small pill of the dough in the cone of the dop and another small bit pressed against the face of the stone. Press the parts together and get the best metal-to-surface contact possible. Lay away to dry for 24 hours, then proceed to cut one side. Soak the dop stick and the stone in acetone in a small, closed jar until it loosens naturally, and repeat for the other side. No other way of making the transfer has been worked out, as it is difficult to dissolve the old compound and at the same time try to make a new bond on the other end.

CUTTING THE GIRDLE

Place the dopped stone in the chuck of the faceting head and tighten. Lower the handpiece angle marker until it reads 90° and back the staff far enough that the edge of the preform rests close to the outer edge of the cutting lap. If your head is equipped with a stop, this is set at 90°, and no steady-rest or roller-rest is needed. Other types of heads have a roller or V-rest which can be set to hold the handpiece horizontal. If the edge of the cutting lap is below the rim of the splash pan and the latter is not notched to accommodate this need, the surface of the lap can be raised by inserting a filler lap between it and the master lap. A disk of plywood will serve.

Lower the setting of the mast until the edge of the preform just touches the cutting lap. Free the trigger so that the handpiece can be rotated freely with the fingers. Lift the stone from the lap, start the water, and lower slowly, at the same time starting to twirl the stem with the fingers of both hands so as to maintain a continuous rotation. Keep this up until the edge no longer is being ground. Examine the edge, and if it has been ground all around, the preform is now a true circle and is concentric both on the

dop and in the chuck. Do not remove it or loosen it in the chuck from this point on, but see that the V-groove in the dop is properly engaged in the V-guide, if your machine provides for such a setting. Restore the mast to its original position and raise the head to cutting position at about 45°. Restore the diamond lap to cutting position on the master lap, coarse side up, and you are ready to begin cutting the facets on a round brilliant (fig. 10–30).

CUTTING THE GIRDLE ON A STEP-CUT STONE

Proceed the same as for a round stone, but bring one of the longer sides of the preform to rest on the lap in setting the 90° angle, and do not use a roller rest. Grind one of the long sides, setting the trigger at No. 32 for this facet. Then turn to No. 16 and grind this side flat and parallel with the opposite edge. Now index No. 8, which will bring one of the short ends of the rectangle into position on the lap, but the extra height will change the angle, which will now need to be reset to bring it to 90° again. Grind this side, then index No. 24 and grind the opposite short end.

To cut the corners, first index No. 4 and set the angle indicator again to exactly 90°, as any change in height alters this reading. Carefully grind a face that is about one fourth of the length of one of the long sides, and set this length on a pair of steel dividers. Next, index No. 12 in rotation and grind to exactly the same length, checking with the dividers. These must match. Then index No. 20 and No. 28 in that order, grinding the corners off.

The preform is now ready for cutting the facets on a step-cut stone. A cushion shape can be achieved accurately from a rectangular stone by cutting the eight edges as above. Then release the trigger to free-wheeling and carefully rock the

Fig. 10–30 One of several methods for grinding a brilliant preform round. (*Courtesy, Lee Lapidaries*)

corners back and forth on the cutting lap until they are uniformly rounded all around the stone. In this way, you are more likely to get a uniform shape than if it is done by freehand grinding.

ADJUSTING THE ANGLES AT WHICH FACETS ARE CUT

Almost all books containing faceting designs (such as *The Book of Gem Cuts,* which has been issued in Vol. 1 and a more advanced Vol. 2, see appendix) contain sets of angles that were devised for *quartz* gems that have a refractive index of 1.531–1.539. As you will not be concerned with very many gem materials which have a lower refractive index, we will deal mainly with those in common use which have higher refractive indices. These should be cut at other angles which will make full use of the power which the gem material possesses of bending and returning flashes of light to the eye of the observer.

Most authorities give sets of angles for cutting the various gemstones, and these will be found in a set of tables in the back of *The Book of Gem Cuts* recommended previously. These angles are the result of both experience and scientific determinations of all the properties involved, which include (1) the *refractive index* of the material, (2) the *dispersion* or property of some gemstones to break up light into its prismatic colors (usually called "fire"), (3) the *clarity* of the material, and (4) the perfection of the *polish.*

The angle at which the pavilion main facets are cut for quartz will be 43°, while the crown mains will be cut at 42°. The pavilion girdle facets will be cut at about 2° to 3° *higher,* or 45° to 46°. With the crown mains at 42°, the crown girdle facets will be cut from 1 1/2° to 3° higher, depending somewhat on the proportion of the stone, or from 43.5° to 45°. The star facets, next to the table, are generally cut near a figure 15° lower than the crown mains, or approximately 27°. This figure may vary up or down as the proportion of the gem requires and must be found by trial cuts, which will be explained later in this text.

By way of comparison, the angles for titania, a man-made double-refractive synthetic with a very high dispersion and refractive index of 2.61–2.90, are given by the most experienced cutters as crown mains at 30°, star facets at 15°, crown girdle facets at 35°, pavilion main facets at 40°, and pavilion girdle facets at 41.5°. The figures were first given in the April 1949 issue of the *Lapidary Journal,* when the material first came on the market, and have been confirmed since by the Titanium Pigment Corporation, a subsidiary of National Lead Company, one of the manufacturers of titania boules.

In this book, no attempt will be made to give more than one or two fundamental "recipes" for standard brilliant and step-cut stones, for this would only clutter the pages with previously published and readily available charts. Once the standard cuts have been mastered and the manipulation of the controls on the facet head thoroughly understood, the following of any set of instructions becomes a step-by-step procedure.

PLANNING THE CORRECT PROPORTIONS FOR THE GEM

The original cutters of brilliants, largely diamond, were working entirely by trial and error, but they eventually arrived at certain proportions and angles that have survived to this day and are still in use. However, gems cut with the proportion of one third of the height in the crown and two thirds in the pavilion will ordinarily yield a stone that has a rather small table. Among diamond cutters, these are known as "old mine cuts." Modern experimenters have found that a proportion of 25 percent of the height in the crown and 75 percent in the pavilion yields a stone with more brilliance, and this is now called the "American cut" in diamonds.

When cutting for color rather than brilliance, the proportion of one third crown to two thirds pavilion will yield an attractive stone, but in making preforms for gem materials with a higher refractive index, it is well to make the crown more shallow.

In making preforms for step-cut stones, especially those which have paler color, greater depth of the pavilion will yield a deeper-colored finished gem. On the other hand, some gems (such as tourmaline) are cut primarily for *color* rather than brilliance, and since they are very dichroic (darkening greatly if viewed lengthwise of the crystal), they should be laid out with these properties in mind. The table will therefore be parallel to the length of the crystal, which is the direction in which the color of the stone is lightest, and should be cut quite shallow in the pavilion. However, in the case of some rubellite colored tourmalines and other fancy-colored nodules, in which it is desired to retain and enhance the beauty of color attained when the crystal is viewed from the end, the table is placed across this plane of the material. Andalusite and certain other gems possess this same property of dichroism to a marked degree. The eye of the cutter will serve as the best criterion.

In laying out the correct proportions for the gem, do not rely entirely on your eyes and judgment of proportion and distance, but use a vernier caliper rule capable of being read to one tenth of a millimeter. Having determined the width of a brilliant *after the girdle edge has been ground truly round,* take seven tenths of this dimension, which will be the approximate depth of the gem when finished. If you desire a proportion of one third crown to two thirds pavilion, you would, therefore, take the first dimension, the diameter (say it was 10 mm), for ease of illustration. Seventy percent of this is 7 mm—and one third of that is 2.33 mm. Set this amount on the caliper rule and transfer the measurement to a small pair of needle-point steel calipers. With one edge of the caliper resting on the edge of the table, the other point will make a slight mark on the *edge* of the preform. Do this all around, and keep the distance set on the calipers. With it you can tell exactly how deep to cut the mains, and you will, therefore, be certain that the finished gem will come out to the correct proportion which is desired. In a step-cut stone, the same method is used to determine the depth to which the first facets next to the girdle, in both crown and pavilion, will be cut.

The thickness of the girdle, which will vary with the size of the stone, should be about 1 percent of the depth and should never be allowed to disappear into a "knife-edge," for this may cause the gem to be damaged while being set.

STEPS IN CUTTING A BRILLIANT

As previously outlined under the heading Indexing and here repeated entirely for complete clarity, step by step, a round brilliant of quartz is cut in the following manner:

Set the 400 side of the diamond lap upward on the master lap and fasten it. Fill the drip can with water. Place the preformed and girdle-rounded stone on its dop into the chuck of the faceting head handpiece, engaging any device such as a groove or bevel designed to aid in matching up facets, and tighten the chuck. Set the index at No. 32 and the degree pointer to approximately 44.5°, to allow for swing-down in reaching a final cut of the desired 43° (fig. 10–31a). Turn on the drip water, letting it drip on the back side of the lap, away from the cutting. Holding the handpiece lightly in the fingers, touch down the bottom of the preform to the diamond lap and cut until the edge of the oval so produced just touches the metallic mark you have previously made with the metal dividers as the position of the eventual girdle. Rotate the index to No. 16—and now is a good time to give some advice: **always, without exception, double-check yourself as to the correctness of the setting before proceeding.** You will be surprised how easy it is to get into the notch next to the one desired without realizing it, and that mistake can ruffle the temper no end!

Proceed to cut the second facet to the same depth on the girdle, checking with the dividers to make sure. Next turn the index to No. 8 and cut this facet to the same depth, by careful measurement. Now index No. 24, which is directly opposite No. 8, and cut it, until the *point* of this facet just meets the other three you have cut (fig. 10–31b). At this stage you have a direct method of checking the accuracy of all of your work up to this stage—preforming, dopping, and girdling—for if all of these have been done correctly, the girdle edge of the last facet you have just cut will check out to be the exact distance down from the table as the first three facets you cut. If

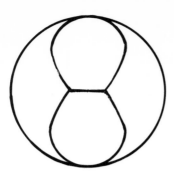 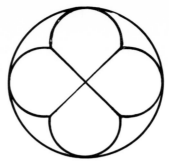 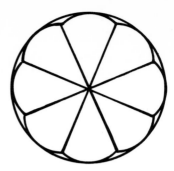

Fig. 10–31a Step 1: Cut two opposite facets on the pavilion or bottom of the stone. Index 32—16.

Fig. 10–31b Step 2: Cut the opposite corners 8—24.

Fig. 10–31c Step 3: Then cut off the remaining four corners, indexing 4—12—20—28.

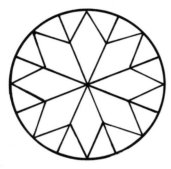 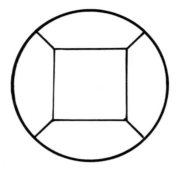 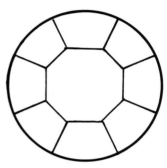

Fig. 10–31d Step 4: Raise the angle (see text) and index the number either side of each main pavilion facet, as 31—1, etc., around the gem. These are the pavilion girdle facets. When you have finished cutting all facets, change to the polishing lap and polish the girdle facets first, then the mains (see text).

Fig. 10–31e Step 5: After redopping to change ends with the stone, set the correct angle on the mast and cut 32—16, then 8—24, leaving a hairline girdle, 0.08 to 0.04 cm (.03″ to .015″).

Fig. 10–31f Step 6: Cut off the corners evenly to obtain eight crown mains, indexing 4—12—20—28.

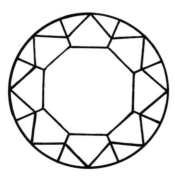 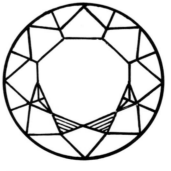 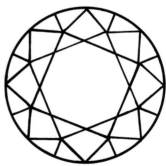

Fig. 10–31g Step 7: Now cut the crown girdle facets (see text), indexing one notch on either side of each crown main setting.

Fig. 10–31h Step 8: Cut the star or "skill" facets by indexing halfway between each crown main, as 2—6—10—14—18—22—26—30. The angle is quite low (around 27° to 30° on most gems).

Fig. 10–31i Step 9: The finished brilliant.

there is any great discrepancy at this point, some one of the jobs was not done correctly—either the stone is not level on the dop and in full contact (but you have had a visual method of checking to see that it is) or the girdling has not produced a fully round preform (this will show up as one facet longer and wider than the rest). If this should happen, it can be corrected at this point by going back to the instructions for grinding the girdle and repeating the process to take out any eccentricity, without harm to the job. Having made this accuracy check, which we will presume you pass with flying colors and evenly cut facets, proceed to cut away the corners of the square you have formed.

Index No. 4 and cut until the *point* of the facet is completed—no more. Change to No. 20 and cut likewise. Next index No. 12 and finally No. 28 (fig. 10–31c). When the last of these has been completed, check very carefully to see that all of the eight main facets you have cut are now exactly the same depth at the girdle and are the same width, using the dividers to assure your eye of this fact. A very slight touch-up may be needed on one or more. The point, or cutlet, will now be an exact meeting place of eight facet edges.

The next step is to cut the pavilion girdle facets. This is done by indexing the number on either side of the main setting for each facet you have already cut, but raise the angle setting on the mast by about 3° to 46°. This will be a preliminary setting only, and is done by *lowering* the head on the staff slightly and locking it into position (fig. 10–31d).

Set the index at No. 31 and touch down very, very lightly for the briefest possible time, wipe the facet so cut, and examine it closely with a magnifying glass. It is sometimes difficult to get the light just right so that these small cuts can be seen against the ground surface of the main facet out of which they are

being cut. Here is a trick that will aid you; provide yourself with a piece of aluminum stick or wire; rub the area you have cut with this, and it will define the edges of the cut area clearly. In cutting these girdle facets, it is desired that they be cut at an angle which will carry them up at least one half the length of the main facet edge, while spreading at the girdle edge to just one half of the width of the main facet. Study the diagram and note what shape they should assume. If your first trial cut is *too broad at the base* and would therefore reach center before it got high enough, your angle setting is *too low* and will need to be raised slightly; if you are at 45°, try a slightly higher setting to 45.5°. Now, change the index setting to the notch the other side of that at which the main was cut, or to No. 1, and again touch down with the very lightest and shortest touch possible. Examine this partially cut facet very closely. If it is the correct height and width to complete a pavilion girdle facet, such as that shown in the accompanying diagram, set the index back in No. 31 and touch down again, correcting that facet *but not completing it*. Now, reset in No. 1 and touch it again, and go back to No. 31. In this way, you approach the completion of the first pair of pavilion girdle facets very gradually, in order to secure the correct setting of height on the mast at which all 16 of the girdle facets in this row will be cut. Once attained, the same setting will be used on all of these facets. Care must be observed at this stage not to *overcut,* and caution is the watchword. **Cut a little and look a lot** is very good advice until you become expert.

If the first pair of facets have been completed until they touch at the center of the main where it touches the girdle, the work on them would be presumed to have been completed at this stage. However, experience has shown that, when the center diamond-shaped main facet is polished, the beautiful needle-sharp point is lost where it contacts the girdle. To avoid this, experience has again taught a little secret that makes it possible to come up with *precision-polished facets that will remain needle-sharp through the polishing stages.* This is accomplished by slightly overcutting the base of the girdle facets *intentionally,* until they overlap very slightly to form the small "tail" shown in fig. 10–32. This is done by *lowering* the setting on the mast very slightly with the microheight adjustment and just barely touching the facets on No. 31 and No. 1 until the desired result is attained.

Having mastered the method by first getting the pair correctly cut, then slightly overcut at the girdle edge, leave this angle setting on the mast and proceed to cut the other 14 girdle facets in pairs. Index by turning to No. 3, then to No. 5 for the next pair, hence around the gem, *one notch on either side of each main position.* One does not need to remember the numbers after the operation has been done one time.

When this series of girdle facets has been completed, make a *written note* on a pad beside the table of the exact angle you have been using—*it is quite easy to forget.* Remove the cutting lap, place the Lucite polishing lap marked for cerium oxide face up on the master lap, and fasten it. Open your container of polishing

powder but do not apply any until needed. Turn on the water drip so that the face of the lap is just wet. It is often wise to add a few drops of a liquid detergent to the drip water, as this breaks down surface tension and enables the lap to present a well-wetted surface at all times. As the polishing lap is usually thicker than the cutting lap, reset the mast height to the angle you noted on your scratch pad for the girdle facets. Reset the gear notch to index No. 31, and touch down to determine where the first contact is made with the girdle facet. This should be at the lower or girdle edge of the facet, and you will probably note that it is at one corner. This is caused by faster cutting toward the outer edge of the diamond lap. Now, make a very slight adjustment of the vernier to move the swing arm pivot of the handpiece to the *left,* if the lap is running away from you and your mast is on your right hand. This will compensate for this circumferential cutting effect, and the one setting will remain for all the facets. If you are left-handed and have the mast at your left, then the adjustment will be in the opposite direction. After polishing the facets on the pavilion, remember to return the vernier setting to zero for cutting the crown.

With contact made across the base of

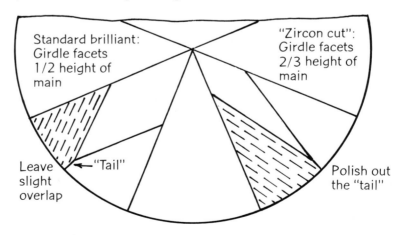

Fig. 10–32 Cutting the pavilion girdle facets. Refer to figure 10–31d.

the girdle facet, move the microheight adjustment up slightly until the entire flat of the facet is being polished equally, and continue until the very tip or point is completely clean of very fine scratches. Examine well with a 10-power glass on every facet *before moving on to the next.* It is always better to do your "cleaning up" as you go, rather than to try to come back and find the exact level later if you have a fuzzy facet tip. Now, proceed around the other 15 pavilion facets, polishing each pair of points so that they match in height. You will of course note that you are leaving a very short "tail" at the intersection of the two girdle facets.

You are now ready to polish the mains. Set the height adjustment to 43° and the index at No. 32. Touch down so that the tip or culet portion of the main pavilion facet makes contact first, then *lower* the setting on the mast slightly with the microheight adjustment until the portion of the "diamond" nearest the girdle is taking most of the polishing effect. As you do so, you will note that the "tail" you left is being polished away, leaving it needle-sharp at the girdle. In this manner you secure precision polished facets on the finished gem—the sort which, when offered for inspection to the critical eyes and loupes of fellow-faceters, will stand their closest scrutiny and gain that "good clean job!" exclamation. To the amateur faceter, it is the love of doing the job right, even though no one else may know it at a casual glance, which drives him to seek perfection.

The mains are polished in this manner, one after another around the gem, rather than in the order in which they were cut, and at the same index numbers with which they were cut. When the polishing is finished, carefully clean the bottom of the stone while it is still in the chuck, and *check every facet* for possible fuzzy tips or scratches. If any shows up, go back to the correct setting

which you have noted on the pad beside you for each type of facet and touch the offending spot gently to the lap, in order to remove the last blemish. When you are satisfied that all are perfect, release the dop from the chuck, place it in the V-way dopping block, and proceed as described earlier for turning the stone and affixing it to another dop.

CUTTING THE CROWN FACETS

Having turned the gem and checked the table against the face plate, to make sure that it has been turned without getting the table out of alignment, make a small mark at the girdle edge with a bronze or aluminum pencil, at the exact point at which one of the mains (the diamond-shaped facets) touches the girdle. If your head does not have the V-grooved or beveled dop sticks to help you align the crown facets with those already cut on the pavilion, this mark and the diagram shown in figure 10–33 will show how this can be accomplished. Set the mast height so that the angle pointer reads about 43° (you are going to cut down to 42° on the finished facets) and place the dop in the chuck with your index at No. 32 and the mark *straight down.* Make a preliminary cut across this mark and check with the dividers to see that the cut is bisected by the mark. If it is not, loosen the chuck slightly, move in the direction necessary to bring it to

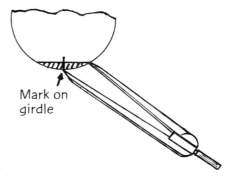

Fig. 10–33 Means for aligning crown and pavilion facets.

center position, and retighten the chuck. When you are sure that it is accurately positioned, complete the cutting of this first crown facet, checking also to see that you have come down to the 42° reading desired (see fig. 10–31e).

Next, index No. 16 directly across from the first facet cut. All these are cut down to the point where they leave just a wide hair's breadth at the girdle—about 0.04 cm. After this, cut No. 8 and then No. 24, at which time the table will present a square appearance. If your work has been accurate, it will measure the same distance with the dividers on each side. Now turn to No. 4 and cut off the first corner of the square, being careful not to cut too deep at the girdle (see fig. 10–31f). Index No. 20 next and cut in a similar manner. No. 12 comes next, then No. 28. At this time the table assumes an octagonal shape. Each of the crown mains so cut should measure exactly the same width at the girdle edge, and this can be checked with the dividers. Any discrepancy in this width should be corrected at this point by taking just a little more off the narrower facets *on either side* of the wider one that has been overcut. Thus, by judicious touching up, all can be made to come out to exactly even size. If your preform was "ovaled" rather than being a true circle and you are cutting the crown first rather than the pavilion, this is the point at which you would return the gem to the 90° position and, using the roller-rest if one is needed, regrind the preform edge until the stone is truly round. This is your *second check point*—the one for the crown.

CUTTING THE CROWN GIRDLE FACETS

Set the mast height so that the reading of the pointer is about 3° higher than that at which the mains were cut,

or approximately 45°. Index No. 31 and touch down to the cutting lap with great delicacy. If the shape of the girdle facet is too broad, as shown in the top diagram in fig. 10–34, then you should *raise* the mast height very slightly with the microadjustment. Shift to index No. 1 and again touch down. The shape of the starting facet so cut may now be like that shown in the middle diagram, in which case it was adjusted too high, and the mast should be lowered. When you attain a height adjustment which will produce a girdle facet such as that shown on the third diagram, which reached *two thirds of the way up the edge of the main facet* on which it is superimposed, it is correct. Note that the bottom corners at the center are very slightly overcut to leave a "tail" which can be polished out later in order to produce perfectly pointed facets at the girdle edge.

Once the proper height setting has been achieved to cut a perfect pair of these crown girdle facets, proceed around the stone, *cutting in the notch on either side of each main facet.* This will produce 16 girdle facets (see fig. 10–31g). In cutting these, proceed with great caution, so that in touching down you do not overcut. If this happens to you, however, during the process of learning, do not despair. You learn only by making errors and then finding your way out of them. To correct such an error, you manifestly cannot cut deeper into the girdle depth in order to recut all the eight crown mains at 42°. However, the crown main angle is not so critical that you cannot lower this to 40.5° or 41°. Return to the main index setting of No. 32 and very carefully recut *all eight* of the crown mains to the same angle, even though an error of overcutting has spoiled only one facet. You will therefore index 32, 16, 8, 24, then 4, 20, 12, and 28 as you did with the first set of crown mains, exercising care not to cut into the girdle width in doing so. Having made the correction, return to the

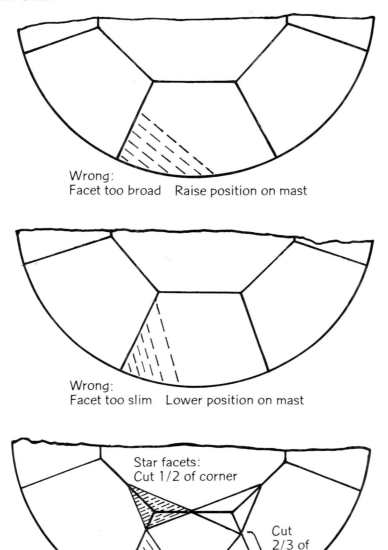

Wrong:
Facet too broad   Raise position on mast

Wrong:
Facet too slim   Lower position on mast

Star facets:
Cut 1/2 of corner

Cut 2/3 of facet

— Slight "tail"

Correct: "Tail" is polished out

Fig. 10–34 Cutting the crown girdle facets. Refer to fig. 10–31g.

mast height setting which you found proper for the crown girdle facets, index at No. 31, and start over, taking No. 1 next and so around the gem in the notch each side of the main crown facet. The cutting of these sets of facets requires the greatest exercise of patience, careful touch, and methodical procedure. It is no wonder that they are sometimes called the "skill facets," although this term is also applied to the next set which is to be cut, called the "star" facets. These are the eight triangular facets which touch the table.

CUTTING THE "STAR" FACETS

Raise the height of the head on the mast until it reads about 15° less than that at which the crown mains were cut, or approximately 27°. This setting must be found by careful trial. The objective is to cut a triangular-shaped facet which will just meet the topmost point of the pairs of crown girdle facets, while at the same time it is spreading equally wide to cut off a corner of the presently existing octagon table and make a new octagon shape. The star facets are cut on a setting *halfway between* those at which the crown mains were cut, or index 2, 6, 10, 14, 18, 22, 26, 30 (see fig. 10–31h). Having set in the first of these index positions, touch down very lightly and examine the shape of the facet which results, less than half of the eventual size. If the facet is "reaching too wide" while not progressing downward properly to meet the point of the pair of girdle facets, then the height on the mast should be lowered. In order to test this result, move to the next uncut position and make a tiny trial cut and such additional close adjustments of height on the mast as are necessary, and then complete the cut. On the other hand, if it is found that the lower point of the triangular star facet being cut is reaching the girdle facets before it is spreading to take up *just half of the width of the main on either side of it,* then it is necessary to raise the height on the mast, thus lowering the angle of the cut until the proper "spread" has been attained. The left and the right points of each triangle will just meet those of the similar facets on either side of them, *when they are polished.* In cutting them, do not *quite* complete them, leaving just a hair's breadth. Since the polish is likewise abrasive, it will remove the minute amount of material necessary to bring the points to a "meet." A faceter is judged by the exactness of his "meets."

Do not be the least dismayed if you make slips in cutting your first dozen stones. Use quartz for practice material and keep at it, doing the same cut until you have "licked" it and are satisfied with your own product. You will learn more by making errors and correcting them than in any other manner. You will learn all the adjustments that can be made on the faceting head and the effect of each move—how much and how little a change is necessary in order to secure a given result. When you have mastered the physical moves of adjusting mast height and indexing to enable you to place angles and facets where you want them to go, and to make them the size and shape you want them to be, you will have become a real faceter.

POLISHING THE CROWN FACETS

Remove the diamond lap and replace it with the Lucite lap, cerium oxide side up. Return the mast height to that at which the crown girdle facets were cut, and index No. 31. Start the drip water, allowing it to drop just enough on the inner portion of the lap to keep it slightly wet, applying polish when needed very sparingly with the fingertip of the left hand. Touch down and adjust the mast height so that the base of the girdle facet next to the girdle edge is starting to polish, then make a very slight upward adjustment of mast height with the microadjusting screw until the whole facet surface is being polished out to its point. When it is completed, examine it very closely with a 10-power glass for scratches, especially at the sharp tip. Then index No. 1 and polish that facet. Remember that it may be, and often is, necessary to take a bit of *left* vernier adjustment in order to compensate for the rotational cutting effect, as explained earlier. Proceed, indexing the notch either side of the main position, around the gem until all 16 crown girdle facets are finished.

Now raise the mast height to the figure at which you cut the star facets (which you should have noted on a scratch pad on your table at the time the set of facets was being cut). This indexing starts at No. 2. Proceed to polish the star facets to a "meet" with the girdle facets. This does not require much time as they are small. Avoid too much polish, for it tends to *fuzz* the edges of the neighboring polished areas on the table if too much "turbulence" is created at the edge of the facet being polished by an excess of polish on the lap, or if it is run too wet.

POLISHING OUT THE "TAIL" ON THE CROWN MAINS

The next and final step is to set the mast height back at 42°, index No. 32, and touch down to the polish lap. Allow the polishing to start heaviest at the outer end of the kite-shaped crown main facet, thus polishing away the "tail" that you intentionally left at this point. As the polish reaches the upper point of the kite, watch closely to see that it "cleans up" this area and does not leave a fuzzy point—a common error often overlooked until the stone is off the dop stick and it is too late to remedy. Proceed around the main settings with the polishing; when you come to the last one, clean the face of the crown thoroughly and go over every facet on the stone, one by one, with the 10-power glass, to make sure that there are no scratches left anywhere. If you find any area that does not satisfy this close inspection, return to the mast height and index position at which the polishing was done on that facet and remedy the fault. Make one final check to be sure that you have completed the crown *to your own satisfaction.* You are the sole judge of the degree to which you have attained your original goal, and much of the real satisfaction of faceting comes from your realization of this perfection.

Take the stone on its dop out of the chuck and place in the right-hand V-groove of the dopping block. Light the jet torch and warm the *stem* of the dop, not the stone, and allow the wax to melt and the stone to fall out of its own accord. Remove while warm and pry away as much of the wax as you can remove with the fingers only. Place the entirely cooled gem in a small jar of acetone or alcohol to soften the remaining wax, but do not scrape it off with a knife. Wipe the gem clean on a small cloth dipped in alcohol and pick it up in the gem tongs, *not in the fingers,* for human skin oil will dull the luster of any stone and reduce the apparent luster and brilliance. There's a real thrill you will never forget in gazing into the beautiful brilliance of your first faceted stone. The eagerness with which you await this moment on every stone you cut thereafter is part of the thrill of learning to cut faceted stones (see fig. 10–31i).

CUTTING THE STEP-CUT GEM

The procedure for making the preform of rectangular or step-cut stones, as well as the first steps in cutting the girdle and the corners, was outlined earlier. If these steps have been done, the procedure for cutting the facets is as follows.

Decide how many steps or rows of facets you will have in the pavilion of the gem you will cut. This varies with the size of the preform—as few as three and as high as six or seven rows of facets are often used. In general, the narrower the facets and the larger the number of rows in a larger stone, the more attractive will be the appearance of the finished piece. The bottom step is determined and is set at an angle which will still reflect light rather than let it leak out the bottom of the gem. For quartz this angle should be approximately 43°. If the proportion of the stone calls for a deep pavilion in order to enhance the pale color of the gem rough, then the first step at the girdle will be set at least 63° or even as much as 68°. The first figure leaves a difference of 20° between the two. Starting at the bottom facet of 43°, if we use a 5° difference between steps, the next row will be at 48°, counting from the bottom. The third row will then be at 53°, the fourth row at 58°, and the last row next to the girdle will be at 63°. For a shallower stone, to lighten up a dark material (dark amethyst, for example), start at 43° as before but use only 3° of difference between each row, as follows: 43°—46°—49°—52°—55°. In proportioning the crown, start with 42° for quartz and use at least three rows of facets, the last one just around the edge of the table being pencil-line-thin. This helps to prevent wear of the gem at the edge of the table. The angles would be approximately 42°—37°—33°.

The first row of facets to be cut is the one on the pavilion nearest to the girdle, hence the one with the highest angle figure. Set the mast height to this figure; place a long edge of the preform on the cutting lap and the stem end in the chuck, which is left untightened. Have the index gear read No. 32. Now push the stem into the chuck and tighten hard, making sure that the edge of the gem preform as it rests on the lap is truly in contact. The vernier adjustment should be at zero, for the vernier will be used a great deal in cutting this type of stone. Swing the handpiece up to the inspection position and with the dividers set a distance which has been determined by calculation as the depth of preform to be used for the crown, the balance going into the pavilion. This will vary from 25 to 33 percent of the height of the preform from table to culet. This is determined by the type of material being cut and whether a shallow or deep stone is desired. Mark the girdle edge with a metallic line, which the point of the steel will make on the ground surface of the girdle edge.

Start the motor, set the drip can going, and touch down the edge of the preform to the cutting lap for a test cut. At this time you will be able to determine whether the edge is truly parallel; if one end is wider than the other, adjust the vernier slightly to bring the two edges into completely parallel position and proceed to grind the first pavilion facet down to the girdle mark you have made. Index right around the gem in order: Nos. 4, 8, 12, 16, 20, 24, 28. Watch the width of the facet, but particularly watch the edge next to the girdle, to see that it matches up as you go. The test of your dopping procedure will come when the last facet in the row is cut; it should come out very close to cornering with the first one cut. If it does not, check to see which facet is "climbing" (caused by rotational cutting effect) and compensate by moving the vernier adjustment and slight recutting. Having arrived at a true set of eight facets in the first row, which meet at all the corners, index 32° and change the height on the mast to reach the next lower angle to be cut. If you started at 63°, the next step might be at 58°. Cut each row, making the width of the facet whatever your eye judges to be about one fifth of the span of distance to bring you to the last facet. If any facet is wider than the others, it should be the first step at 63°, and they should diminish in width as the steps are cut, the narrower ones being in the lower portion of the pavilion for most attractive appearance.

You will note as you cut rows in succession that the corner facets will "cut out" about the third row down, and thereafter only the four main facets will be indexed. On the last of the three corner steps that generally are cut, a neater job is obtained if the angle of the corner facets is altered slightly to bring the point of this triangle facet, which will terminate the corner, to intersect exactly with the main facets on its left and right.

As you proceed with the rows, your

principal job is keeping the rows exactly parallel as you cut. Use of the dividers will aid you in doing this. Measure down from the table to the various facet corners to determine whether you are staying level all around.

When you reach the last four facets at the lowest setting of 43°, the cutting of the pavilion will be completed. Step-cuts are not difficult, once you learn to make the facet head do your bidding in keeping the edges of the facets truly parallel.

POLISHING THE PAVILION FACETS

Remove the cutting lap and place the Lucite polishing lap in position. Return to the first angle setting for the row next to the girdle and start polishing on index No. 32, and so around the first row of facets in order, using the abrasive action of the polish to correct any very minor deviations from exact cornering. "English," or pressure exercised with the wrist on the handpiece, can save a lot of resetting of various vernier adjustments in bringing all areas of a facet to equal brilliance in polishing. **Do not use too much polish** or get the lap too wet, for so doing will cause either balling up of polish and scratches, or else "fuzzing" of neighboring polished facet edges. *Examine each facet before you change the setting to move to the next.* That is the time to make sure of a complete and scratch-free polish. When all are completed, examine the entire pavilion area before you remove the dop stick from the chuck.

CUTTING THE CROWN OF A STEP-CUT STONE

Having turned the stone by the method outlined under Dopping the Brilliant Preform, set the index again at No. 32 and line up a long edge of the preform on the cutting lap, then tighten the chuck very tightly.

Proceed to cut the first row of facets next to the girdle at 42° all around, leaving a girdle thickness of about 0.04 cm on small stones, or proportionately wider for larger stones, but try to get it exactly even all around.

The next set are cut at 37°, and the final set at 33°. Allow the width of the second row of facets to be proportionately smaller than the first row cut at 42°. The width of the final row should be just as narrow as you can make it. Remember that the polishing powder will also do some cutting, so just barely get these started. A single touch will tell you whether you are parallel to the edges and the girdle, and another after any needed adjustment of the vernier will finish the cutting operation on these facets. Try to see that the corner facets of each of the four corners are the same length.

Replace the cutting lap with the Lucite polishing lap and start with the row of facets nearest the girdle, proceeding in order to that nearest the table. When the last of these facets has been done, the polishing is finished. Clean the surface with alcohol and very carefully check every facet, paying special attention to the corners to see that there are no scratches or fuzzy areas. If the gem passes close inspection, remove the dop from the chuck, place it in the V-block, and heat the stem of the dop until the wax softens, allowing the stone to fall out. Clean it of wax, allow it to cool, and soak it in a small amount of alcohol to complete the removal of the wax. Your gem is then finished.

CUTTING THE DOUBLE-MIRROR BRILLIANT

This is *a needed improvement on the standard brilliant cut for gemstones of lower refractive indices.* One of the principal faults of the standard brilliant cut when used with materials of low to medium refractive index is that when viewed at any angle other than perpendicular to the table, the gem has a tendency to "blank" out and reveal large areas which are apparently lacking in brilliance.

Long experimentation with many different combinations of angles and various cuts brought about the designing of the *double-mirror brilliant* now presented here (fig. 10–35). It is particularly useful for the lower and middle-range varieties of gemstones in which the low refractive index and moderate dispersion need all the help they can get from the gemcutter in order to present their best appearance in the finished stone.

The principle of the double-mirror cut is relatively simple. Opposite the crown mains, there are opposed directly beneath in the pavilion a set of facets that are the direct *mirror-images* of the same facets that are above them—in other words, in reverse position from the girdle. Hold a mirror at a 90° angle at the girdle of an illustration of a standard brilliant crown, and you will have an almost exact image of the facets that are used in this cut.

In order to achieve these results, the preform must be made with the eventual gem in mind. First, grind the table area on a piece of gem material and polish this in the usual manner. Then, grind it to a circular outline of the size desired and to the depth needed, keeping in mind that the finished gem will be somewhat deeper than a normal brilliant. Keep the edges of the preform at a right angle to the table, then mark off a tentative girdle position, with 25 percent of the height of the preform in the crown and 75 percent in the pavilion area. Grind the bottom portion into a fat turnip shape, taking care to leave ample depth. Dop the preform with the table to the metal dop and check to see that it is truly flat and centered. Then, place the dopped preform in the chuck of the faceting head, set it down to the 90° girdling position, and turn until the

stone is truly round and concentric on the dop.

Now, proceed to cut the set of eight pavilion mains marked A in figure 10–35, at 53°, using a 64-gear. The individual numbers are not given, as they are the same as for the standard brilliant. Extra care should be taken that each and every one of these mains is exactly the same width at the girdle. This is an important item; if not attended to at this time, it will come back to plague the faceter later. Use a sharp-pointed pair of dividers; *don't guess.*

Having completed this set of eight mains, cut the eight mains of the lower set marked B in figure 10–35 on 43° for quartz, on 40.5° for topaz, tourmaline, or other gems in the 1.63–1.64 range of refractive index. This angle may be altered slightly *upward* between 40.5° and 43°, but go no lower than the 40.5° figure. The angle for the bottom facets will depend on the R.I. of the individual gemstone being cut. The angle 40.5° has been found by long trial to be particularly effective with blue or white topaz. These finished facets, when completed later, are directly under the table and add greatly to the brilliance of the finished stone if carefully placed, cut, and polished.

Having ground all of the two sets of mains on the pavilion, the height is next set at approximately 58.5°, one notch either side of the main settings, and the girdle facets P^1 and P^2 are cut, reaching two thirds of the length of the side of the main A, exactly the same as if the crown facet C were being cut. It is very necessary that these reach the same height all around and meet accurately at the center. Use a pair of sharp-pointed calipers kept whetted sharp by honing the inner edges of the points. Be sure—do not guess; the eye will fool you in different angles of light.

Next comes the cutting of the principal facets which make this design work—those marked M^1 and M^2. These

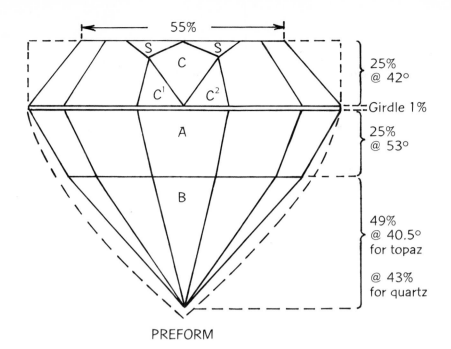

55%

25% @ 42°

Girdle 1%

25% @ 53°

49% @ 40.5° for topaz

@ 43% for quartz

PREFORM

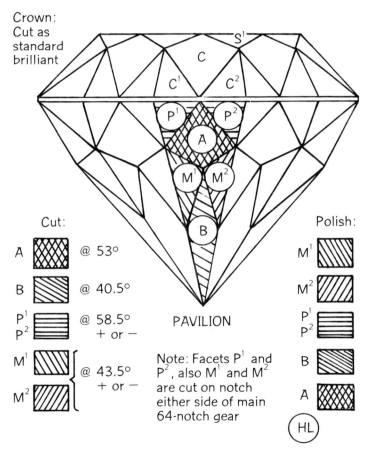

Crown: Cut as standard brilliant

PAVILION

Cut:

A @ 53°

B @ 40.5°

P¹ P² @ 58.5° + or −

M¹ M² } @ 43.5° + or −

Note: Facets P¹ and P², also M¹ and M² are cut on notch either side of main 64-notch gear

Polish:

M¹

M²

P¹ P²

B

A

HL

are cut at a plus-or-minus figure of approximately 43.5°, but this angle will be found to be a compromise between the 53° of facet A and the 40.5° of facet B for topaz (or the 43° of facet B, if quartz is being cut) and will actually be found by test only. *Cut a little and look a lot* until you get it going right, so that it will meet the points of the kite A (lower drawing, fig. 10–35), while at the same time meeting accurately at the topmost point of the diamond-shaped facet B (lower drawing, fig. 10–35). These facets are cut on a setting one notch either side of each main, exactly as the girdle facets.

Start to polish by doing M^1 and M^2 first, then the girdle facets P^1 and P^2, letting the polish cause each to overlap and create a tiny "tail" where they meet the girdle in the case of the facet A and at the top of the diamond B. Then, when you polish B, this tiny "tail" can be polished out and needle-sharp facets obtained. Now, polish the main facet A in the same manner, starting the contact at the "tail" next to the girdle.

Turning the gem accurately, make certain that the center of one of the top mains lines up *very accurately* with the point of one of the mains A in the pavilion, for there is no reason for making this cut at all if the reflection is lost in opposed facets of similar size.

The crown is exactly the same as that on a standard brilliant, the cutting of which has previously been described.

POLISHING FACETED STONES

Examples of polished and even engraved diamonds which bear the names of rulers of much earlier eras are well known, and some of these come down to the present time to make us ponder the skill and the persistence of those first gemcutters. The Romans of Pliny's time (A.D. 23–79) are recorded as having known and used numerous polished gems, many of which came to Rome, already cut, through the medium of the caravan routes and the sea voyages around Arabia to the gem-yielding lands of India and Ceylon. It is in Pliny's writings that we get our first inkling of the methods of the lapidaries of that time in the cutting of cameos, intaglios, and engraved gems, and in the polishing of various gems, among them the carbunculus, the peridot, and the adamus (long thought to have been diamond, but now believed to have been sapphire). Amethysts were cut, some into cups supposed to possess the boon of warding off the effects of too much wine.

It is known that the lapidaries of those times used both diamond and corundum for engraving. Emery, found plentifully in Greece and Syria, was used as a grinding agent. Mention is likewise made of several polishing agents then in use, all of them similar or identical to present-day materials. Their "German tripoli" is the same that we use today. Their "Damascus ruby powder" was a natural corundum powder very similar to our present-day synthetic Linde A powder. That they even knew the effect of the addition of acidic liquids to the polishing agent in order to secure a better polish on peridot is indicated. Today, we know that these things simply break down surface tension and expedite polishing in certain instances.

Suffice it to say that the polishing of fine gems, thus rendering their luster more brilliant and their colors more entrancing, was an extremely ancient art which has progressed through the ages into the very fine and precise lapidary practices with which modern-day gemcutters release the beauty and the fire of hidden gems for the world to enjoy.

The cutting of gems to geometrical pattern is simply a grinding process, entirely simple in its fundamentals, except perhaps in the case of diamond. It is the *polishing* of these flat planes in the faceted stones which alone is responsible for the beauty of the finished gem, and it is with these fundamentals that we are now concerned.

What are these fundamentals? The true nature of the polishing process is both a technical and a scientific problem, varying somewhat with each different type of gem material, and there are two points of view as to how polishing is achieved. We should realize that most gem materials are combinations of the oxides or silicates of many metals. One of the theories below was first expounded while the polishing of metals was under scientific observation, as a matter of fact. These two theories are:

1. That the polishing process is merely a matter of very fine grinding which so reduces the presence of very fine parallel striations that the eye can no longer see them. The polishing of diamond is done in the same operation by which the facets are first ground.

2. That the polishing process in a great many substances other than diamond consists of the abrading of the surface to fineness by a combination of friction and heat, so that a flow of the surface takes place. This has been ascribed to a combination of chemical action, local heating of minute high points of the material being polished with the polishing lap, and the molecular disturbance of atoms, causing the formation of an amorphous surface layer—the so-called and much debated *Beilby layer*.

The differences between grinding and polishing are sometimes very fine. For instance, it has been found that when a fine emery paper is backed with glass or a firm backing, it can impart only a dull finish, but with a flexible backing, a polish can be achieved on certain materials.

As all cutting or grinding of gems is in effect a minute chip-removing process, (*a*) polishing must be regarded as the end process in a progressive smoothing of the surface layer—that is, grinding with successively finer agents until the undisturbed base material is reached. Minute striations are left by this process, but they are merely rendered submicroscopic in size and therefore not visible to the unaided eye. This is far from being a true *luster*—"radiant and luminous brightness, the quality of shining by reflected light." However, in the polishing of gemstones with diamond powder, such materials as sapphire, ruby, and the synthetics of the same, the apparent polish obtained is often sufficiently good to pass muster and frequently is used. The fact that such polished gems can be improved in brilliance by the application of polishing techniques depending on the second method (*b*) is sufficient to indicate that simply *superfine grinding* is not the final and ultimate in polishing.

When the method of Sir George Beilby was first brought forward in 1921, there were proponents, and also others who argued that such a flow of matter was not possible. However, with the coming of the electron microscope and by electron diffraction methods, it has now been proved beyond a doubt that in all gemstones except diamond, the final polish is caused by a momentary fusion and flow of submicroscopic surface projections, spreading a "liquid-like" Beilby layer over the polishing plane. Minerals tested by these methods are divided into three groups:

1. Those in which the layer remains amorphous (spinel and zircon)

2. Those in which the layer generally remains amorphous but recrystallizes on important crystal planes, such as cleavage planes (kyanite, calcite, etc.)

3. Those in which the layer recrystallizes in conformity with the substratum in all planes (corundum)

This brings us to the realization that *polishing is not grinding*, but that in various gem materials, a "flow" of the surface layer occurs to a greater or less degree. Some evidence of this is given by the fact that a hard material can be polished by a *softer* powder, which must, however, have a *higher melting point* than the gem being polished. For instance, sapphire (hardness 9, Mohs scale) can be polished with tripoli, tin oxide, titanium oxide, or rouge, which vary from 7 down to 6 in hardness. A fairly recent investigation has revealed that this polishing action (the *results* of which have been known to man for a long time, without his knowing the *reason why*) is actually accomplished with polishing powders which invariably have a higher melting point, so that at the points of minute contact of irregularities with the face of the lap, the projections may melt locally. Extreme pressures are also exerted on these tiny projections above the general level of a facet, and on the surface of a convexly curved cabochon with only a small area of contact. Very high local temperatures are thus generated, and without doubt, superficial melting of the surface takes place. In the final polishing of topaz, if the table is quite large, the lap is sometimes allowed to become quite dry after it has been properly charged with polishing agent and scored, and it is at this point that the very best brilliance of polish is achieved.

Many lapidaries have experienced the difference in the *feel* of the stone on the lap at the instant when a brilliant polish is attained—how it gets "slick" all in a moment. Sometimes reversing the direction of attack will make the polish fill the surface and result in a quick polish when it has been eluding the faceter, perhaps because he has been trying to polish against the grain of the particular material.

Likewise, it has been noted that the speed of the lap has a great deal to do with attaining a good polish quickly. Often the ability to press hard enough to momentarily "stall" the lap, thus lowering the speed, or otherwise to control and slow down the speed with pulley changes will result in a quick polish.

Sometimes, on the other hand, the reverse may be true. Where heavy pressure and lower speed have been used and the result is not satisfactory, a lighter touch and higher speed may generate the very heat and molecular disturbance that will bring about a good polish.

It is also known that the final layer of polish is somewhat harder than the gem material itself. For instance, in retouching the polish on a facet, experienced faceters often note that it is easier to grind away the old polish entirely and start over than to try to repolish over the old layer.

The polishing process is essentially affected by (*a*) the material of the lap, (*b*) the polishing agent, (*c*) the lubricant used (water, kerosense, oil, detergent, acid, etc.), and (*d*) the speed of rotation and the amount of pressure with which the gem is applied, and that indefinable something called "touch" which the skilled lapidary develops from experience and which varies with different gem materials.

A list of the various laps which it is desirable for the lapidary to have was given earlier. We will here discuss the uses of each type of lap and the proper polishing agents, the speed, and the type of gem materials for which they are best suited.

THE LUCITE LAP

Mention of this lap has already been made a number of times. It is very widely used for quartz materials and is excellent for beryl, when used with cerium oxide. One side of the lap should be marked for such use, and the other side scored and used for Linde A powder. This side may be used for polishing the harder-stone girdles after the faceting job is finished, for to do so on the regular lap tends to depress a mark into the face of the lap which is not very good for its continued use on flat facets.

The Lucite lap must always be used wet and *never* allowed to get dry, for it heats very quickly, and this will cause the dopping wax to become warm, the stone will tilt, and you have real trouble on your hands. In a case of this sort, the stone must be entirely redopped and the position of a main facet redetermined in relation to the index gear—a time-consuming task.

THE PURE TIN LAP

This is the most useful and versatile of all the laps and the one on which the faceter should lavish the best of care, to keep it completely free of contamination. The surface is turned on a lathe set to run very fine at the start. If the lap should later become gouged or so badly contaminated with grit that this is again necessary, it can be done in any machine shop, provided that it is impressed upon the operator to keep the new surface untouched with the fingers or any grit. A single-edged razor blade should be kept on the faceting table with the other tools, to be used for scraping the surface as the lap spins, to remove any ordinary contamination that may be producing a scratch. The tin lap is crosshatched by tangential knife cuts placed close together from two directions, producing a diamond-hatched surface, or else with a knurled wheel described earlier, run in two directions.

The tin lap is most useful with Linde A powder, and this combination will be found suitable for a great many of the gems up to sapphire in hardness. Generally speaking, it will do its best polishing when a light drip of water is applied at the back edge about halfway in from the outer edge, and the end of the fingertip of the middle finger on the left hand is used to spread the water inward and maintain a half-wet, half-dry condition. Additional polishing powder can be applied with the fingertip as needed, by touching the moistened finger to the dry powder or by moistening the powder to a heavy cream in a small opal glass ointment jar kept on the faceting table. It should always be kept covered except when in use.

For large table surfaces, after the preliminary polishing of the area has reduced the frosted appearance, the best results with many gem materials will be had when the stone is held in the fingers and applied to an almost dry lap. The polish thus achieved is very brilliant and free from streaks.

THE TIN–TYPE METAL COMBINATION LAP

For such stones as zircon, a harder lap is needed and can be used with Linde A, chromium oxide, tripoli, or diamond powder, the latter generally of 6,400 grit or finer and used only on a lap especially reserved for it. Diamond should not be mixed on a lap on which any other polishing agent has been or is intended to be used. Diamond *cuts*, while other powders *polish*.

By working down the surfaces of a sapphire on diamond powder on a tin–type metal lap and following with tripoli on another lap of similar hardness, the best results can be obtained. Some companies produce a quite hard metal lap especially suited to this use.

THE HARDWOOD MAPLE LAP

On soft materials, it has been found that a good polish can be secured with a wood lap, the surface of which has been pretreated with paraffin or beeswax to prevent water from swelling it. The drip water should be softened by using a few drops of detergent liquid to help break the surface tension.

THE MUSLIN-FACED WAX LAP

Probably the most useful lap for polishing very soft, fragile gem materials is the one which is made on a metal base by adding a layer of muslin which has been stretched over the warmed lap, to which a small amount of beeswax mixture has been added. After this has been stretched and trimmed at the edge with a razor blade, more wax is sparingly applied from the bowl of a warmed spoon and rubbed in until the surface is smooth. Such a lap will almost "polish the unpolishable," provided that it is used with detergent-treated water, thin polishing powder mixtures, and patience. Exact directions for its making can be found in *Gem Cutting. A Lapidary's Manual,* by John Sinkankas (see appendix).

THE LINOLEUM LAP

A most useful lap for polishing the tops of buff-top stones, those which have rounded tops, as some hearts, and the girdles of various gems after they have been faceted can be made by cementing a round piece of battleship linoleum to a wood block (the waterproof veneer kind). Cerium oxide, tripoli, or tin oxide can be used as the polishing agent. Any depression in the rim caused by polishing the girdle of a stone soon returns to shape, a peculiar property of the linoleum.

FLAT LAPPING ON A STEEL PLATE

Where a very large surface, too large to be flat lapped on the ordinary laps, must be reduced to a good polish, a piece of hardened steel plate, which is itself flat, can be used with grits of successive fineness until 1,200 is reached, the work being rubbed by hand against the plate. Water is used as a lubricant. After each operation, workpiece, plate, and hands should be scrubbed diligently with a hand brush. When the lapped surface shows no scratch under close examination, polishing powders may be

applied which are suitable for the material and the work of flat lapping completed by hand rotating the piece. Some workers use a piece of plate glass rather than steel for the plate. A very high polish can be obtained in this manner if the work is diligently done and the operator has the patience.

CERAMIC LAPS

Another recent type of lap is the ceramic lap, which is designed as a polishing lap to be used with diamond compound as a polishing agent. It has a hardness of 9 and is a carborundum in composition. Because it is a ceramic lap and 9 in hardness, it is brittle as well as hard; therefore, it is necessary to handle it with care to prevent any chipping or breakage. The manufacturer recommends that it be handled as you would fine china. The laps are 8″ (20.3 cm) in diameter, with one side diamond-polished to a precision flat surface for the final polishing. The other side, which is the semipolishing side, has a fine satin finish. It is strictly a polishing lap.

The laps should be kept very clean and should be recharged as necessary when they are being used. They should be cleaned each time before they are put away or stored. They are easy to clean, since they can be washed in lukewarm or tepid water with Lava soap. The bar of Lava soap can be handled as you would a sanding block. If some of the diamond remains or sticks to the laps, any of the prepared diamond compound thinners can be used to remove the diamond that will not wash off.

These laps are designed primarily for use with diamond compounds, and the sizes recommended are 50,000 (0.5 micron) and 100,000 (0.25 micron) diamond compound packaged in the aerosol-type pressure bottle so that very small amounts can be sprayed on. After the diamond polish has been sprayed on, start the lap revolving and, with a soft tissue, remove any excess, since very small amounts of diamond polish are required. While the lap is still revolving, take a soft lead pencil and mark the lap by starting in the center and gradually working toward the outer rim so that you create a coil effect of concentric circles on the lap. Then, while the lap is still revolving, start again from the center and draw cross marks from the center to the outer rim of the lap so that the lap is marked off in small, curved, rectangular sections. Then, as you polish your stone, you can see the areas where you have used the diamond and can move to other areas of the lap. The graphite deposited from the soft pencil also seems to provide a slight lubricating effect. The recommended speed for the lap is 50 rpm or less. It is a good lap for the harder gem materials, but any gemstone 7 in hardness or less must be handled with extreme care. When polishing any of the soft gemstones, do not turn the lap on but simply polish the stone by hand without any power by just swinging the faceting arm back and forth over different areas of the lap. Very little pressure is required. The softer the gemstone, the finer the diamond compound you should use. No water is necessary. This lap will produce extremely flat facets (almost optically flat surfaces).

If you have not used one before, remember that everyone has a different touch. Proceed cautiously and experiment a little until you get the feel of the lap and can determine how much or how little pressure is needed. This will depend upon each individual and is an important factor.

FACETER'S TRIM SAWS

Trim saws were discussed previously in chapter 5; however, very little comment was made concerning the need of the faceter. Since faceting material is often very expensive and rare, as well as being composed of quite small pieces, it is necessary to conserve as much of the material as possible. This can also apply to those cabochon materials that are rare and expensive, for example, a fine piece of fire opal.

Often an expensive piece of faceting rough will have a healed fracture or a feather which runs through the stone, or there will be an inclusion of some foreign material which could not be seen when the purchase was made. This may prevent the faceter from cutting one single stone without a good bit of loss of material, especially if it has to be ground away. In such instances, if a very thin saw cut can be made through the inclusion or following the direction of the fracture or feather, two smaller stones can be cut rather than one large stone, and a greater amount of material can be used instead of having to be ground away. By doing so, sometimes one larger and one smaller stone can be cut for use in different pieces of jewelry or for different purposes. This allows the faceter to get the most he can from the material with a minimum of weight loss.

Several equipment manufacturers have realized this particular need and have designed small, compact trim saws specifically for this purpose (figs. 10–36, 10–37, and 10–38). Moreover, the blade manufacturers have produced suitable very thin blades for the saws. Saw blades can be purchased in 4″ (10.2-cm), 5″ (12.7-cm), and 6″ (15.2-cm) diameters in either a steel core or a copper core. The core thickness is usually 0.010″ (.25 mm), 0.012″ (.30 mm), or 0.025″ (.60 mm). A core thickness of 0.010″ (.25 mm) will usually have a rim thickness of 0.020″ (.50 mm). Some 5″ (12.7-cm) diameter saw blades can be purchased with a core thickness of 0.012″ (.30 mm) and a rim thickness of either 0.020″ (.50 mm) or 0.022″ (.56 mm), depending upon the brand of blade you purchase. The 6″ (15.2-cm) diameter saw blades

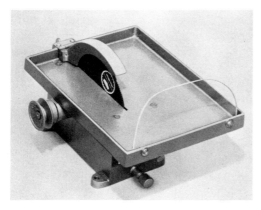

Fig. 10–36 The Highland Park 6TS facketer's trim saw, which will handle either a 4, 5, or 6″ (10.2, 12.7, or 15.2-cm) saw blade, is simplified and compact. A similar model can be obtained which has a vise, motor, pulley, and belt with a belt guard all mounted on its own base. Both are designed to give the faceter maximum efficiency. (*Courtesy, Highland Park Manufacturing Co.*)

are usually available in core thicknesses ranging from 0.012″ (.30 mm) to 0.040″ (1 mm). The accompanying photographs show some of the trim saws designed specifically for the faceter. Some of them have small vises, or other models can be purchased with vises. Many times the rough faceting materials must

Fig. 10–37 The Covington Faceteer's trim saw is compact and easy to use. It has a blade guard and a splash guard at the front of the saw table. It will accommodate either the 4, 5, or 6″ (10.2, 12.7, or 15.2-cm) very thin saw blades. (*Courtesy, Covington Engineering Corp.*)

be hand held in order to place the saw cut exactly where it is needed. Remember, it is necessary to be exceptionally careful to hold the material firmly and steadily, making only straight cuts, and not to force the material through the blade. They are very thin blades, and curves or side pressure will warp the blade or loosen the diamond in the blade. If your dealer cannot give you the information you need concerning the operation of your faceter's trim saw and blade, then do contact the manufacturer of the saw you have for advice.

Fig. 10–38 The Crown faceter's trim saw will accommodate the 4, 5, or 6″ (10.2, 12.7, or 15.2-cm) very thin saw blades. It is compact and has a vise which can be pulled to the front of the saw table if you do not wish to use it. Also, an accessory cross feed vise can be added at any time; this saw is very versatile. (*Courtesy, Crown Manufacturing Co.*)

SUMMARY

This chapter has presented the basic steps in learning to facet. The perfection and skill that can be obtained are entirely dependent upon the individual desire and imagination. Some individuals like to try all types of gem materials; others prefer to facet as many new designs as they can find. The gem and mineral magazines, especially those which specialize in or stress lapidary techniques, often publish new designs or modifications of some of the standard designs.

There are individuals who prefer the

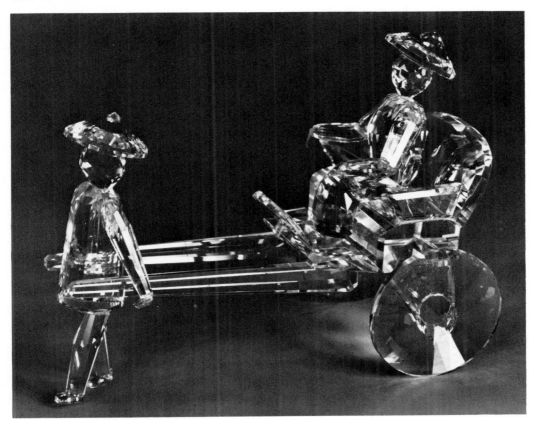

Fig. 10–39 "The Rickshaw" is one of the latest quartz novelties completed by Jerry Muchna of Phoenix, Arizona. (*Courtesy, Jeffrey J. Kurtzeman,* Lapidary Journal)

challenge of working out new designs that have not been tried before. You are limited only by your imagination and your desire to accomplish something different. Jerry Muchna of Phoenix, Arizona, is an individual who had the desire to carry his hobby a little further than the usual type of faceting. He specializes in faceting novelties from Brazilian quartz and has developed his own individual techniques. He likes to work with the Brazilian quartz because he is able to obtain large pieces that are free of inclusions and flaws. His collection of faceted novelties now totals 78 different pieces requiring over 5,000 hours. His projects range from animated objects to still lifes. His finished novelties are amazingly fine reproductions of real life objects, and all of them are easily recognizable even without titles. In order to

get a graceful curved effect on some of his figurines, he developed his own method of cutting concave facets. His basic faceting unit is that made by MDR Manufacturing Company. The tools necessary for faceting concave facets were devised by using sewing machine parts, a vibrator, and some computer parts.

He does not always try to design his novelties on paper but usually works them out as he goes. Instead, he models them out of clay first; once he has the clay model, he can facet it in the quartz. He completes each facet as he works; that is, once he has his indexing and degrees set, he does not change them until the facet is ground, sanded, and polished to a completely finished facet. Then he goes to the next facet. By working this way, he does not have to worry about resetting the exact same angle and degrees a second time. Among his faceted novelties are a complete little crystal city, a helicoptor, a rickshaw, and a faceted rose.

The rickshaw (fig. 10–39) has a total of 34 parts; the coolie and his passenger, "Suzy," each have 11 parts and each required 48 hours to complete. The coolie is 2″ (5 cm) high, weighs 40 carats, and has 380 facets. "Suzy," the passenger, is almost 1³/₄″ (4.5 cm) high, weighs 36 carats, and has 380 facets. The rickshaw is 3″ (7.6 cm) long, 1³/₄″ (4.5 cm) high, 1¹/₂″ (3.8 cm) wide, weighs 160 carats, and has 230 facets and a total of 12 parts. It required 60 hours to complete.

The faceted rose shown in the color section is made of 18 pieces, all faceted, weighs 732 carats, is approximately 3″ (7.6 cm) tall, and required 140 hours to complete. The outer sides of the petals have concave facets to help achieve the graceful appearance of the flower. Each row of petals is graduated in height to give the proper depth perception; the center of the rose has a teardrop-shaped piece. The bud part of the rose is half of a faceted sphere. (See color insert.)

Jerry Muchna is mentioned here to show that the faceter need not be restricted to the standard published designs; he is limited only by his own desires, techniques, abilities, ingenuity, and imagination.

11 · Collecting the Rare, the Unusual, and the Beautiful in Faceting Materials

Generally, the very first material a beginning faceter starts working with is some form of quartz. After a while, when he has cut enough of this to master the mechanics of the art and is used to manipulating the controls of his facet head, he feels ready to branch out and try other materials. He ventures into cutting one of the harder and more valuable gem materials, cuts a few of these—and then he is on his way—with growing confidence in his technique, probably reinforced by reading every book on the subject of gem materials he can get his hands on.

He starts a collection of gem materials—the standard gem materials first, a bit of this and that picked up from dealers' and importers' advertisements in the lapidary magazines. These first materials are quite likely to be garnet in some of its several colors; topaz, both the local and the imported varieties of which are moderate in cost; the beryl family with its pale blue, sea green, and pink or salmon-colored types; and perhaps a boule or two of the synthetic corundums to get a touch of cutting and polishing the harder materials.

About this time, it is very likely that a dealer will tempt him with a truly fine and more costly piece of rough gem material, sent along on approval with a packet of more prosaic material. He buys it. It is rushed to the lap and cut. It's a pretty thing—his appetite is whetted.

Before long he is seeking all the colors of some particular gem—for instance, tourmaline, the chameleon of the gem world, with its great variety of available colors. Then if he already has a few of the more common types, he will perhaps turn his search to the harder-to-acquire members of a group, such as the spessarite, rhodolite, and demantoid garnets. Group after group is at least started—the vacant spaces noted as future "wants."

As different gems are faceted, different hardnesses and crystal structures encountered, cleavage mastered, and cutting and polishing techniques varied to meet each new material—by trial and error, and by study of the methods of others—the faceter begins to open up for himself a vast new field of interest. As we have previously said, in this book we shall make no attempt to give the reader a course in gemology. If that is the direction in which his hobby takes him after he has learned the practical ways of cutting gems, there are several excellent texts of great detail and accuracy which he can use for the study of this subject, and these have been listed in the appendix.

From this point, stretching over a

period of years from his first effort at gem cutting, the urge to learn and keep learning grows apace, along with the urge to acquire still more varieties of gem material. Swapping with other gem faceters is a very fruitful source of additional acquisitions as the list of gem materials grows. The collector lets duplicates pile up, always in the hope of getting a better piece of rough than the first amateurish purchase. Swapping also helps someone else along the line to get his start in a particular group of gem materials. So it spreads.

We would like to give this word of advice at this point. Your collection should be housed in "papers," which have the merit that you can make them yourself. Fold letter-size paper inward $2^1/_2''$ (6.4 cm) from each long edge, then upward one fourth of the length. Drop the gem material into this fold, and make three additional upward folds. Another merit to this method is that all packets are the same size, and can be stowed, for

lack of a better container, in an ordinary box such as index cards come in.

Be sure to label the packet with the name of the material, the date acquired, from whom, the cost (coded), the unit of weight by which purchased (gram, carat, pound, etc.), the locality from which the material came (quite important later), and if you desire to do so to add to your own knowledge, the properties of the material—hardness, specific gravity, refractive index, peculiarities of cleavage, and other such properties.

It is a fascinating phase of the gemstone hobby, collecting and faceting the rare, the unusual, and the beautiful. Best of all, you are not likely to exhaust the opportunities for acquisition, study, or cutting in the average lifetime. Herewith is a list for collectors' guidance, not complete by any means, but containing the principal varieties of gem materials that can be faceted:

GEM FACETING MATERIAL

Variety	Colors	Minimum Refractive Index	Maximum Refractive Index (Where only one is given, the gem is singly refractive)	Hardness
Fluorite	White, yellow, purple, blue, green, brown	1.434		4
Opal	Clear, yellow, cherry	1.454		6
Sodalite	Blue	1.483		5
Obsidian	Brown, green	1.495		$5^1/_2$
Pollucite	White	1.521		$6^1/_2$
Feldspar (orthoclase)	White, yellowish	1.522	1.53	6
Apophyllite	White	1.535	1.537	$4^1/_2$–5
Iolite	Grayish blue, purple (trichroic)	1.534	1.599	7–$7^1/_2$
Quartz	White, smoky, yellow (citrine), purple (amethyst), green (treated)	1.553	1.544	7
Scapolite	White, pink, yellow, green	1.545	1.555	6
Beryllonite	Clear to yellowish	1.553	1.577	6
Beryl	White (goshenite), blue, green (aquamarine), yellow green, pink, salmon (morganite), green (emerald)	1.575	1.582	$7^1/_2$
Hambergite	White, yellowish	1.556	1.628	$7^1/_2$

Gem Faceting Material—*(Continued)*

Variety	Colors	Minimum Refractive Index	Maximum Refractive Index	Hardness
			(Where only one is given, the gem is singly refractive)	
Brazilianite	Yellowish green	1.598	1.617	$5^1/_2$
Prehnite	Light green (rarely clear)	1.615	1.645	6
Lazulite	Electric blue	1.61	1.64	5
Danburite	White, yellow	1.630	1.636	7
Topaz	White, yellow, red, pink, blue, sherry, pale green	1.630	1.638	8
Tourmaline	White, green, blue, red, orange, yellow green, brown, black	1.622	1.640	7
Andalusite	Red green, brown	1.634	1.644	$7^1/_2$
Apatite	Yellow, white, green, blue, purple, brown	1.637	1.640	5
Datolite	Yellowish white	1.625	1.669	$5^1/_2$
Phenakite	White	1.654	1.670	$7^1/_2$
Euclase	Blue, white, yellow	1.658	1.677	$7^1/_2$
Fibrolite	Light blue	1.658	1.677	$7^1/_2$
Spodumene	Lilac (kunzite), white (triphane), green (hiddenite)	1.660	1.675	7
Dioptase	Blue green	1.651	1.703	5
Enstatite	Green	1.665	1.674	$5^1/_2$
Kornerupine	Yellow brown, sea green	1.667	1.680	6
Peridot	Yellow green, bottle green	1.658	1.696	$6^1/_2$
Sinhalite	Yellow brown	1.667	1.705	$6^1/_2$
Axinite	Clove brown, honey yellow	1.679	1.690	7
Rhodizite	Rose, yellowish, greenish	1.69		8
Diopside	Bottle green	1.686	1.712	5–6
Willemite	Yellow green	1.691	1.719	$5^1/_2$
Idocrase	Green, brown, yellow, light blue	1.708	1.716	$6^1/_2$
Spinel	Red, bluish red, lilac, brown, black, blue	1.717		8
Taaffeite	Lilac (very rare, only two known stones)	1.718	1.723	8
Kyanite	Blue, green	1.712	1.728	4–7
Rhodonite	Ruby red	1.733	1.744	5–6
Garnet (grossular)	Greenish, pink	1.744		$7–7^1/_4$
Garnet (pyrope)	Red	1.747		$7^1/_4$
Rhodochrosite	Red orange	1.601	1.821	$3^1/_2–4^1/_2$
Epidote	Greenish brown	1.733	1.768	$6^1/_2$
Chrysoberyl	Yellow, brown	1.745	1.768	$8^1/_2$
Alexandrite (variety of chrysoberyl)	Red green	1.745	1.768	$8^1/_2$
Sapphire	Blue, pink, yellow, green, orange, white	1.761	1.769	9
Ruby	Red	1.761	1.769	9
Benitoite	Blue, white	1.757	1.804	$6^1/_2$
Azurite	Blue	1.730	1.838	3–5
Garnet (almandine)	Red, red brown	1.781		$7^1/_2$
Garnet (spessartite)	Orange red, reddish	1.80		7
Zircon (low)	Red, reddish brown, yellow	1.81		$6^1/_2$

Gem Faceting Material—*(Continued)*

Variety	Colors	Minimum Refractive Index (Where only one is given, the gem is singly refractive)	Maximum Refractive Index	Hardness
Zircon (intermediate)	Leaf green, bluish green			7$\frac{1}{2}$
Zircon (high)	Yellowish green, sky blue, white	1.928–1.987		7$\frac{1}{2}$
Garnet (uvarovite)	Green	1.87		7$\frac{1}{2}$
Garnet (andradite) (demantoid)	Yellowish green	1.888		6$\frac{1}{2}$
Sphene	Yellow, green, brown	1.900–2.02		5$\frac{1}{2}$
Cassiterite	White, yellow, brown	1.997–2.093		6–7
Zincite	Red, orangeish yellow	2.013–2.029		4–4$\frac{1}{2}$
Sphalerite	Yellowish brown, red	2.369		3$\frac{1}{2}$–4
Diamond	White, yellowish white, blue, pink, red, brown, green, gray, black, canary	2.419		10
Anatase (octahedrite)	Brown to black, yellow, blue	2.493–2.554		6–6$\frac{1}{2}$
Brookite	Yellowish to black	2.583–2.741		6–6$\frac{1}{2}$
Rutile (natural)	Red	2.616–2.741		6–6$\frac{1}{2}$

RARE GEMS

(Seldom-faceted materials that are collector's curiosities, some very difficult to obtain, some very hard to cut)

Variety	Colors	Minimum Refractive Index	Maximum Refractive Index	Hardness
Moldavite	Brown, green	1.48	–1.52	2$\frac{1}{2}$–3
Tektite	Brown, green	1.48	–1.52	2$\frac{1}{2}$–3
Leucite	White	1.508	–1.509	5–6
Cleavelandite	White	1.525	–1.536	6–6$\frac{1}{2}$
Oligoclase	White	1.525	–1.536	5–6
Bytownite	White, yellowish	1.525	–1.536	5–6
Anorthite	White, grayish, reddish	1.575	–1.588	6–6$\frac{1}{2}$
Tremolite-actinolite	Emerald green	1.613	–1.614	6
Celestite	Sapphire blue, white, pink	1.622	–1.631	3–3$\frac{1}{2}$
Barite	Blue, brown	1.636	–1.648	2–2$\frac{1}{2}$
Gadolinite	Black	1.77	–1.82	6$\frac{1}{2}$–7
Cerussite	White	1.80	–2.07	6–6$\frac{1}{2}$
Vanadinite	Ruby red, straw yellow	2.29	–2.35	2–2$\frac{1}{2}$
Wulfenite	Reddish orange	2.304	–2.402	2$\frac{3}{4}$–3
Stibiotantalite	Brown, reddish yellow	2.39	–2.46	5$\frac{1}{2}$
Greenockite	Yellow	2.506	–2.529	3–3$\frac{1}{2}$
Proustite (ruby silver)	Red	2.79	–3.08	2–2$\frac{1}{2}$
Cinnabar	Ruby red	2.91	–3.27	2–2$\frac{1}{2}$
Marcasite	Metallic	—		6–6$\frac{1}{2}$

(This list might be extended to all minerals that occur in transparent form and which are compact enough to be cut, but these are collector's items and not gemstones.)

SYNTHETIC GEM MATERIALS

Variety	Colors	Minimum Refractive Index (Where only one is given, the gem is singly refractive)	Maximum Refractive Index	Hardness
Corundum (sapphire)	White, blue, red, green (red green alexandrite type), yellow, orange	1.762	1.770	9
Corundum (ruby)	Red, color never quite like natural ruby, which is purplish red	1.762	1.770	9
Spinel	Great variety of colors, many not found in natural spinel	1.728 or 1.731		8
Titania (rutile)	Red, yellow, blue, orange, white (pale yellowish white)	2.62	2.90	$6^1/_2$
Fabulite (strontium titanate)	White	2.41		6
Chatham emerald (cultured)	Green	1.561	1.564	$7^1/_2$
Gilson created emerald*	Green	1.561	1.564	$7^1/_2$
Igmerald	Green	1.559	1.566	$7^1/_2$
Quartz	White, light yellow, light green, light blue, light brown	1.553	1.544	7
New Synthetics Now Available				
Linobate (lithium metaniobate)	Green, red, blue, blue violet, yellow, colorless	2.21	2.30	$5^1/_2$
Yttrium Aluminate (a derivative of YAG)	Pink	1.94	1.95	$8^1/_2$
YAG (yttrium aluminum garnet)	Colorless, pale yellow green, yellow, pink, pale green, purple (lilac), green	1.83		$8^1/_4$–$8^1/_2$
G.G.G. (gadolinium gallium garnet)	Colorless	2.03		8
Chrysoberyl* (alexandrite)	Has color change: green in daylight to purplish red in incandescent light	1.747	1.757	$8^1/_2$
Linde star (ruby)†	Red	1.762	1.770	9
Linde star (sapphire)†	Cornflower blue, azalea pink, shell white, honey, black, claret red	1.762	1.770	9
Turquoise† (Gilson-created)	Blue	1.60	1.62	$5^1/_2$–6

*These gem materials are currently available only in cut stones. It is not known if or when gem rough will be available.

†At present a limited supply of these gem materials is available in either boule sections or slabs for specific mm-size cabochons.

12 · The Lapping Process

Essentially, the same sort of cutting of flat surfaces by grinding, then polishing, that is done in the faceting of gemstones is that which produces the large, flat areas needed for book ends, slabs, pen sets, table tops, and so forth, the only difference being that it is accomplished with different equipment and with more economical loose grits rather than with a diamond-impregnated lap.

EQUIPMENT NEEDED

Depending on the size of the work to be done, a lap kit should be purchased which consists of a cast iron or mild steel lap plate with a flange on its underside by which it can be attached to a central vertically mounted axle; this is fitted with an upper sleeve-type bearing and a lower cup or thrust bearing that can be mounted on the floor or a cross brace (fig. 12–1). It is very convenient and comfortable to mount the mud pan, which catches the water and grit slung off the lap, into a round hole cut into a waterproof piece of plywood which will become the lap table top. This gives a rest for the arms and makes a far neater arrangement, which can be covered with another flat board when not in use, giving the space double utility.

Units may be purchased which have

lap plates from 10″ (25.4 cm) to 24″ (61 cm) in diameter. A size of around 14″ (35.6 cm) or 16″ (40.6 cm) is ample for ordinary needs. This size can be driven by a ¼ H.P. motor of the type suited for vertical mounting. A V-belt

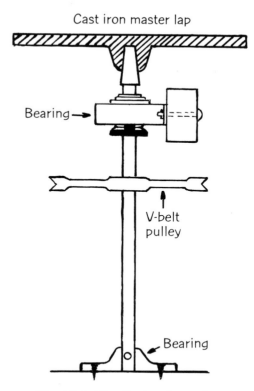

Fig. 12–1 The flat lapping unit.

pulley of 2″ (5.1-cm) diameter on the motor and a 10″ (25.4-cm) pulley on the shaft will give 385 rpm. It is desirable that the lap not rotate too fast so that it will not throw off the abrasive. A table showing the relation of spindle to pulley sizes and resultant speeds is given in the appendix.

A cross bar mounted across the face of the lap, and just clearing it, is very helpful. One end is hinged to the table itself and notched to clear the rim of the mud pan. The other end rests on the opposite rim of the mud pan. By its use a number of small flats can be lapped at once with little attention, while the operator goes about other work. This bar should be of wood. If you are the type of person who likes to build your own equipment, lap kits are available so that all you have to do is set them up wherever you prefer to have them and assemble the parts.

SIZE AND KIND OF GRITS TO BE USED

For most lapping of gemstone materials, only a few grit sizes are necessary, and the most useful are 100, 220, 400, 600, and 1,200-grit silicon carbide. For very large pieces with rough faces, 60 or 80-grit may be indicated at the beginning, in order to increase the speed of leveling the surface. Do not buy too much of any size at the start. You will of course use more of the coarser grits than the fine ones, for very little of the latter is needed for good work. Label the grits and store them in screw-lid open-mouthed jars. Use cheap paint brushes, one for each grit size, with which to apply the grits to the lap. **Never mix grits or the brushes with which you apply them.**

THE LAPPING OPERATION

The sawed slab of gemstone material which is to be flat lapped should first be examined closely for any "spurs" left at the edge by the slabbing operation. These should be ground off square with the surface on the grinding wheel, but do not overdo it or you may prolong the lapping operation in order to lap down to the bottom of the grinding wheel marks. Very obvious "high spots" can likewise be ground down on the wheel before starting if a rough rather than a sawed surface is to be lapped.

While a few hobbyists will use clay or other vehicles to make their grits adhere to the lap and not sling off, you will find that very shortly after the lapping operation is started with the coarsest grit, a "mud" will be formed which is generally sufficient to do this job. If there is too much sling-off of the abrasive, the lap speed should be cut down by changing to a different size pulley, or by a "jack-shaft" arrangement under the lapping table, by means of which an auxiliary shaft is interposed between the motor and the spindle.

At first, apply just enough grit and water to make the stone start to grind with a scratching sound. When this diminishes to a low swishing sound, add more abrasive and water with the brush. Try to keep the mud just wet enough to flow, but not wet enough to flow off the lap. Rotate the position of the stone regularly so that it grinds in all directions. The grinding is actually done by the rolling action of the innumerable small grains of abrasive, the sharp corners of which take out very minute chips from the surface, rather than by plowing a furrow across the face of the material. If the slurry, or mud, gets too stiff for the grit to rotate, scratching may result, prolonging the operation.

After this operation with the coarsest grit has proceeded for a time and the grinding has reduced the surface to a semblance of flatness, remove the rock from the lap. Wash it in a pail of water or in the shop sink and dry thoroughly, so that you can see the surface clearly.

Examine it closely for any dull patches or scratches, and if any are present, return the stone to the lap for further grinding. Make sure at each stage that the surface is completely uniform and lacking in visible scratches. When the first stage has been done to your satisfaction, remove the stone and wash it carefully, then wash the lap completely, using a small, wood-backed scrub brush to make sure that none of the grits adhere. If your starting grit size was 100 grit, you can now shift to 220 and recharge the lap with this. Continue to grind until the new surface is uniform all over when tested dry. Then clean up again thoroughly, shift to 400 grit, and grind at that stage until there is no ves-

tige of a dull spot left from the 220 grit.

After the 400-grit lapping is finished, usually you can go directly to the 1,200 grit. However, on certain types of slabs, such as unakite, variscite (fig. 12–2), or any of those ornamental stones or special gem materials which are listed in chapter 8, you may need to include a 600-grit grinding step before proceeding to the 1,200-grit step.

When you think that you are through, and before you go to the final lapping with 1,200 grit, be very careful that you have left no scratches. Sloppy cleaning up after the various steps can cause more grief than anything else. Be sure to clean under the fingernails, and use a different brush with which to apply

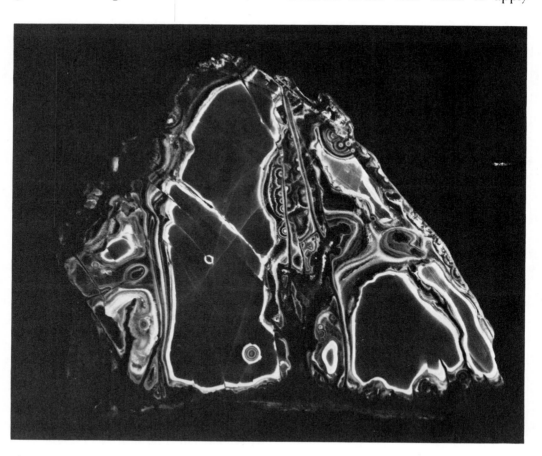

Fig. 12–2 Variscite from Fairfield, Utah, has interesting patterns of yellow and tan veining and circular spots in a soft, delicate, apple green basic color. (*Photo by Pansy D. Kraus,* Lapidary Journal)

each size grit. Some lapidaries will line the edge of the splash pan with paper or light cardboard and remove this each time they change grits, in order to prevent possible contamination.

In grinding the last stages, you will note that the piece tends to grip tight to the lap and may try to "sling." Your cross brace will help, but the remedy is to add a little more water and hold tightly to the piece in the last stages. When the 1,200-grit stage is completed to your satisfaction, clean up everything, *even your apron front,* and especially the hands.

If the piece is very large, an optical polishing technique is indicated, and this involves the use of a somewhat flexibly mounted round wood disk to the face of which old manila rope has been coiled and fastened with waterproof cement. Insert a ferrule and stem ½" (1.3 cm) off the center of the back with a short stem of about 8" (20.3 cm) and ½" (1.3 cm) in diameter. Insert this in a drill press or other revolving chuck—even an electric drill will do. Fasten the block down tightly to a base by casting it into a shallow cardboard box with plaster of paris. This block can then be held firmly by C-clamps on the flatbed of the drill press, especially if you first place a small piece of ¼" (0.64-cm) plywood in the bottom of the cardboard box before pouring in the plaster of paris.

Apply wet sanding paper sheets to the rope-faced disk, using plastic tape, and sand the surface of the block with this, keeping it quite wet. Often 600-grit speed-wet cloth is better than paper.

Move the disk over the face of the block until the entire surface shows no evidence of any scratch; in fact, it will begin at this point to assume a gloss. Persevere in the sanding until you have no uneven areas left.

Remove the sanding cloth from the rope polishing "dop." Then clean up and apply a slurry of cerium oxide to the face of the block to be polished and proceed to bring all parts of the surface into contact with the polishing dop. If you are working with an electric drill as the power for turning the polishing dop, the block can be mounted on a low box and some pressure exerted as you polish. The polishing agent will need to be suited to the material being flat polished. For travertine onyx, ricolite, and any of the softer materials that contain calcium, the addition of a little oxalic acid to the mixture will aid in the polishing. This is a *poison* and should be handled accordingly. Jade should be handled in the manner indicated in chapter 8, and a mixture of chromium oxide and Linde A should be used for the polishing agent. The old techniques call for the use of tripoli, while levigated alumina is often used in modern stone polishing of harder materials. The technique given here is simply a duplication of the methods of stonecutters of monuments and such.

ALTERNATE METHODS

When a large number of small pieces are to be polished, they can be laid face down on a sheet of plate glass over which a piece of newspaper has been placed. Place the hardest rocks around the outside edge. Make a rim of cardboard about 2" (5.1 cm) high and tape it together to make a square or rectangle surrounding the stone slabs or pieces. Brace the edges with blocks. Pour over the entire lot a loose mixture of plaster of paris and allow it to set hard. Then remove the rim and soak the newspaper off the face. Proceed to lap the whole as if it were one piece, and polish in the same way, then break apart to get out the individual pieces.

Today, we do not need to resort to homemade equipment, for we now have available several models of flat lapping and polishing machines (fig. 12–3). One of these supplies a spindle turned by a motor, on which the cast iron grinding

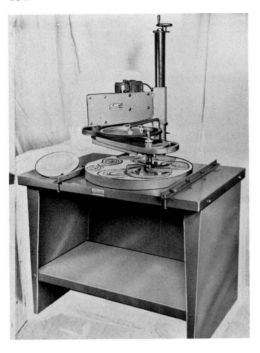

Fig. 12–3 Covington automatic slab polisher has an 8″ (20.3-cm) lapping head and
a leather polishing head. (*Courtesy, Covington
Engineering Corp.*)

Fig. 12–4 Vi-Bro-Lap, a vibrating lap that
can handle several slabs at one time. (*Courtesy, Highland Park Manufacturing Co.*)

lap or the rope-faced polishing dop can
be rotated, while the work remains stationary.

Another type of lapping machine uses
a vibratory principle to accomplish the
lapping (figs. 12–4, 12–5, and 12–6).
The base of the lapping surface is a
quartered casting in which grooves hold
the grit mixture while the lapping is
being done. Rubber shock absorbers are
placed around each of several slabs or
pieces to prevent them from bumping
each other harshly, and they are simply
laid on the table, which is actuated by a
motor into a vigorous lateral vibration.
This accomplishes the same type of
grinding that is done by a rotary lap.

SANDING AND POLISHING
ON DRUMS

It is possible to take flat lapped
smaller pieces directly from the lap to a

3″ (7.6-cm) wide drum sander, used with
wet sanding cloth, using the finer
grades, and reduce the surface to a condition almost as good as flat polishing
techniques will yield. After sanding
through each stage, wash the pieces and

Fig. 12–5 The Rociprolap lapping and polishing machine does not vibrate but revolves two or three times a minute and re-
ciprocates about 600 times a minute; it is
available in an 18″ (45.7-cm) or a 20″ (50.8-
cm) unit. (*Courtesy, Rose Enterprises*)

Fig. 12–6 Raytech 15″ (38.1-cm) or 10″ (25.4-cm) Hustler vibrating laps are available with polishing pad and bumper ring and have a built-in motor. (*Courtesy, Raytech Industries*)

the hands carefully and proceed to the next stage. Final polishing is usually done with a felt wheel and cerium oxide, unless some other wheel and polishing agent are indicated by the nature of the material. This method requires a good deal of care and patience if a truly uniform polish is to be achieved.

Very few hobbyists resort to finishing flat pieces by hand, especially with the newer type laps that provide for a final polish, as well as the fine lapping. The major factor in obtaining a final polish is cleanliness. Everything should be cleaned thoroughly between each stage.

The new vibratory lapping units are available in sizes ranging from 10″ (25.4-cm) to 20″ (50.8-cm) laps.

FILLING PITS IN FLATS

Some of the new epoxy cements are very useful in filling pits in large surfaces which otherwise might be marred. This can be done after the pieces are lapped and polished. The pit, or hole, is scrubbed clean, possibly stained dark, and then filled with the transparent material. A final polishing over the fill will finish it.

13 · How to Carve and Engrave Gems

In earliest times few men knew how to read or write. Education was limited principally to priests, scribes, and rulers. An often repeated reference in the Bible mentions "the scribes and Pharisees," the latter term meaning the priests who believed in the strict observance of the religious laws of the Hebrews. Some of the earliest forms of writing that were not simply picture symbols were impressions made on clay tablets by a three-cornered stylus. This was cuneiform writing. It was done on soft clay tablets by scribes or learned men who performed the services of a public stenographer to the people of earlier times. In order that the recipient of such a message might have some means of knowing that it was really from the person whose name was given, some means of identification was necessary. When a letter or document was written, it was impressed on a flattened pillow of moist clay and, when completed, was wrapped in an outer covering of thin clay about which a strip of reed was tied two ways and knotted. Atop the knot, another button of clay was pressed, and into this the impression of a seal was made. "With my hand and seal ..." is a phrase that comes down to us from earliest times, as a means of validating a document.

THE FIRST SEALS

These seals were carved from softer materials, such as alabaster, soapstone, and other materials which were more easily worked, but as man's ability to grind harder materials progressed, we find hundreds of examples of seals made of harder materials, such as agate, carnelian, turquoise, and beryl, which have been turned up by excavations in the almost forgotten cities of the ancient Far East.

The first seals took the form of elongated cylinders with bulgy sides, into which various designs were engraved. For ease of carrying, they were pierced by means of a tubular reed rotated between the hands or by a bow-drill, with water and sand as the abrasive agents. These were drilled from each end to meet in the center. The cylinder seal could then be strung on a knotted thong or on a chain around the neck of the owner and kept secure from loss. In use, it was removed from the neck and grasped at both ends by the knots in the thong, then pressed against the wet clay and rotated.

Other than for weapons, the use of hard materials for seals is one of the first instances of the cultivation of the lapidary art by man. As time went along, the artistic urge which is inherent in man also found these seals being carved with increasing skill and the resulting forms made more and more beautiful. More colorful materials were sought and rubbed into shape on gritty rocks, then on leather to secure a polish. After that the design was engraved by incising with the point of a sharp piece of harder rock, such as flint, "by means of reed arrows tipped with flint, sharpened to a point, by means of which they engrave their seals" (Herodotus, in his description of the Ethiopian contingent in the army of Xerxes).

The actual invention of the true art of gem engraving (the incising of a gem by means of a drill charged with the powder of a harder material) is undoubtedly to be credited to the seal-cutters of Nineveh, and that at a date shortly preceding the times of Sargon; that is, as early as the year 729 B.C. This is the period when cylinders began to make their appearance in the so-called "hard stones"—the *pierres fines* of the French—which were onyx, agate, chalcedony, carnelian, and crystal.

The delicate execution of the archaic Greek intaglios, marked by the minuteness of detail and elaborateness of finish, is evidence that the artisans who made them had already invented the use of the *diamond point* applied in the manner described by Pliny: "These minute splinters of crushed diamond, gem engravers greatly value and mount them in an iron tool; there being nothing so hard that they will not hollow out with facility."

The same instrument is distinctly referred to in the Bible: "The sin of Judah is written *with a pen of iron and a point of diamond;* it is graven on the table of their heart" (Jer. 17:1). The passage (evidently alluding to the stones in the breastplate of the High Priest) is rendered by Jerome as "Stylo ferreo in ungue adamantino." There is some room for doubt that actual diamond was among the stones used in the breastplate, for the word *adamus* of those primitive times has been shown to have been the corundum or sapphire, as we know it now, while the Sanskrit word *sapphirus* then used probably meant the lapis lazuli which we know today.

In later times the Greek, and then the Roman, artisans reached a perfection in the engraving of gemstones which has never been equaled. Cabinets of the gems of those times fill the great museums of Europe, and many books have been written which are filled with line engravings of these intaglios. The cameo form of raised carving came along later.

HOW THE AMATEUR MAY DO CARVING

The past is interesting, but it is with the present that we are concerned. How can the materials available to the amateur hobbyist be used to create carved objects of beauty and utility?

The raw materials are abundant and, for the most part, very moderate in cost. Some of the softer materials which should be used for your first carving projects are:

Material	Qualities	Hardness
Soapstone	Sometimes dyed to imitate jade in color, but can be scratched with the fingernail or carved with a pocketknife	1–1 1/2
Alabaster	A pure white or slightly stained type of translucent gypsum	2
Satin spar	Another attractive variety of gypsum, with satiny luster	2

Material	Qualities	Hardness
Ivory	An organic material which carves very beautifully and has been used since remote times for that purpose. Several varieties, taken from tusks of the elephant, teeth of the walrus and hippopotamus, and so forth, are available	$2^{1}/_{2}$
Amber	The fossilized resin of ancient trees. Not a mineral	$2^{1}/_{2}$
Ricolite	A banded green variety of serpentine	$2^{1}/_{2}$–3
Serpentine	Also called bowenite, ricolite, williamsite, chrysotile, and verd-antique. All of the serpentines have long been carved readily due to their softness and excellent colors available	$2^{1}/_{2}$–3
Jet	A fossil carboniferous material, compact black, carved readily, but somewhat brittle	$2^{1}/_{2}$–4
Travertine onyx	A calcite mineral which comes in many colors, especially yellow with white bands. It carves well, may be dyed, as much Mexican onyx has been	3
Howlite	A hydrous calcium borosilicate	$3^{1}/_{2}$
Lepidolite	A lilac-colored mineral sometimes used for carving, when massive	4
Obsidian	This natural volcanic glass has been carved into a number of very effective pieces. Somewhat brittle, chips easily	5–$5^{1}/_{2}$
Lapis lazuli	A very beautiful cerulean blue mineral with specks of included pyrite. Rather high priced but can be used for small objects	5–$5^{1}/_{2}$
Hematite	Commonly used for intaglios in men's rings. Very messy to carve and polish because of the red oxide staining everything	$5^{1}/_{2}$–$6^{1}/_{2}$
Turquoise	Infrequently carved in modern times, but often used by the Chinese, and very fine when well done. Lends itself readily to carving, and beautiful effects are possible	6
Jade	Two distinct materials, nephrite and jadeite, probably the peer of all carving materials because of its superior toughness. Takes a beautiful polish	N: 6–$6^{1}/_{2}$ J: $6^{1}/_{2}$–7
Quartz, as		
—Crystal	Often used for beautiful carvings	7
—Agate	Many dishes and other objects are carved from agate, especially the banded types from Brazil, often artificially dyed in Germany	
—Carnelian	The red or orange variety of cryptocrystalline quartz	
—Sardonyx	The layered variety, often used for cameos and intaglios where advantage is taken of alternating light and dark layers	
—Sard	The red-brown solid color agate much used for intaglios by the ancients	
—Chalcedony	Often the blue or gray blue varieties have been carved	
—Amethyst	Intaglios were often cut in amethyst	
—Onyx	This is the harder agate onyx, which consists of flat parallel layers of white, gray, black, or colors other than orange, red, or brown. Often dyed black	

Material	Qualities	Hardness
—Citrine	The clear yellow quartz, sometimes carved after cutting into buff-top stones	
—Smoky quartz	Variety of quartz, seldom carved	
—Rose quartz	Very often carved into beautiful figurines, especially by the Chinese	
Quartz, as		
—Rutilated quartz	Offers very interesting material for carving when well filled with the orange red needles of rutile	7
—Tigereye	Very effective results can be secured from this material by taking advantage of the chatoyant effect and the banding. Blue, red, yellow, and varicolored varieties available	
—Aventurine	A lovely spangled green material that can be carved readily	
—Chrysoprase	The most valuable of the chalcedonies and one that offers a lovely blue green	
—Chrysocolla (silicified)	The highly silicified hard material colored by copper which offers a blue. color without peer. Quite expensive in best grades. Not to be confused with the soft mineral, which is hardly worth carving	
—Jasper	The opaque form of colored chalcedony. Carves and polishes well	
—Petrified Wood	Much of this material offers excellent carving, if solid. Often very colorful	
Dumortierite-quartz	A very beautiful blue mineral of lower cost than lapis lazuli	7
Transvaal "jade"	Really green grossularite garnet in massive form; resembles some jades	7
Tourmaline	The pink crystals were revered by the Chinese, who often carved them into beautiful figurines. Most material is full of fractures but sound enough for carving	$7\frac{1}{2}$
Sapphire	The Indian carvers have long made use of both sapphire and ruby crystals for carvings. Recently in America a series of "Heads of the Presidents" has been done by Harry B. Derian and Norman Maness of Los Angeles for Kazanjian Bros. (see fig. 13–5). Requires great skill and diamond tools	9

EQUIPMENT NEEDED FOR CARVING

The *point carver* is a machine which can readily be made from any good, light running spindle with a small high-speed motor and pulley at one end and a small $\frac{1}{4}''$ (0.64-cm) chuck at the other end of the shaft. The spindle should be fastened to a board which can be tilted downward toward the operator at an angle from 30° to 45°. In fig. 13–1 the downward tilt is apparent if it is noted that the back side of the machine is mounted on a box, the top of which slopes. This machine was designed and built by Maury G. Maline, of Sunnyvale, California. There are now a number of machines built specifically for carving. Like many other lapidary processes, the practice of the art has created the need for equipment, which has encouraged manufacturers to provide it. The necessary components are available from any lapidary equipment manufacturer, and their assembly is not a difficult matter

Fig. 13–1 A point carving machine made by Maury G. Maline, of Sunnyvale, California. Some of his finished pieces are in the foreground. (*Courtesy, Lockheed Bulletin*)

for anyone with a mechanical knack.

What is needed is a variable-speed spindle operated by a high-speed motor which can be controlled by a foot-treadle rheostat such as that used on a sewing machine. No great amount of power is needed for small carving, but it is necessary that the rig should be capable of high speeds and be relatively free of vibration. You will note that in the type of machine shown, a form of hand rest is provided with which the work can be steadied as it is held in the fingers of both hands. The cutting bit remains in one spot, while the work is moved against it.

TOOLS NEEDED

Some carvers who work with larger objects make use of a drill press with which to drive the cutting tools. In one such case, the "carving" is accomplished by cutting the head from a $\frac{1}{4}''$ (0.64-cm) bolt, so that the lower end with a bolt, then two washers and another bolt, can provide a spindle on which round, 3″ (7.6-cm) wet standing cloths, which have been cemented back-to-back with Peel 'Em Off cement and pierced at the center with a $\frac{1}{4}''$ (0.64-cm) hole, can be fastened. The edge of such a flexible cloth disk can do a very good cutting job by taking material off certain shapes of carved pieces. Smaller pairs of disks down to $1^1/_2''$ (3.8 cm) can be used for closer work.

Still another method, and one favored by several champion carvers, is to make, or have made, a number of soft iron tools of various shapes, such as thin-slitting, knife-edged, blunt-end cone, inverted cone, ball end, pointed cone, cylinder, tube, and broad-face grinder. These are used with carborundum or silicon carbide grits in grinding away excess material on the harder gemstones out of which some carvings are made. These tools are like those used by R. S. Harvill, of Sinton, Texas, winner of the Parser Award in 1958, in carving "The Genie and the Lamp," pictured in fig. 13–2.

Another type of equipment which is sometimes used is the flexible shaft device. This can be used with the smaller pieces of work which can be readily held and controlled with one hand. At the same time, the other hand manipulates the handpiece in which is fixed a drill or tool of steel, or possibly a diamond-charged tool. Different types of carving require different techniques, and some of the techniques used by several of the most accomplished carvers in the country will be discussed.

SAWING OUT THE BLANK

The shape of the object to be carved must be determined and a piece of rough found which is free of flaws or cracks that are likely to interfere with or spoil the work later. Careful measurements should be made and set up on the block of material as pencil sketches, one on the front and one on a side at right angles to it. Make the first cuts with either the slabbing saw or the trim saw after carefully planning to make sure you are not removing any material you will need later. A perfectly flat base is made with the first cut; then by clamping with triangular wood blocks in the vise of the saw, each cut is laid out with

pencil lines, and these are lined up with the projected path of the saw blade. Every bit of material you can remove with the saw saves that much later effort in grinding it away more slowly. A flat dish shown in figure 5–2, chapter 5, shows how much work can be done with the edge of the trim saw blade alone.

ROUGH GRINDING TO GENERAL SHAPE

With the outlines roughed in by sawing, the piece is then taken to the coarse wheel of a wet grinder and the exterior excess that can be reached with the wheel removed. We will presume that you are doing a piece "in the round"— that is, a free-standing piece which is to be cut around on all sides and is not to be hollowed out. The grinding wheels are very effective in taking off comparatively large amounts of material and for smoothing cuts on large surfaces left by the saw. They are not for getting into narrow crevices or cutting fine lines, because the edge of the wheel breaks down too fast.

For the working out of moderate-sized hollows, smaller abrasive sheels which are chucked in a drill press or a horizontal shaft are used, with water if necessary to aid the grinding. When as much material has been removed as your grinding wheels will take off, chuck the properly shaped soft iron tool in the horizontal chuck and apply grit and water.

About this time, you will learn that *patience,* and a lot of it, is the one essential without which good carving cannot be done. The soft iron tools can be re-shaped, or new ones made in the horizontal spindle, by using a file. If you are not adept at making tools, any nearby machine shop can make any size or shape desired. These tools will have as many shapes and sizes as the jobs you are doing, and will gradually get smaller from wear. If it is a thin-edged tool, it

Fig. 13–2 "The Genie and the Lamp," carving in green and black Wyoming nephrite jade, by R. S. Harvill, of Sinton, Texas. (*Photo by Will Thompson*)

will gradually get more blunt as it is used, and a new one may have to be made to preserve the original shape or thinness of section. It is a very good idea to make several tools of the same type at one time; then as one loses its shape, another can be substituted. Even when apparently worn out, lay them aside, for they may fit some other job later.

Make these soft iron tools in the various shapes mentioned previously: thin-slitting, knife-edged, inverted cone, blunt-end cone, pointed cone, ball end, cylinder, tube, and broad-face grinder. These tools are always used with water, oil, glycerine, or some fluid to carry the grit under them and do the actual cutting, Fine needle-tooth and very thin tools work better with the fine 400 and 600-grit abrasives. The broader the tool, the larger the diameter. The grit size can be increased up to 60 grit for roughing, but finer grit is used for finishing, to avoid scratches. Always use light pressure against the tool so that the grit can be carried under; otherwise, the tool and not the work will be cut.

In the last five years, gemstone carving has become so popular that many tools which previously had to be made can now be purchased. A variety of silicon carbide points and tips, as well as diamond tips, are available to the hobbyist at a reasonable cost.

Good eyesight is not an absolute necessity in carving, because the work is often covered with mud or, if dry, with dust, so *feel* is more important. The hands do not have to be small and delicate, but they must be trained to do your bidding and should be strong. Do not grip a piece with all your might, but hold onto it firmly and hold it against the wheel or tool *lightly.*

If the design calls for a figure or a handle which must be drilled so that a portion of it stands out from the rest of the object, this should be done with a diamond hole-saw. Sets of these from $1/4''$ (0.64 cm) to $1\,1/2''$ (3.8 cm) in size can be procured at a nominal cost, or made from tubing, the edges of which are nicked with a dull knife blade, filled with diamond grit in lipstick, and hammered shut. The piece should be set in plaster of paris on a board so that it is firmly held in place, and drilling should be started on a surface that is flat to the drill-edge, to prevent undue wear. If necessary, several holes may be drilled, each slightly intersecting the other, so that a considerable amount of material may be removed before grinding is necessary.

HOW TO HOLLOW OUT A PIECE

If a hollow vase or other object is to be made, one large tubular drill will need to be used for the largest inside diameter with which the neck of the piece will be finished. This is cut by making a diamond hole-saw of a piece of mild steel or brass tubing of the required size, fitted at the back end with a round piece of waterproof plywood to which can be attached a driving stem for use in the drill press.

Another frequently used method is to make the drilling tube as above, but to mount the piece to be drilled in plaster of paris on a wood block fixed in the bottom of a basin to catch drip. Build a dam of modeling clay around the area to be drilled and fill this with water and fairly fine grit (about 200 is fine enough). Start the drill press and gently raise and lower the tool until you get a starting groove made in the correct position on the blank. Set the depth stop on the drill press to the proper depth so that you do not cut too deep. Raise and lower the cutting tool to allow fresh grit to get under the edge and proceed to drill to the necessary depth. When you have finished, you will have a cylindrical cut, but it will be anchored very firmly to the bottom of the parent piece. How to get it out? Change the size of the drilling tool for another much smaller and drill a series of overlapping holes around the circumference until they meet. Now do the same on one side of the center, overlapping so that some tall, thin triangular sections are left. One of these wafers can be broken loose from its anchorage by wedging and prying with a screwdriver or other tool. Enlarge the hole by wedging out pieces next to the hole, until a small saw on the end of a long stem can be inserted to the bottom of the hole. With this, start cutting off other pieces until you can get larger and larger saws into the hole. You will eventually get the entire center out, after which the edge pieces can be undercut with the saw blade and taken out.

It is now possible to purchase core drills in various diameter sizes. This simplifies carving for those who are not adept at building their own tools. Diamond core drills are more expensive, but properly used they last longer.

INTERNAL GRINDING

If the piece being made has a flareout and the diameter further down is larger than the neck, fit small grinding wheels to the end of a long bolt with two nuts and two washers (having cut off the head of the bolt with the hacksaw so that it can be chucked in the drill press or horizontal spindle). With this device, the interior of the vessel can then be enlarged to the proper size and wall thickness desired. By substituting a series of soft iron washers clamped between the nuts at the end and adding grit and water, the surface can be ground finer and finer after the irregularities left by the drill holes have been removed. Internal sanding is done in the same manner, using small wood wheels and fine grit.

The sanding and polishing of a piece often presents the longest and most tedious work, for there are often areas no one can reach, and only strips of wet sanding cloth and patience will get the job done by hand. Sometimes it is better if a portion of the surface of a piece is left with a dull finish and only the highlights are highly polished, especially in figures. Folding or rolling fine sanding cloth around soft wood sticks of various shapes will provide a means of getting into many areas. Fine-grit rubber-bonded abrasive wheels on a flexible shaft will get into some spots and speed the progress of the work somewhat.

Patience and an eye for graceful form, as well as the desire to persevere with the job until no more improvement can be made, are essential.

THE GEM CARVINGS OF MRS. OLIVE M. COLHOUR

In figure 13–3 is shown the combination of good taste and design, coupled with mechanical excellence, that have made the amateur gem carvings of Mrs. Olive M. Colhour, of Seattle, Washington, stand out among the best in the nation. She has often carved small figurines out of fire agate. In each instance, she must design a figurine which best suits the general natural contour of the rough material. This would seem to be a very limiting factor in achieving grace and symmetry of design; however, Mrs. Colhour has been very adept and successful in doing so.

In working this material for carvings, Mrs. Colhour first uses a trim saw to remove all excess, then the edge of a small grinding wheel 6″ (15.2 cm) in diameter by $\frac{1}{2}$″ (1.3 cm) thick to peel away the remaining excess. If a layer of fire agate is apparent beneath the surface, sometimes it is wise to peel away as much of the usual white outer covering as possible, without penetrating too deeply.

A bench-sized machinist's drill press and a motor tool are used with various sized disks of sanding cloth glued back to back and placed on a small $\frac{1}{4}$″ (0.64-

Fig. 13–3 A group of small carvings, shown actual size, executed with great precision by Olive M. Colhour, of Seattle, Washington. *Top center,* A pierced and carved belt buckle in Wyoming light green nephrite jade. *Upper left and right,* Heads carved of Lassen Creek rainbow obsidian, which show several changes of color when moved. *Center,* Pansy of Ellensburg blue agate, with inlay of yellow and black. *Lower left,* Two-toned Wyoming dark green jade. *Lower right,* Wyoming light green nephrite jade. (*Courtesy, Olive M. Colhour*)

cm) bolt head, with washers and nut to hold them in place. This is then chucked in the tool. Disks vary from $1/2''$ (1.3 cm) to as much as $4''$ (10.2 cm) in size. Grit size can be changed as needed for coarse and fine sanding.

Polishing is done with cerium oxide on a $4''$ (10.2-cm) felt disk tapered to a thin edge. To get into small hollows, hardwood sticks are soaked in water and used in the motor tool or drill press with cerium oxide powder.

HOW TO CARVE A CONTINUOUS CHAIN LINK NECKLACE

After the hobbyist has mastered all the intricacies of carving and feels that he can fully control every process of drilling, sawing, grinding, and sanding, then perhaps he may feel like attempting to carve a continuous link necklace (fig. 13–4).

The following is an account in his own words of the methods used by E. B. Bomar, of Phoenix, Arizona, to accomplish the job:

"Many have asked me why I attempted to carve a continuous chain necklace of jade. That is a question I cannot answer. One of my friends said that it was because a Chinese expressed doubt that I could. That is not true, because I hunted for nearly a year for a suitable piece of jade before finding it in the possession of the late Chang Wen Ti of Los Angeles. Mr. Ti did express some doubt and attempted to dissuade me from the undertaking. However, after a discussion of procedure and price, I carried the jade home—to stare at it for several months.

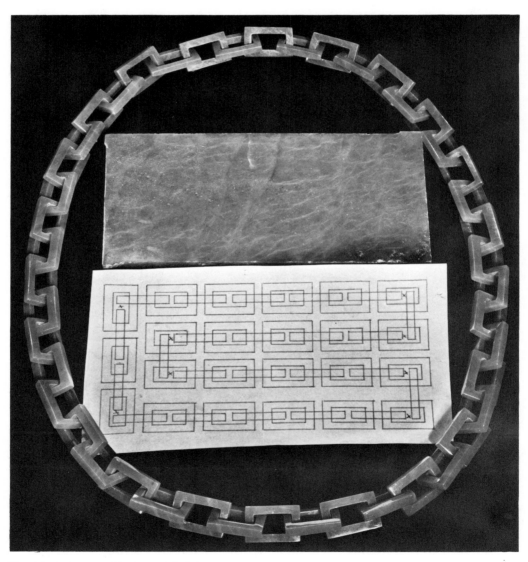

Fig. 13–4 Pattern, block, and finished continuous link jade necklace, made by E. B. Bomar, of Phoenix, Arizona.

"After a time I decided that the necklace should have a total length of 23 inches. Each link would be ¾" [1.9 cm] long, ½" [1.3 cm] wide, and have a square cross section of ⅛" [.32 cm]. With these dimensions, the necklace would have to have 46 links. Using these requirements, a pattern was worked out which seemed the simplest. Examination will show that all links except one are the same length, and that a minimum of blanking cuts dead end at a link. With this pattern, the complete necklace can be cut from a block 2½" wide, 4⅞" [12.4 cm] long, and ½" [1.27 cm] thick.

"The pattern has a long run of links on one side with approximately ⅛" [.32 cm] wider spacing than on the other side. (This is visible on the accompanying drawing as the wider interval between the two front rows on the long side.) This was necessary to make the run of links across one end symmetrical. Because of the offset it is necessary that the pattern be made on tracing paper and a blue-line print be made and the tracing reversed and printed. A pattern for each side of the jade blank is then available without the work of duplicating the tracing in reverse. One pattern is then cemented with waterproof cement to one side of the blank, and three spotting holes are drilled through the tracing and blank. The reverse pattern can then be keyed to the opposite side and cemented down.

"For the blanking out of the necklace, I built a sawing machine on which all cutting could be done on the surface of the work. The diamond blade could be set to make a cut of fixed depth, and in addition, it could be moved from side to side on a pivot point. The work could be mounted on a movable table, controlled by a feed screw, similar to a cross feed on a lathe. With this arrangement it was only necessary to reset the work once on each side to completely blank out the necklace.

"A mounting plate was made. It had four threaded screws spaced to clear the outer edges of the jade blank. The screws were provided with extra nuts, which were used to level the blank and assure that all cuts could vary in depth from the face of the blank, but not to go deeper than the top surface of the horizontal links. This precaution is not necessary if a jade blank is perfectly uniform in thickness. In my own case I was sawing to a depth to maintain ⅛" [.32 cm] thickness, for the links lying horizontally in the blank. The leveling nuts were then adjusted and dopping wax melted over them. The blank was heated (an infra-red heat lamp is excellent for such controlled heating) and pressed down to seat on the leveling nuts. Top hold-down nuts were then applied and waxed into place.

"The mounting plate, along with the blank, was then mounted on the movable sawing table and the depth of cut adjusted. Cuts were made lengthwise following the pattern. This blanking operation sounds simple, but as much as I had worked on the pattern, knowing every little detail, sometimes I couldn't help feeling I'd made a wrong cut. When this happened, I would quit for the night and take a fresh start with a more alert mind.

"The blade I used was 2¾" [7 cm] in diameter; diamond bonded in Bakelite. It runs at about 4,000 rpm. Just a simple twist of the wrist and a link is cut into. The cut, dead-ending at a link crossing the cut, leaves some material that has to be worked out with smaller wheels. If care is used in making each cut, only small ridges are left on the surface of the horizontal links and the sides of the vertical links are very near to size. After all needed cuts are made in the 4⅞" [12.4 cm] length, the mounting plate is rotated 90° in the horizontal plane and cuts are then made to leave all the vertical links standing to size. I did not completely cut through the areas between runs of links for fear of weakening the blank. The blank was then removed from the mounting plate and turned over. I adjusted the leveling nuts and dopped the blank as before, using the holes mentioned before for locating the reverse pattern. The blanking described above was then repeated.

"After all excess materials had been cut away the areas between the long runs of links were cut away, and also that portion between the links across the end and the single-cross link connecting the two inside runs of links. When the above operations were completed the blank became a cross throughout the runs of links with the vertical links cut to length.

"The next procedure was to remove the material between the inside of the vertical links and the horizontal links. To do this job I made a saw blade $1/2''$ [1.27 cm] in diameter, charged on the edge with diamond powder, and mounted it on a mandrel similar to those used with flexible shaft grinders. This blade has to be soldered to the end of the mandrel for two reasons: First, if the blade jams the solder joint will break and not a link. Second, the blade must be in contact with the upper side of the horizontal links. In order that the blade could be easily resoldered and would run fairly true, I soldered the screw, furnished with the mandrel, in place and filed off the head of the screw, leaving approximately $1/64''$ [.04 cm] of the screw projecting from the mandrel. A hole was drilled in the center of the $1/2''$ [1.27-cm] diamond saw, same size as the mandrel screw, and the blade was then soldered to the mandrel. The mandrel was mounted in a vertical drill press, running about 4,000 rpm, and the blank was placed in a shallow pan of water, the water level barely covering the horizontal links. The saw was pulled down to barely touch the horizontal links and locked to this depth. Carefully centering the saw in a vertical link the blank was fed into the saw until the mandrel shank touched the vertical link. This same procedure was followed on the opposite

side of the same vertical link. After all vertical links on the top side of the blank had been cut through the blank was turned over and all vertical links were cut through on the reverse side.

"Refer to the pattern [see fig. 13–4]. At the points marked (x) 1.5-mm [.06''] holes were drilled. Using a soft iron wire in a jeweler's saw, with a paste of 400-grit silicon carbide and water, the material inside the horizontal links at these eight corner links was removed. If you wonder why a longer wire was not used remember you are cutting to a very close tolerance and the short wire is much easier to control. You will do well if you achieve a speed of $1/2''$ [1.27 cm] per hour.

"Due to the cutting arc of the $1/2''$ saw, a small V-shaped piece is left at the inside ends of the vertical links. To remove this is somewhat of a problem. I secured from a cooperative dealer a damaged metal bonded (sintered) diamond saw blade 4'' [10.2 cm] in diameter. Using tin snips the edge of the blade was removed and carefully straightened. A short section of this rim slipped into an X-acto knife handle makes an excellent diamond file with which to remove the V-shaped section remaining in the corner links. A similar tool can be made by spreading diamond grit in lipstick on a hardened steel surface (a very little will do) and hammering all the sides of a squared piece of mild steel into the grit until it is 'charged' with diamond. When all the corner links, both vertical and horizontal, are cleaned out with the diamond file, you are now ready to separate the first links. [Diamond files can now be purchased, and it is not necessary to make your own unless you wish to.]

"After trying drilling to separate the links I gave this up. Other methods were tried, using various types and sizes of wire, and I finally happened to pick up a spool of wire-recorder stainless steel wire which I had on the work table. It is quite strong for its size. When properly handled there are many uses for it in stone carving. Before attempting to use it for separating the links, it is best to master its use. Clamp a small piece of scrap jade 1/8″ [.32 cm] thick between leather jaws in your vise. Place the spool of recorder wire on a nail driven into the edge of the work bench. Tie a slip knot in the free end of the wire and place a small bolt or dowel in the end thus formed, to use a 'handle.' Reel off a couple of feet of the wire and break it off. Make a thin paste of 400-grit silicon carbide and water and add a few grains of a powdered detergent soap to the paste. Use a small brush to dab the paste on top of the slice of jade. Wind several turns of the broken end of wire around another dowel held in the right hand, grasping the other end in the left hand. Drape the center of the length of wire over the jade and through the paste. Bring the hands down until several ounces of pressure are exerted on the wire and *slowly* pull the wire across the jade. If too much pressure is used the wire will be cut into at once. Pressure must be kept on the wire at all times or it will coil into a tangle and new wire must be used. Keep feeding more paste to the cut.

"After some practice you will find that you can make a cut 1/8″ [.32 cm] deep by 1/8″ [.32 cm] wide in about 10 minutes. Practice with the use of the wire until by using a single wire you can make a cut 1/8″ [.32 cm] deep. If you do not you are inviting trouble in separating the links, for if you are unfortunate and break a wire in the cut, it may take six or eight wires and an hour's time to clear the broken wire out of the cut. Sometimes if the second cut is made with a slightly larger sized wire, a smaller wire that has been 'frozen' in a cut can be cleared, or in an emergency a spot of hydrochloric acid will etch the broken piece of steel wire enough to allow it to be removed, even though it is of 'stainless' steel.

"As the cut made by the wire is only approximately 0.005″ [.01 cm] wide it is necessary to make two cuts for separating each link on the inside. Then the 3/64″ [.01 cm] × 1/8″ [.32 cm] × 1/8″ [.32 cm] waste is too large to remove in nearly all cases. Slide the waste up and cut into it with the wire to free it. After separating all of the corner links it is now possible to unfold all the runs of links. Some trimming with a diamond file may be necessary.

"The next procedure is to select one of the long runs of links and cut horizontal links to length. It will be apparent that you cannot turn any of the runs a full 90° to bring the horizontal runs up to vertical position. I lined the jaws of the drill press vise with leather and found that I had enough slack to bring the horizontal links to a vertical position in this manner. Mark the length of each link now in a vertical position and cut the length down to the surface of links now lying horizontal. While still in the vise, transfer the work to the drill press and use the 1/2″ diamond wheel to slot out between the vertical links and horizontal links, making cuts from both sides. Lubricate the saw with water, applied with a small brush. Now that the adjacent runs of links do not interfere, mount a longer piece of the diamond rim materials, previously described, in a jeweler's saw and remove the V-shaped pieces at the end of each link. Turn the run of links upside down and repeat.

"You will now find that the slots cut in the links overlap each other approximately 3/64″ [.1 cm]. Remove this tiny block of material, making two cuts with the wire and cutting into the block where necessary to remove it. Repeat the operation on the remaining runs of links. Grind the exterior surface of the links on the edge of a 220-grit wheel. It is practically impossible to grind the flat sides of the links so that the wheel does not cut into the surface. To overcome this problem, grind at a slight bevel and the wheel marks will terminate at a diagonal across the corner. True up the insides of all links by clamping gently in the leather-lined drill press vise, using some of the diamond 'file' to remove larger amounts of excess materials, or you may use strips of 150 wet sanding cloth mounted on a piece of old hacksaw blade from which the teeth have been removed by grinding. Use a strip slightly less than $1/2''$ wide on the side of the links and $1/4''$ wide on the ends. When the cloth becomes dull, dampen it with water and apply 220-grit powder until you have worn all the grit from the cloth, then replace with a new strip.

"After the links are rough sanded inside you may as well do the finish sanding. For this, use Durite waterproof sanding paper cut into $1/2''$ [1.27-cm] and $1/4''$ [.64-cm] strips. Back these up with pieces of hacksaw blade as before, so that greater pressure can be applied. Finish sanding by using 320, 400, and 600-grit in succession. The final sanding with 600 grit will give a fair polish if the paper is allowed to become well-worn. Use as much pressure as good judgment permits.

"I wanted all the links of my chain to be as flat as possible. It is impossible to sand a flat surface on a sanding wheel backed by rubber. Too much sanding paper would be wasted in using wide strips on a conventional sanding wheel. I used an $8''$ [20.3-cm] maple disk, $3/4''$ [1.91 cm] thick, mounted on a face plate. Cover the periphery of this disk with double-faced adhesive tape, and apply $3/4''$ [1.91-cm] strips of Durite waterproof sandpaper. Cloth is better but it is so stiff it comes loose. The wheel should run as fast as the adhesive bond will permit (approximately 400 rpm).

"Sand all the links except one for at this point you will notice difficulty in locating the point where the last work was done. After all parts have been sanded with the 320 grit, sand with 400 and finally with 600, allowing the grit to become rather worn at the last.

"You should now be ready to polish.

Remove the adhesive tape on the maple wheel and sand off any adhesive that may remain. Increase the speed to about 600 or 800 rpm. Apply chrome oxide polishing powder (adding about 10% of Linde A to 90% chrome makes an ideal mixture), keeping the wheel as wet as possible, and polish the exterior surfaces of each link. Little polishing is accomplished until the wheel starts to dry and maximum polishing action will last for only three or four seconds. You will feel an increase in the drag when this takes place. It is useless to continue trying to polish after the drag has stopped. Apply fresh polishing powder and continue. If you have a 3,600 rpm motor, make a $4''$ maple wheel and use it mounted directly on the shaft. For some reason, the polishing action lasts longer on the smaller wheel. Considerable pressure must be used and it is better to wear gloves as it is difficult to get a good polish on jade unless it becomes uncomfortably hot to the bare hands while polishing. To polish the inside of the links clamp a link at a time in the leather-lined drill press vise and use strips of leather pulled backward and forward through the link, using tin oxide on soft leather. Don't forget to polish the marker link!

"Well, there you are, 46 links in one continuous chain with 736 polished surfaces! Sounds tough, but after reading this over I think I might try it again."

CARVINGS AND SCULPTURES IN GEM MATERIALS

Several years ago the lapidary firm of Kazanjian Brothers, of Los Angeles, California, commissioned the production of a series of "Heads of the Presidents" from a number of very fine large pieces of Australian black and deep blue sapphire which they had acquired (fig. 13–5). To date, four of these have been finished: Washington, Jefferson, Lincoln, and Eisenhower. The first (Lin-

Fig. 13–5 The Kazanjian "Heads of the Presidents," carved in sapphire.

coln) was carved by Norman Maness, a carpenter turned steel engraver because of war injuries. Mr. Maness had to design all the diamond tools used in the work. Harry B. Derian did the other three heads. Several other carvings have also been made by Mr. Derian, one of which was the head of Christ carved from a massive ruby. In technical excellence and artistic portraiture, Mr. Derian has done some of the finest work in these hard materials ever known. He works almost entirely with a flexible shaft and with diamond-charged tools.

The work of Maury G. Maline, of Sunnyvale, California, won him the "Best of Show" award at the annual show of the California Federation of Mineralogical Societies in San Bernardino, California, in June 1958. The point carver which he uses was made by him and is shown in fig. 13–1, along

with a few pieces of his unusual work combining carving with silver work.

Mr. Maline describes a method which he has worked out for faster and easier carving, which uses a dry grinding procedure rather than the usual method of silicon carbide mud applied to cast or soft iron spindles and wheels. The carving is done by using a small type of flexible shaft with a variable-speed-controlled motor and silicon carbide "soft bond" wheels. These wheels purchased unmounted and in quantity are fairly reasonably priced. They are called "heatless wheels" and are made by Mizzy, of New York, in 15 sizes of wheels only, no other shapes being presently available. They are procurable from lapidary supply firms. The largest is $1'' \times {}^3/_{16}''$ (2.5×0.48 cm) and the smallest $^1/_2 \times {}^1/_6''$ (1.3×0.43 cm). These cut every bit as fast as diamond tools—in fact, fast enough so that the worker has to be careful lest too much material is removed in the wrong places. Diamond tools are used for finishing facial features and small detailed work. So far, jade, rhodonite, and obsidian have been carved by this method, and it has proved to be both inexpensive and time-saving.

Sculpture

While hardly a project which an amateur hobbyist is likely to undertake, and requiring professional skill of the highest order, the carving of full-scale statuary and figures from gemstone materials has been accomplished by the late Donal Hord. His famous "Lady Yang," done in precious apple green Wyoming nephrite jade, is world famous and is the largest known figure executed from jade, weighing 161 pounds (72.5 kg) (fig. 13–6). Some of the ancient Chinese "jade mountains" are very large, but these are done in a flamboyant style of ornate relief and cannot be called sculpture.

"La Cubana," executed in black obsidian, is an example of the use of a natural gem material for full-scale sculpture; the material is especially suited to the choice of subject (fig. 13–7).

"Rest on the Flight into Egypt" is done in black diorite, a material not previously thought suitable for sculpture. "Morning" was likewise done in the same type of material.

Before "Lady Yang," the vigorous American Indian figure "Thunder," carved of spinach green Wyoming jade and weighing 105 pounds (47.2 kg) was the largest jade sculpture ever executed (fig. 13–8). It took Donal Hord and his close assistant, Homer Dana, over a year to produce "Thunder," while "Lady Yang" took 15 months. The cost in time alone, not to mention the cost of a 300-lb. (135-kg) block of gem-grade nephrite jade, if such could be found, is representative of some of the obstacles

in the way of the production of such pieces. That is why they will remain unique in the world of sculpture, but a world that is fortunate indeed to have had the stone so beautifully handled by a master of his art.

Carving Amber, Jet, and Coral
Amber

Amber, the fossilized resin of several types of coniferous trees, has been sought by man since the earliest time. It is not truly a mineral but rather an organic substance. Because it was possible to electrify it by rubbing on wool, the ancients referred to it as *electrum,* although this term was also later given to a natural pale yellow alloy of gold and silver. It was used in incense fires in the temples, giving off a pungent odor of pine needles when burned. Because of its warmth to the touch, it was sought for personal wear and became a great rage with the fashionable ladies of Rome. Most of the best material comes from the shores of the Baltic Sea. Many gums, such as copal and kauri gum, look somewhat like amber, but they are not so ancient, nor do they have the same properties. Amber is very easily imitated. One test is to make a saturated solution of salt with water. Genuine amber will float, while the imitations will sink.

Amber comes in colors from creamy yellow to rich brown, with some rare material being red or almost green. Some is quite transparent, sometimes with inclusions of insects, twigs, or other foreign matter. Because amber becomes ductile at a low temperature, it is easily possible to fake inclusions. It can be "reconstructed" by heating and pressing together to secure larger pieces than are commonly found in nature. Much amber used for carving is of such material.

Amber is carved readily with a steel knife, but there is a marked tendency for it to chip at the slightest overuse of pressure; hence, a jeweler's saw is used

Fig. 13–6 "Lady Yang Kuei-fei," carved from gem-quality green nephrite jade (Wyoming) by the late Donal Hord. (*Courtesy, Homer Dana*)

Fig. 13–7 "La Cubana," done in obsidian by the late Donal Hord. (*Courtesy, Homer Dana*)

to get it into general shape, and fine-toothed files are used to shape it more precisely. The sanding of amber to remove the file marks should be done on a flat board to which sheets of coarse, medium, and fine sanding paper are tacked. A large area is desirable in order to avoid heat from the friction. Sand dry with a swiping circular motion, going from the coarse to the medium, then to the fine paper.

Polishing is done with a piece of chamois (tanned sheepskin with the rough side out) tacked to a board, to which tin oxide is applied as a paste. Another piece tacked to a board can be used for the final polish, for which a reportedly good agent is cigarette ash, although dry jeweler's rouge will do.

Amber can be drilled readily with ordinary steel drills, dry, using low speed and very little pressure so as not to heat or crack the material. A hand drill is excellent for this use. When beads are being made, a centering jig or cone device is desirable to get the holes accurately placed (see figs. 13–9 to 13–15).

Jet

Jet is a natural carbonaceous substance which came originally from wood or vegetation that was covered by muds that became shale. This was subjected to heat and pressure without oxygen until it became a dense solid. It takes a very nice polish and produces a very black ("jet black," in fact) object. Since it carves very easily and can be drilled readily, it attracts the amateur carver at once. Do not attempt to work it with power tools. They are too fast, generate too much heat, and cause a black dust which is disagreeable.

The equipment needed is identical to that described above for amber, with the exception of a common kitchen paring knife. A different set of sanding boards should be made and reserved for jet so that the black pigment from it will not get into the sanding boards used for

amber. The edge of the paring knife should be kept sharp *and rough* with a coarse file, so that it can be used with a slanting sawing motion to remove material.

Saw out the blank which has been marked with a lead pencil, using a fairly coarse-toothed jeweler's saw and patience. The saw may tend to bind because of the seemingly oily nature of the material, but persevere and prevent it from cracking in the process. When the blank has been roughed out, place it flat near the edge of the work table; using a sawing motion of the knife blade, shape the piece as desired. Use files to aid the shaping.

In sanding jet, hold the jet in the left hand and use the sanding board against it with the right hand. Strips of 1″ (2.5-cm-) wide sanding cloth or paper cemented to ¼″ × 1″ (0.64 × 2.5-cm-) wide laths, such as are sold for use in sanding silver, are excellent for this, and the square edges will get into most corners. When all but the finest of scratches have been removed, the piece is ready for polishing, unless there is drilling to be done. Always provide a flat or seat for drilling edgewise into the material, as in a heart, and predrill other holes before shaping to final form, to avoid the chance of chipping at the edges of the drilled hole. Ordinary steel drills turned very slowly will do this job, and epoxy cement will hold the piece to its fastening.

To polish jet, have a chamois-covered board ready and apply red rouge generously to the skin on the board. Rubbing the piece of jet with this board will bring up a high luster. Tin oxide will also serve as the polishing agent. Jet does not rub off when worn, and the polish is quite lasting. When made into modern pieces in which the somber black of the jet can be set off against the color of turquoise, chrysocolla, carnelian, or a host of colorful gem materials, it offers a great many opportunities for

Fig. 13–8a A series of eight stages in the carving of a jade sculpture, "Thunder," by the late Donal Hord. Carved from spinach green jade. The work required over a year to complete. (*Courtesy, Homer Dana*)

Fig. 13–8b (*Courtesy, Homer Dana*)

Fig. 13–8c (*Courtesy, Homer Dana*)

Fig. 13–8d (*Courtesy, Homer Dana*)

Fig. 13–8e (*Courtesy, Homer Dana*)

Fig. 13–8f (*Courtesy, Homer Dana*)

Fig. 13–8g (*Courtesy, Homer Dana*)

Fig. 13–8h (*Courtesy, Homer Dana*)

Fig. 13–9 Covington gem drill designed for use with silicon carbide or Norbide abrasives. (*Courtesy, Covington Engineering Corp.*)

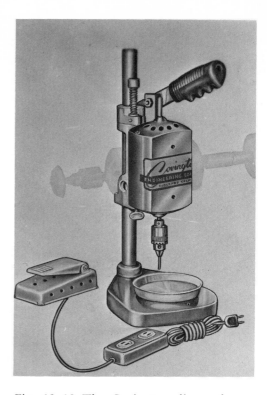

Fig. 13–10 The Covington diamond gem drill can be rotated and used also as a buffer or a gem carver. (*Courtesy, Covington Engineering Corp.*)

Fig. 13–11 The Imahashi ultrasonic drill has a steel wire drill vibrating in an abrasive medium. It will penetrate very hard materials and is used to drill all types of gemstones. (*Courtesy, Highland Park Manufacturing Co.*)

Fig. 13–12 The Crown bead pot has a bed of clay which holds each bead, thus eliminating the need for clamping each bead individually. (*Courtesy, Crown Manufacturing Co.*)

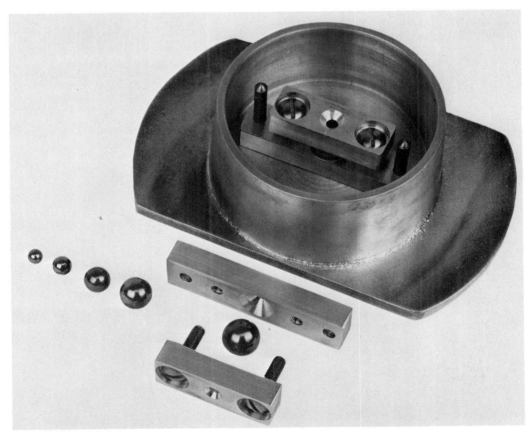

Fig. 13–13 The Crown bead gripper, in which each bead is clamped individually. (*Courtesy, Crown Manufacturing Co.*)

Fig. 13–14 The Imahashi bead mill laps and grinds rough gemstone material that has been preshaped. The top lap is a slower turning rubber-covered lap, while the bottom lap is a faster turning iron lap. Beads must be polished by an additional step, usually using a tumbler. (*Courtesy, Highland Park Manufacturing Co.*)

the designer with imagination. "Faceted" beads of flattened jet between other colored stones can enliven the whole and provide contrast that is pleasing. Jet is a neglected material at present, but it should not be. The best material comes from Whitby, England, but it may also be obtained from Colorado and Utah. Some of the better gem dealers stock it regularly.

Coral

The beautiful red coral of commerce grows under the sea in various parts of the world, but the best of it comes from the Mediterranean Sea and from Japan. The variety most sought is *Corallium rubrum,* which is branched, seldom over ¼" (0.64 cm) thick, and of a pink to tomato red color, with some of the finer types a deeper red. It takes an excellent polish. It is rather brittle, and care must be used in sawing it or in drilling. All of the best material is imported and can be secured from gem supply firms.

The tools are somewhat the same as those used in working jet and amber.

Fig. 13–15 The Crown bead mill is a self-contained, friction drive unit which will form 20 or more beads at a time. The plates, as well as the pot, are removable for easy cleaning. It has two size-forming plates. (*Courtesy, Crown Manufacturing Co.*)

Because of the brittle nature of the coral, it is better to clamp the saw in a vise, blade up, and hold the branch of coral between the fingers, pulling it gently toward you (the saw teeth should point away from you). By rotating the branch between the fingers, it can be partially sawed through without chipping the edges of the cut. It is then shaped with files to the selected design, after which it is well sanded by holding in the left hand and using a sanding board with the right hand. When all scratches have been removed, rub the piece on a board with fine tripoli, then on another to which a paste of tin oxide has been applied. Rub briskly and a fine brilliant polish will be the result. To finish, rub on a board to which red rouge has been applied.

Drilling coral can be accomplished by driving a needle into a small block of hardwood to serve as a handle, then filing off the head or eye end of the needle to leave two prong ends. A stroke of the triangle file inside these will sharpen them to a cutting edge at their outer side. Rotating such a drill slowly by hand will enable a slender hole to be drilled in many of the materials that are softer than steel. Coral, jet, and amber all yield readily to drilling with such a tool.

The authors are indebted to Henry H. Cox, Jr., of Chicago, editor and amateur lapidary hobbyist, for excerpts from his *Lapidary Journal* articles on the cutting and polishing of amber, jet, and coral, portions of which are used in this chapter.

$14 \cdot$ The Making of Gemstone Novelties

We have previously described in chapters 6 and 10 how to cut cabochons and how to facet gems, respectively. In other chapters, we have discussed the special techniques for special cabochons, how to carve and engrave gems, and how to cut star and cat's-eye gems. There comes a time when the earnest amateur will wish to depart from the conventional gem cutting and dare to create something in stone for himself— to make some good practical use of his acquired lapidary knowledge—to spread himself as an artist.

This is the time when a gemcutter, who has really learned his gemcraft, starts to adapt his knowledge and machines to the problems that confront him in working out his ideas. No book can give one directions for solving all these problems, for it is doubtful if any one person has had to solve all of them. Anything that approaches the gadget term in gemstone craft is called a novelty, and the ultimate in the creation of these things finally gets into the field of sculpture. In the following pages we present a few of the thousands of projects that have come to the authors' attention during the last ten years which would fall into this gemcraft category. Their story is told principally in their illustration, and it is hoped that they will inspire the reader to go down side paths in the gemcutting hobby and achieve more fun and happiness than he can in just turning out gemstones intended for jewelry and adornment.

MAKING BOOKENDS

The first novelty that the gemcutter usually turns to is creating a very practical set of bookends. There is nothing difficult about this, once the careful selection of solid colorful material has been made. The best and cheapest materials for making bookends are the many varieties of petrified wood, travertine (so-called onyx), rhodonite, obsidian, jasper, marble, and jade. However, jade is now expensive.

The making of bookends is principally slab sawing and lapping, the procedures for which are adequately described in chapters 4 and 12, respectively.

It is a sad fact that almost all book ends offered in the market do not serve the purpose for which they were intended—to hold up books. The reason for this is that the books are usually heavier than the materials designed to hold them. The artist in stone, however, has no excuse for making inefficient bookends, for he is dealing with heavy materials. Therefore, the lapidary should select two chunks of good material weighing about 10 pounds (4.5 kg) each if he wants bookends that will hold upright from five to ten volumes. Smaller bookends will serve only an aesthetic purpose rather than a utilitarian purpose and will hold only a volume or two.

Petrified wood makes interesting and beautiful bookends. Select it as slices of a log section if you find such material available. There are many advertisers in all issues of the magazines serving the field who offer these massive materials on a satisfaction or money-refunded basis. Petrified wood bookends should be no less than 2″ (5.1 cm) and up to 4″ (10.2 cm) in thickness. Do nothing to the outside but leave the interesting bark untreated. Slab the chunks so that there is a perpendicular face that holds the books and a flat face that rests on the desk or table. Many operators never polish these faces but cover them with felt to protect the furniture and books from scratches. Actually, one never sees these surfaces when they are in use. The front

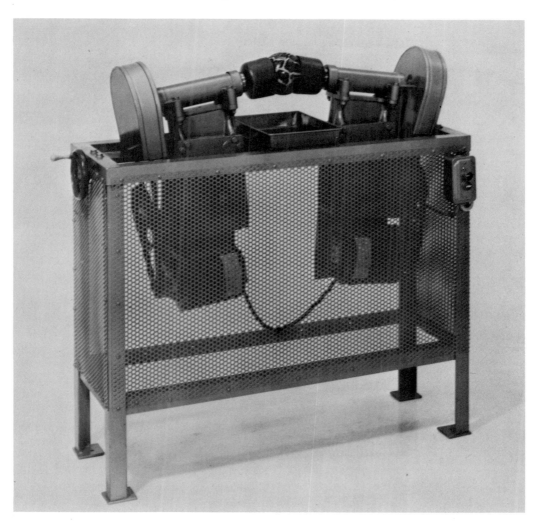

Fig. 14–1 The Highland Park sphere machine is semiautomatic and will grind spheres from 1″ (2.5 cm) to 6″ (15.2 cm) in diameter.

and the back of the bookends should be lapped and polished on the lapping machine. (See color insert.)

SPHERES

A great area of interest at any of the gem and mineral shows given each year by the 1,222 gem and mineral clubs or their Federations is a display of spheres. There is no better way in which a great variety of beautiful gem materials can be seen in their various colorings and markings. Spheres are not difficult to make, and most of the drudgery in their preparation has been eliminated since sphere-cutting machinery has been devised. Several of these machines are shown in figures 14–1, 14–2, and 14–3.

However, if one wishes just a few spheres, the cost of a machine is not indicated, and the operator can do fine work with an inexpensive gadget consisting of two pieces of pipe machined to a 45° angle on the inside. One piece of pipe is attached to the arbor shaft and the other piece is held in the hand, the sphere revolving between the pieces as it is ground to shape. The operator should have several sets of these pipes

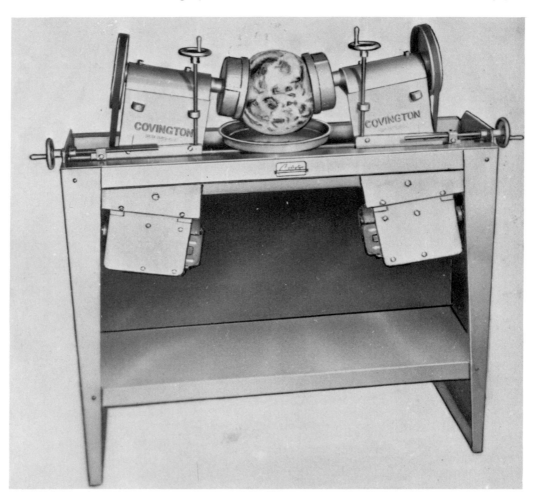

Fig. 14–2 Covington automatic-feed sphere machine. Cup arms slant down and run the sphere in a bath of grit slurry. Spheres from $1^{1}/_{4}''$ (3.2 cm) to $9''$ (22.9 cm) in diameter can be made. (*Courtesy, Covington Engineering Corp.*)

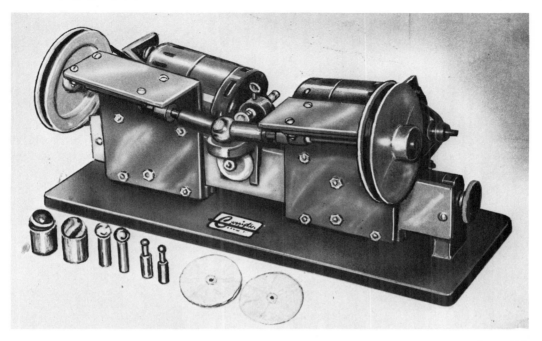

Fig. 14–3 Covington automatic Little Sphere Maker will cut and polish spheres from ¼″ (0.64 cm) to 1″ (2.5 cm) in diameter. The arms and cups also run on a downward slant. (*Courtesy, Covington Engineering Corp.*)

or pipe bushings. The resulting sphere will always be one third larger than the diameter of the pipes used (fig. 14–4).

After the material is selected, it is cut to a cube in the slabbing saw. Then the corners are sawed off. After these operations, the cutter has a roughed-out ball. This is then taken to the coarse grinding wheel, and the projections are ground until a better sphere is attained.

Mix grits and water in a fruit jar or some other handy receptacle—100 grit for large hard spheres, 220 grit for smaller or softer spheres. Stuff some paper or rags in each piece of pipe and soak them with the grit mixture. As the grit falls into the splash pan it should be replaced with the free hand, the engaged hand meanwhile turning the pipe it is holding so as to distribute the pressure. Keep the sphere moving and keep it grinding. When a perfect sphere that is scratch-free is finally attained, the paper or rags can be removed. The

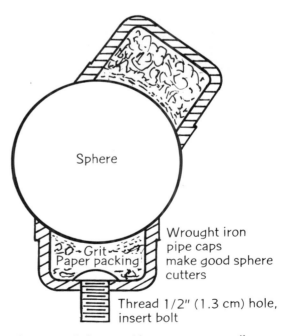

Fig. 14–4 Sphere-making cups are easily made.

pipes and sphere are thoroughly washed, and the sphere is then ground further with 400 or 600 grit. After again washing the pipes and sphere, tie a piece of felt or canvas over each pipe. Leave enough slack so that there will be room for the sphere to revolve in the two depressions in the pipes. Final polish is accomplished with the conventional tin oxide or cerium oxide slurry. An interesting way to display a sphere is shown in fig. 14–5.

In the following pages we offer many illustrations of the best lapidary work turned out by amateurs all over America (figs. 14–6 to 14–10). The ex-ception, of course, is the work of Donal Hord and his assistant, Homer Dana, shown in the previous chapter. Hord's work is known throughout the world, and he is regarded as one of the greatest of modern sculptors, especially in hard gem materials. The progressive studies of some of his work indicate the beginning imaginings and the final result. In a smaller way, the cutter of novelties must operate in the same manner even if the gemcraft project is only a set of gemstone buttons for a dress or a bola tie for himself. This is one branch of the lapidary art where you must "plan your work and work your plan."

Fig. 14–5 Bronze dragon balancing a sphere of brecciated jasper from California. Made by Leo J. Houlihan, of Conesus, New York.

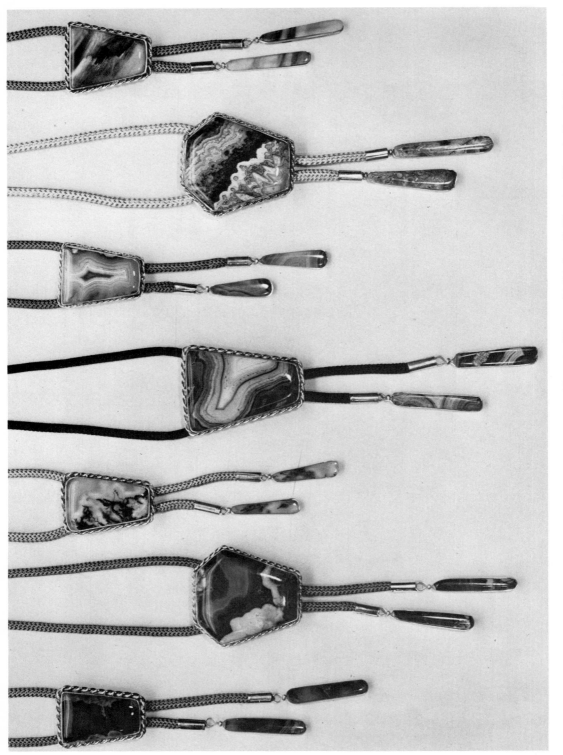

Fig. 14–6 Bola ties in various gemstone materials by J. Alden Houlihan, of Whittier, California. (*Photo by Frank Hewlett*)

Fig. 14–7 "The Old Spinning Wheel," made entirely of Montana moss agate by Claire A. Kennedy, of Milwaukie, Oregon.

Fig. 14–8 Flower picture in various gems by Genevieve Colony, of Sacramento, California.

Fig. 14–9 "Geisha," a combination intarsia and carving by Olive M. Colhour. The finished size of the picture is 18″ (45.7 cm) × 22″ (55.9 cm) and consists of 154 pieces. Three meters of jade strips were used in the shoji (screen). Three hundred slices were cut for the selection, approximately 1,100 saw cuts were made, and the entire piece took 436 hours of work. Fourteen types of materials were used, among them verd antique from Canada for ceiling and floors; black jade from California for shoji strips and hair; green nephrite jade from Canada for the pedestal; carnelian from Washington in the flower; howlite from California for cuffs and neckpiece; jadeite from California under the pedestal; jadeite from Burma for the leaves and Alaskan green nephrite jade for the stem of the flower; opal from Australia for the flower center and hair comb; clear agate from Oregon for the shoji panes; brucite from Washington for the underdress; wonderstone from Nevada for the kimono; and fossil ivory from Alaska for the hairpins. The frame is combed gumwood and copper, with Japanese characters for the word "Geisha" in copper.

Fig. 14–10 "The Fringed Lily," a combination intarsia and high relief carving made by Olive M. Colhour, is made of abalone shell and brucite and is inlaid, rather than appliquéd, with cement.

15 · An Introduction to Mosaic and Intarsia in Gems

There is a growing interest in the field of mosaics and intarsia among advanced lapidaries today. With the prevalence of modern architecture in office buildings, churches, schools, and public buildings, architects are calling more and more upon the services of skilled artisans in stone to create and execute these forms of gemcraft for architectural embellishment. Many of the new buildings in the last five years have included extensive and elaborate use of these ancient art forms. Probably the most notable example of this is the use of mosaics in the outer walls of the University of Mexico in Mexico City, said to be the most modern and the most beautiful university in the world. The opportunities for gemcutters who can master these branches of the lapidary art are unlimited, for there is a crying need for competent artisans. If any readers progress in gemcraft to the point where they are proficient in these media and they want to pursue a career in this field, they should show examples of their work to leading architectural firms in the large cities, accompanied by sketches for larger projects.

Roughly speaking, mosaics are pictures made up of pieces of colored glass and other materials, while intarsias are made up strictly of cut stones. Intarsia is far more difficult to achieve because each piece that is inlaid must be cut and ground to exactness and must be absolutely the same thickness, while pieces of glass are broken and uneven and sometimes vary a great deal in thickness.

Mosaics are among the very oldest of the world's art forms, probably preceded by established forms of architecture, painting, and music. One of the most famous of the ancient mosaics has been buried in the ashes of Vesuvius for more than 2,000 years. It portrays a dog on a doorstep with the admonition *cave canem,* or "beware the dog." Almost the entire interior and much of the exterior of the Cathedral of Saint Mark in Venice is covered with elaborate mosaics. The Venetians particularly were the world's greatest mosaic artists because they possessed the secrets of making fine colored glass. Even today mosaics made anywhere in the world depend on Venetian glass for their materials. Florence became a rival of Venice, and since the Venetians would not give their glass to the Florentines, because of jealousy the Florentines turned to stone and intarsia work in which they became highly skilled.

Today's methods of making mosaics are the same as those of old Venice, except that today the artisan has the advantage of wire saws and motors. Hours of work were formerly required for

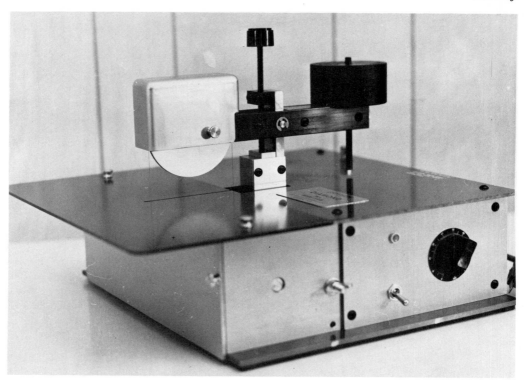

Fig. 15–1 The Gryphon diamond Micro Wire Saw is now used throughout the United States, Mexico, Australia, and Japan. The saw operates in a manner similar to a sewing machine. (*Courtesy, Gryphon Corp.*)

tasks now accomplished in a few minutes by the use of the trim saw. In addition to the regular trim saws and wire saws that are used with loose abrasives, some hobbyists are now using the more recent diamond wire saw (fig. 15–1). The diamond wire saw will permit very intricate shapes to be sawed, and the mosaic and intarsia pieces can be fitted more accurately with less grinding to achieve the proper fit to the joining piece. Both professionals and hobbyists are using the diamond saw even though it is fairly expensive. The art had deteriorated in the 1930s to the point where only one apprentice was learning the trade instead of the 30 or 40 who were previously allowed to learn it. These men learned the trade not so much to create new mosaics as to keep in repair the precious inheritance of the old mosaics.

After the war, John B. Skupen, Jr., of San Francisco, went to Italy and studied the craft under several masters. He has since taught the craft to many students in the San Francisco Gem & Mineral Society until that Society has become famous for its mosaic and intarsia work. This is only one of the factors that makes this group probably the most advanced of any of the lapidary groups in America today. Many of their members also excel in carving.

The first step in mosaic or intarsia work is to draw the design and cut it up into pieces which are glued to slabs of stone. Each piece is then cut out and fitted into the design as a whole, as in putting together a jigsaw puzzle. After the pieces have all been cut and put into place, they are cast as a unit into cement. The whole picture is then lapped and polished using conventional lapidary procedure, as described in chapter 12.

As Mr. Skupen reported in an early

Lapidary Journal article, "One of the most important considerations in stone mosaics is the design with which you begin. A poorly thought out design can cause much extra work later on in cutting the stones. A good design will anticipate the problem points and eliminate them. In the basic approach to the problem of design one can say: 'Well, I have a lot of slabs to use, what can I do with them?' or, 'I find the suggestion of a picture in this piece, and if I cut it here and put something there, etc. . . .' Each approach has its own problems, but the second is the most difficult, mostly because it is a cut and fit method.

"The limitations to design are due primarily to cutting the size of stones desired to make a picture as you want it to be. Very small pieces are easily lost or broken, large pieces are hard to handle.

Long thin pieces are difficult to work, and inside curves are touchy."

The thickness of the saw blade makes sharp inside corners almost impossible if the angle is small. Cutting outside corners requires a very steady hand. Successful stone mosaics should rely on the contrast of adjoining pieces of material rather than on the pattern contained in the stone.

In the accompanying illustrations (figs. 15–2 to 15–7) some very simple mosaic work—just the gluing of pieces of unpolished stone in a design—is shown. Also there are examples of designs made by cementing baroques (tumbled stones) into patterns and designs, a mosaic, and the incomparable intarsia of Joseph A. Phetteplace, as well as a map intarsia made by a group of gem and mineral club members.

Fig. 15–2 Colored bits of gemstone materials cemented to a backing to create a design. Made by Geraldine Schidlowski, of La Mesa, California.

Fig. 15–3 "Midsummer Bouquet," a crude but highly interesting mosaic of unpolished chips from Indian arrowheads assembled with great imagination by Josephine Roberts, of Duchwater, Nevada. Such work provides a source of pleasure and sense of achievement for someone with rocks but no machinery for polishing them.

Fig. 15–4 A floral picture in tumbled gemstones. Made by Henry and Carol Green, of Hawthorne, California.

Fig. 15–5 A portion of a 30-m mural in glass and gemstones representing a Balinese festival. Made by Mary Bowling for the Bali Room of the Beverly Hilton Hotel in Beverly Hills, California.

Fig. 15–6 Intarsia of "Man o' War," by Joseph A. Phetteplace, of Wauzeka, Wisconsin. This picture is one of the greatest intarsias ever created by an American. More than 3,000 hours of work were spent in cutting and polishing the 1,000 individual gems that make up the work, in what is termed *pietre dure* mosaic.

Fig. 15–7 A gemstone map of the United States. This was a pooled effort of the members of the San Fernando Valley Mineral & Gem Society, of North Hollywood, California. Each state was carved by a different member out of a gemstone material from that state.

Appendix
Useful Tables and Bibliography

As we have stated earlier in this book, it is not necessary for the reader to know that amethyst is only purple quartz in order to have wholesome fun and recreation in the hobby of gemcraft. However, as in all forms of endeavor, knowledge is power, and the gemcutter who comes to know the characteristics of his gem materials is certainly bound to appreciate them better. It is inevitable, once machinery has been acquired and some cutting has been done, that the novice will want to acquire information that will guide him in his purchases of materials and take him to places where he can gather his own rocks. Therefore, we list in the following pages most of the books that are currently available on subjects allied with the rockhounding hobby. These books can be purchased from almost any dealer advertising in the pages of the magazines serving the hobby. Most of the magazines maintain a Book Department for the convenience of readers, many of whom are far removed from book shops or rock shops. A list of these magazines will be found in chapter 2.

Books do go out of print, but this is the book situation as of May 1975. Prices have not been included because of frequent changes.

OTHER BOOKS ABOUT GEM CUTTING

Balej, Ronald J. *Gem Cutter's Guide.* Minnesota Lapidary Supply, 524 North Fifth Street, Minneapolis, Minnesota 55401, 1963.

Balej, Ronald J. *Tumbler's Guide.* Minnesota Lapidary Supply, 524 North Fifth Street, Minneapolis, Minnesota 55401, 1963.

Baxter, William T. *Jewelry, Gem Cutting & Metalcraft.* New York, McGraw-Hill Book Co., 1950.

The Book of Gem Cuts. Vols. 1, 2 & 3 (loose leaf). MDR Manufacturing Co., 2686 South LaCienega Boulevard, Los Angeles, California 90034, 1971.

Cox, Jack R. *A Gemcutter's Handbook: Advanced Cabochon Cutting.* Mentone, California, Gembooks, 1971.

Dake, Henry C. *The Art of Gem Cutting.* Mentone, California, Gembooks, 1963.

Giacomini, Afton. *Trophy Winning Facet Cuts.* Mentone, California, Gembooks, 1973.

Hoffman, Douglas L. *Comprehensive Faceting Instructions.* Spokane, Washington, Aurora Lapidary Books, 1968.

Hoffman, Douglas L. *Comprehensive Gem Diagrams.* Spokane, Washington, Aurora Lapidary Books, 1967.

Hoffman, Douglas L. *Star Gems.* Spokane, Washington, Aurora Lapidary Books, 1967.

Kennedy, Gordon S., et al. *The Fundamentals of Gemstone Carving.* The Lapidary Journal, 3564 Kettner Boulevard, P. O. Box 80937, San Diego, California 92138, 1967.

Leiper, Hugh, and Kraus, Pansy D. *Gem*

Cutting Shop Helps. The Lapidary Journal, 3564 Kettner Boulevard, P. O. Box 80937, San Diego, California 92138, 1964.

O'Brien, Dan, and O'Brien, Marie. *How to Cut Gems.* O'Brien's, 1116 North Wilcox, Hollywood, California 90038, 1953.

Ritchie, Carson I. A. *Scrimshaw.* New York, Sterling Publishing Co., 1972.

Sinkankas, John. *Gem Cutting: A Lapidary's Manual.* New York, Van Nostrand Reinhold Co., 1962.

Soukup, Edward J. *Facet Cutters Handbook.* Mentone, California, Gembooks, 1962.

Sperisen, Francis J. *The Art of the Lapidary.* Milwaukee, Bruce Publishing Co., 1961.

Vargas, Glenn, and Vargas, Martha. *Faceting for Amateurs.* Glenn Vargas, P.O. Box 56, Coachella, California 92236, 1969.

Victor, Arthur, and Victor, Lila. *Gem Tumbling & Baroque Jewelry Making.* The Victors, South 1709 Cedar, Spokane, Washington 99203, 1962.

Walter, Martin. *Gem Cutting is Easy.* New York, Crown Publishers, 1972.

Walter, Martin. *Gemstone Carving.* Radnor, Pennsylvania, Chilton Book Co., 1977.

BOOKS ON MINERALS

American Geological Institute. *Dictionary of Geological Terms.* New York, Doubleday & Co., 1976.

Arem, Joel. *Rocks and Minerals.* New York, Bantam Books, 1973.

Cormack, M. B. *The First Book of Stones* (for children). New York, Franklin Watts, 1950.

Dana, E. S., and Ford, W. E. *Dana's Textbook of Minerology.* New York, John Wiley & Sons, 1949.

Dana, E. S., and Hurlbut, C. S. *Dana's Manual of Minerology.* New York, John Wiley & Sons, 1971.

Desautels, Paul E. *The Mineral Kingdom.* New York, Grosset & Dunlap, 1968.

Desautels, Paul E. *Rocks and Minerals.* New York, Grosset & Dunlap, 1974.

English, George L. *Getting Acquainted with Minerals.* New York, McGraw-Hill Book Co., 1958.

Fenton, Carroll Lane, and Fenton, Mildred Adams. *Rocks and Their Stories.* New York, Doubleday & Co., 1951.

Gait, Robert I. *Exploring Minerals and Crystals.* New York, McGraw-Hill Book Co., 1972.

Jones, Robert W., Jr. *Nature's Hidden Rainbows.* Ultra-Violet Products, 5114 Walnut Grove Avenue, San Gabriel, California 91778, 1970.

Leiper, Hugh, ed. *The Agates of North America.* The Lapidary Journal, 3564 Kettner Boulevard, P.O. Box 80937, San Diego, California 92138, 1966.

MacFall, Russell P. *Collecting Rocks, Minerals, Gems and Fossils.* New York, Hawthorn Books, 1963.

MacFall, Russell P. *The Gem Hunter's Guide.* Binghamton, New York, Thomas Y. Crowell Co., 1975.

Pearl, Richard M. *How to Know the Minerals and Rocks.* New York, McGraw-Hill Book Co., 1955.

Pearl, Richard M. *Rocks & Minerals.* New York, Barnes & Noble, 1956.

Pough, Frederick H. *A Field Guide to Rocks and Minerals.* Boston, Houghton Mifflin Co., 1976.

Quick, Lelande. *The Book of Agates and Other Quartz Gems.* Radnor, Pennsylvania, Chilton Book Co., 1963.

Roberts, W. L., Rapp, G. R., Jr., and Weber, J. *Encyclopedia of Minerals.* New York, Van Nostrand Reinhold Co., 1974.

Sinkankas, John. *Gemstone & Mineral Data Book.* New York, Winchester Press, 1972.

Sinkankas, John. *Prospecting for Gemstones and Minerals.* New York, Van Nostrand Reinhold Co., 1970.

Spreckels, Milton L. *The Complete Guide to Micromounts.* Mentone, California, Gembooks, 1965.

The Story of Fluorescence. Raytech Industries, River Road, P.O. Box 84, Stafford Springs, Connecticut 06076, 1965.

Vanders, Iris, and Kerr, Paul F. *Mineral Recognition.* New York, John Wiley & Sons, 1967.

Zimm, Herbert S., and Shaffer, Paul R. *Rocks & Minerals.* Racine, Wisconsin, Golden Press, 1957.

BOOKS ON GEMOLOGY AND THE PROPERTIES OF GEMS

Anderson, B. W. *Gem Testing* (American Edition). New York, Emerson Books, 1964.

Desautels, Paul E. *The Gem Kingdom.* New York, Random House, 1971.

Gubelin, Edward J. *Internal World of Gemstones.* ABC Edition, Zurich, Switzerland. Available in U.S. from The Lapidary Journal, 3564 Kettner Boulevard, P.O. Box 80937, San Diego, California 92138, or Los Angeles, Gemological Institute of America, 1973.

Hansford, S. Howard. *Chinese Carved Jades.* Greenwich, Connecticut, New York Graphic Society, 1968.

Kalokerinos, Archie. *Australian Precious Opal.* New York, Arco Publishing Co., 1971.

Kraus, Edward H. *Gems and Gem Materials.* New York, McGraw-Hill Book Co., 1969.

Leechman, Frank. *The Opal Book.* Ure Smith, Sydney, Australia. Available in U.S. from The Lapidary Journal, 3564 Kettner Boulevard, P.O. Box 80937, San Diego, California 92359, 1973.

Liddicoat, Richard T., Jr. *Handbook of Gem Identification.* Los Angeles, Gemological Institute of America, 1975.

Mae, Edna, and Bennett, John F. *Turquoise Jewelry of the Indians of the Southwest.* Colorado Springs, Turquoise Books, 1973.

Parsons, Charles J. *Practical Gem Knowledge for the Amateur.* The Lapidary Journal, 3564 Kettner Boulevard, P.O. Box 80937, San Diego, California 92138, 1969.

Pogue, Joseph E. *Turquois.* Memoirs of the National Academy of Sciences. Glorieta, New Mexico, Rio Grande Press, 1975.

Pough, Frederick H. *The Story of Gems and Semiprecious Stones.* Eau Claire, Wisconsin, Harvey House, 1967.

Shipley, Robert M. *Dictionary of Gems & Gemology.* Los Angeles, Gemological Institute of America, 1974.

Sinkankas, John. *Gemstones of North America.* New York, Van Nostrand Reinhold Co., 1976.

Smith, G. F. Herbert. *Gemstones.* New York, Pitman Publishing Corp., 1972.

Spencer, L. J. *A Key to Precious Stones.* New York, Emerson Books, 1971.

Vargas, Gelnn, and Vargas, Martha. *Descriptions of Gem Materials.* Glenn Vargas, P.O. Box 56, Coachella, California 92236, 1972.

Webster, Robert. *Gems, Their Sources, Descriptions, and Identification.* 3d ed. Hamden, Connecticut, Shoe String Press, 1975.

Webster, Robert. *Practical Gemology.* London, N.A.G. Press. Available in U.S. from The Lapidary Journal, 3564 Kettner Boulevard, P.O. Box 80937, San Diego, California 90049. 1973.

Whitlock, Herbert P. *The Story of Gems.* New York, Emerson Books, 1936.

BOOKS ON WHERE TO GO FOR ROCKS

Abbott, A. L. *Gem Trails in California.* New York, John Wiley & Sons, 1976.

Bitner, Fred H. *Arizona Rock Trails.* Bitner's, P.O. Box 9367, Phoenix, Arizona 85020, 1957.

Brown, Vinson, and Allan, David. *Rocks and Minerals of California and Their Stories* (Guide). Healdsburg, California, Naturegraph Publishers, 1972.

Henry, Darold J. *California Gem Trails.* Gordon's, P.O. Box 4073, Long Beach, California 90804, 1974.

Hutchinson, Bill, and Hutchinson, Julie. *Rockhounding & Beachcombing on Vancouver Island.* The Rockhound Shop, 850 Tolmie Avenue, Victoria, B.C. Canada, 1975.

Johnson, Cy. *Western Gem Hunters Atlas.* Scenic Guides, Box 288, Susanville, California 96130, 1976.

Johnson, Paul Willard. *A Field Guide to the Gems & Minerals of Mexico.* Mentone, California, Gembooks, 1965.

Pearl, Richard M. *Colorado Gem Trails & Mineral Guide.* Chicago, Swallow Press, 1965.

Simpson, Bessie W. *Gem Trails of Arizona.* Glen Rose, Texas, Gem Trails Publishing Co., 1974.

Simpson, Bessie W. *Gem Trails of Texas.* Glen Rose, Texas, Gem Trails Publishing Co., 1975.

Simpson, Bessie W. *New Mexico Gem Trails.* Revised Edition. Glen Rose, Texas, Gem Trails Publishing Co., 1974.

Strong, Mary Frances. *Desert Gem Trails.* Mentone, California, Gembooks, 1971.

Willman, Leon D. *Gem and Mineral Localities of Southeastern United States.* Dr. Leon D. Willman, Dean of Students, 1006 Pine Drive, Jacksonville, Alabama 36265, 1963.

Zeitner, June Culp. *Appalachian Mineral & Gem Trails.* The Lapidary Journal, 3564 Kettner Boulevard, P.O. Box 80937, San Diego, California 92138, 1968.

Zeitner June Culp. *Midwest Gem Trails.* Mentone, California, Gembooks, 1964.

Zeitner, June Culp. *Southwest Mineral & Gem Trails.* The Lapidary Journal, 3564 Kettner Boulevard, P.O. Box 80937, San Deigo, California 92138, 1972.

MISCELLANEOUS BOOKS ABOUT ROCKS

Fenton, Carroll Lane, and Fenton, Mildred Adams. *The Fossil Book.* New York, Doubleday & Co., 1958.

Fenton, Carroll Lane, and Fenton, Mildred Adams. *The Rock Book.* New York, Doubleday & Co., 1940.

McFall, Russell P., and Wollin, Jay C. *Fossils for Amateurs.* New York, Van Nostrand Reinhold Co., 1972.

Schneider, Herman, and Schneider, Nina. *Rocks, Rivers and the Changing Earth.* New York, William R. Scott, 1952.

Von Bernewitz, M. W. Revised by Harry C. Chellson. *Handbook for Prospectors and Op-*

erators of Small Mines. New York, McGraw-Hill Book Co., 1973.

BOOKS ON JEWELRY MAKING

Adair, John. *The Navajo & Pueblo Silversmiths.* Norman, Oklahoma, University of Oklahoma, 1944.

Bovin, Murray. *Centrifugal or Lost Wax Jewelry Casting.* Murray Bovin, 68-36 108th Street, Forest Hills, L.I., New York 11375, 1971.

Bovin, Murray. *Jewelry Making.* Murray Bovin, 68-36 108th Street, Forest Hills, L.I., New York 11375, 1971.

Bovin, Murray. *Silversmithing and Art Metal.* Murray Bovin, 68-36 108th Street, Forest Hills, L.I., New York 11375, 1971.

Choate, Sharr. *Creative Casting.* New York, Crown Publishers, 1966.

Choate, Sharr. *Creative Gold- and Silversmithing.* New York, Crown Publishers, 1970.

Franke, Lois E. *Handwrought Jewelry.* New York, Taplinger Publishing Co., 1962.

Hardy, R. Allan. *The Jewelry Repair Manual.* New York, Van Nostrand Reinhold Co., 1967.

Hunt, W. Ben. *Indian Silversmithing.* New York, Macmillan Publishing Co., 1960.

Pack, Greta. *Jewelry & Enameling.* New York, Van Nostrand Reinhold Co., 1941.

Pack, Greta. *Jewelry Making for the Beginning Craftsman.* New York, Van Nostrand Reinhold Co., 1958.

Shoenfelt, Joseph F. *Designing and Making Handwrought Jewelry.* New York, McGraw-Hill Book Co., 1960.

Untracht, Oppi. *Enameling on Metal.* Radnor, Pennsylvania, Chilton Book Co., 1957.

Von Neumann, Robert. *The Design and Creation of Jewelry.* Radnor, Pennsylvania, Chilton Book Co., 1972.

Weiner, Louis. *Hand Made Jewelry.* New York, Van Nostrand Reinhold Co., 1960.

CONVERSION TABLES

Carat—one carat = 0.200 milligram by the International metric standards. This should not be confused with the word Karat, which is a measure of the fineness of gold.

1 gram	= 5 carats
1 carat	= 200 milligrams
1 kilogram	= 1000 grams
1 avoirdupois ounce ≐ 141.75 carats	= 28.35 grams
1 troy ounce	= 37.8 grams
1 avoirdupois pound = 2268 carats	= 453.6 grams
1 kilogram (1000 grams)	= 2.203 pounds
1 grain ¼ of a metric carat	= 0.05 metric grain
1 pearl grain (*not* the equivalent of the avoirdupois grain)	= ¹/₂₀ gram = ¼ carat
1 carat	= 4 pearl grains
1 troy ounce	= ¹/₁₂ pound

(Most opal is sold by the troy ounce)

CLARK STANDARD SIZES FOR ROCKS

1 mm (about ¹/₂₅″) or less	particle
1 mm to ¹/₈″	fragment
¹/₈″ to 2¹/₂″	pebble
2¹/₂″ to 10¹/₂″	cobble
over 10¹/₂″	boulder

ABBREVIATIONS

Carat—ct   Grain—gr   Ounce—oz   Gram—g
Pound—lb   Pennyweight—dwt   Millimeter—mm
Avoirdupois—avoir

SUGGESTED DIAMOND SAW SPEEDS

6″ diameter—2,500 rpm   14″ diameter—950 rpm
8″ diameter—2,000 rpm   16″ diameter—850 rpm
10″ diameter—1,500 rpm   20″ diameter—800 rpm
12″ diameter—1,200 rpm

CONVERSION TO THE METRIC SYSTEM

AREA
1 square inch = 6.5 square centimeters
1 square foot = 0.09 square meter
1 square yard = 0.8 square meter
1 square mile = 2.6 square kilometers
1 acre   = 0.4 hectare

LENGTH
1 inch = 2.54 centimeters
1 foot = 30 centimeters
1 foot = .30 meter
1 yard = 0.91 meter
1 mile = 1.61 kilometers

TEMPERATURE
212°F   = 100°C (boiling point)
194°F   =   90°C
176°F   =   80°C
158°F   =   70°C
140°F   =   60°C
122°F   =   50°C
104°F   =   40°C
 98.6°F =   37°C (normal body temperature)
86°F   =   30°C
68°F   =   20°C
50°F   =   10°C
41°F   =   5°C
32°F   =   0°C (freezing point)

To convert Fahrenheit to centigrade, subtract 32 from the Fahrenheit reading and multiply the result by the fraction $5/9$.

To convert centigrade to Fahrenheit, multiply the centigrade reading by $9/5$ and add 32 to the result.

VOLUME
1 teaspoon   = 4.92 cubic centimeters
1 tablespoon = 14.78 cubic centimeters
1 fluid ounce = 29.57 cubic centimeters
1 cup   = 0.24 liter
1 pint   = 0.47 liter
1 quart   = 0.95 liter
1 gallon   = 3.8 liters
1 cubic foot   = 0.03 cubic meter
1 cubic yard = 0.76 cubic meter

WEIGHT

1 ounce = 28 grams avdp. or 31.1 Troy
1 pound = 0.45 kilogram
1 ton   = 0.9 ton

DIAMOND ABRASIVE CHART*

Use	Grit	Microns
Rough or very coarse grinding or fast removal of material	100	150
	120	120
	170	90
	230	60
	325	45
Fast grinding for roughing out and shaping	600	30
Removal of scratches from coarse grinding and shaping	1,200	15
Very fine sanding and removal of small or shallow scratches	1,800	9
Prepolishing or extremely fine sanding	3,000	6
Semipolishing to polishing; will polish some of the harder gemstones	8,000	3
Polishing; will polish most of the harder gemstones	14,000	1
Polishing on most gemstones; used mostly by faceters	50,000	0.50
Very fine polishing on brittle or very soft gemstones; primarily for faceting	60,000	0.25

*This chart, by no means complete, shows only those diamond abrasives of primary importance to the lapidary. Color coding has not been shown, since there are slight variances between different manufacturers.

TABLE OF FACETING ANGLES

Gem	Angles		Kind of Lap				
	Crown	Pavilion	Tin Lap	Tin–Type	Lead	Type	Lucite
Andalusite	45°	41°	Tin oxide*				
Apatite	43°	39°	Tin oxide		Linde A	Linde A*	
Benitoite	37°	42°	Tin oxide / Linde A*				
Beryl	42°	43°	Tin oxide	Cerium oxide		Linde A / Tin oxide*	Cerium
Corundum	37°	42°	6,400 diamond* (kerosene)		Tripoli	Chrome oxide	
Epidote	37°	42°	Tin oxide*				
Garnet							
various types	37°	42°	Tin oxide				
darker types	43°	40°	Linde A*				
Peridot	43°	39°	Linde A* (detergent)			Linde A	
Phenacite	43°	39°	Tin oxide*				
Quartz	42°	43°	Tin oxide			Tin oxide	Cerium*
Spinel	37°	42°			Tin oxide	Linde A*	
Spodumene	43°	39°	Tin oxide			Linde A*	
Titania	34°	41°	Linde A / 6,400 diamond	Linde A*		Linde A	
Topaz	42°	40.5°	Linde A*			Linde A	
Tourmaline	43°	39°	Tin oxide	Tin oxide		Linde A*	
Zircon	43°	40°				Linde A*	

*Indicates preferred method, lap and polishing powder.

Note: In some cases the above is a close approximation, and variations may be called for by variation in the material. In dealing with colored stones the angles of the facets are not so important from an optical standpoint, as a large part of the light entering a gem is absorbed and not returned through the crown. The deeper the color, the lower the angles need be in the pavilion area of the stone in order to make it more shallow and thus enhance the color. Cut for beauty of form and shape.

RPM SPEED TABLES*

Here is a table of rpm speeds in relation to pulley sizes that will be useful to all machine operators. The speed of the motor used is 1725 rpm. These pulley sizes shown in centimeters are based on standard direct conversion of 2.54 cm per 1″ and do not reflect standardized metric pulley sizes.

Diameter of Pulley on Machine in Inches (cm)

Diameter of Motor Pulley in Inches (cm)	1¼ (3.175)	1½ (3.81)	1¾ (4.44)	2 (5.08)	2¼ (5.72)	2½ (6.35)	3 (7.62)	4 (10.16)	5 (12.7)	6½ (16.51)	8 (20.32)	10 (25.4)	12 (30.48)
1¼ (3.175)	1725	1437	1232	1078	958	862	718	539	431	331	269	215	179
1½ (3.81)	2070	1725	1478	1293	1150	1035	862	646	517	398	323	258	215
1¾ (4.44)	2415	2012	1725	1509	1341	1207	1006	754	603	464	377	301	251
2 (5.08)	2760	2300	1971	1725	1533	1380	1150	862	690	530	431	345	287
2¼ (5.72)	3105	2587	2217	1940	1725	1552	1293	970	776	597	485	388	323
2½ (6.35)	3450	2875	2464	2156	1916	1725	1437	1078	862	663	539	431	359
3 (7.62)	4140	3450	2957	2587	2300	2070	1725	1293	1035	796	646	517	431
4 (10.16)	5520	4600	3942	3450	3066	2760	2300	1725	1380	1061	862	690	575
5 (12.7)	6900	5750	4928	4312	3833	3450	2875	2156	1725	1326	1078	862	718
6½ (16.51)	8970	7475	6407	5606	4983	4485	3737	2803	2242	1725	1401	1121	934
8 (20.32)		9200	7885	6900	6133	5520	4600	3450	2760	2123	1725	1380	1150
10 (25.4)			9857	8625	7666	6900	5750	4312	3450	2653	2156	1725	1437
12 (30.48)					9200	8280	6900	5175	4140	3184	2587	2070	1725
15 (38.1)							8625	6468	5175	3980	3234	2587	2156
18 (45.72)								7762	6210	4776	3881	3105	2587

Courtesy, Lapidary Journal.

Speed of Driven Pulley Required

Diameter and speed of driving pulley and diameter of driven pulley are known.

Rule: Multiply the diameter of the driving pulley by its speed in revolutions per minute and divide the product by the diameter of the driven pulley.

Example: If the diameter of the *driving* pulley is 12″ and its speed is 1725 revolutions per minute, and the diameter of the driven pulley is 6.5″, then the speed of the driven pulley is $\dfrac{12 \times 1725}{6.5} = 3184$ revolutions per minute.

(This rule and example apply to the chart above.)

Diameter of Driven Pulley Required

Diameter and speed of driving pulley and revolutions per minute of driven pulley are known.

Rule: Multiply the diameter of the driving pulley by its speed in revolutions per minute, and divide the product by the required speed of the driven pulley.

Example: If the diameter of the *driving* pulley is 1.5″ or 1½″ and its speed 1725 revolutions per minute, and the driven pulley is to rotate 862.5 revolutions per minute, then the diameter of the driven pulley is $\dfrac{1.5 \times 1725}{862.5} = 3″$ diameter pulley.

Diameter of Driving Pulley Required

Diameter and speed of driven pulley, and speed of driving pulley are known.

Rule: Multiply the diameter of the driven pulley by its speed in revolutions per minute, and divide the product by the speed of the driving pulley.

Example: If the diameter of the *driven* pulley is 5″ and its required speed, 1035 revolutions per minute, and the speed of the driving pulley is 1725 revolutions per minute, then the diameter of the driving pulley is $\dfrac{5 \times 1035}{1725} = 3″$ diameter pulley.

GEMOLOGICAL MEASURES*
Comparative Sizes of Gemstones

Stone Size (ss)	Pearl Size (ps)	Millimeter (mm)	Inch (″)	Carat (ct)	Point (pt)
1	4–5	1	$^3/_{64}$	$^1/_{200}$	$^1/_2$
2	6–7	$1^1/_8$		$^1/_{100}$	1
3	8–9	$1^1/_4$		$^1/_{64}$	
4	10	$1^1/_2$	$^1/_{16}$	$^1/_{50}$	2
5	11–12	$1^3/_4$			
6	13–14	2		$^1/_{25}$	4
7	15–16	$2^1/_8$	$^5/_{64}$	$^1/_{20}$	5
8	17–18	$2^1/_4$	$^3/_{32}$	$^1/_{16}$	$6^1/_4$
9	19–20	$2^1/_2$		$^1/_{10}$	10
10	21	$2^3/_4$	$^7/_{64}$		
11	22–23	3	$^1/_8$		
12	24–25	$3^1/_8$		$^1/_8$	$12^1/_2$
13	26	$3^1/_4$			
14	27	$3^3/_8$	$^9/_{64}$		15
15	28–29	$3^1/_2$			
16	30	$3^3/_4$		$^1/_5$	20
17	31–32	4	$^5/_{32}$		
18	33	$4^1/_8$		$^1/_4$	25
19	34	$4^1/_4$			30
20	35	$4^3/_8$	$^{11}/_{64}$	$^1/_3$	$33^1/_3$
21	36–37	$4^1/_2$		$^3/_8$	$37^1/_2$
22	38–39	$4^3/_4$			40
23	40	5	$^3/_{16}$		
24	41–42	$5^1/_4$		$^1/_2$	50
25	43–44	$5^3/_8$	$^{13}/_{64}$		
26	45–46	$5^1/_2$		$^5/_8$	$62^1/_2$
27		$5^3/_4$		$^3/_4$	75
28–29		6	$^{15}/_{64}$	$^7/_8$	$87^1/_2$
30		$6^1/_4$		1	100
31		$6^1/_2$	$^1/_4$	$1^1/_8$	1.125
32		$6^3/_4$		$1^1/_4$	1.25
33–34		7	$^9/_{32}$	$1^1/_2$	1.50
35–36		$7^1/_2$		$1^3/_4$	1.75
37		$7^3/_4$		$1^7/_8$	1.875
38		8		2	2.00
39		$8^1/_4$		$2^1/_4$	2.25
40		$8^1/_2$		$2^1/_2$	2.50
41		$8^3/_4$		$2^3/_4$	2.75
42		9		3	3.00
43		$9^1/_2$		$3^1/_4$	3.25
44		10		$3^1/_2$	3.50
45		$10^1/_4$		$3^3/_4$	3.75
46		$10^1/_2$		4	4.00
47		11		$4^1/_4$	4.25
48		$11^1/_2$		$4^1/_2$	4.50
49		$11^3/_4$		$4^3/_4$	4.75
50		12		5	5.00

*Courtesy, *Lapidary Journal.*

BIRTHSTONES THROUGH THE AGES*

Month	Jews	Romans	635 A.D. Isidorus, Bishop of Seville	Arabians	Poles	Italians	18th to 20th Century	Encyclopedia Britannica "Current Acceptance" 1947	Webster's Unabridged Dictionary	Present Popular List	Synthetic Stones
January	Garnet	Garnet	Hyacinth	Garnet	Garnet	Jacinth Garnet	Hyacinth Garnet	Garnet	Garnet	Garnet	Garnet
February	Amethyst	Amethyst	Amethyst	Amethyst	Amethyst	Amethyst	Amethyst Hyacinth Pearl	Amethyst	Amethyst	Amethyst	Amethyst
March	Jasper	Bloodstone	Jasper	Bloodstone	Bloodstone	Jasper	Jasper Bloodstone	Bloodstone	Jasper Bloodstone	Bloodstone Aquamarine	Aquamarine
April	Sapphire	Sapphire	Sapphire	Sapphire	Diamond	Sapphire	Diamond Sapphire	Diamond	Diamond Sapphire	Diamond	White Sapphire
May	Chalcedony Carnelian Agate	Agate	Agate	Emerald	Emerald	Agate	Emerald Agate	Emerald	Emerald	Emerald	Green Spinel
June	Emerald	Emerald	Emerald	Agate Chalcedony Pearl	Agate Chalcedony	Emerald	Emerald Agate Cat's-eye Turquoise	Pearl	Agate	Pearl Moonstone	Alexandrite
July	Onyx	Onyx	Onyx	Carnelian	Ruby	Onyx	Turquoise Onyx, Ruby	Ruby	Turquoise	Ruby	Ruby
August	Carnelian	Carnelian	Carnelian	Sardonyx	Sardonyx	Carnelian	Sardonyx Carnelian Moonstone Topaz	Sardonyx	Carnelian	Sardonyx Peridot	Peridot
September	Chrysolite	Sardonyx	Chrysolite	Chrysolite	Sardonyx	Chrysolite	Beryl Chrysolite	Sapphire	Chrysolite	Sapphire	Sapphire
October	Aquamarine Beryl	Aquamarine Beryl	Aquamarine Beryl	Aquamarine Beryl	Aquamarine Beryl	Beryl	Aquamarine Beryl, Pearl Opal	Opal	Beryl	Opal Tourmaline	Rose Zircon
November	Topaz	Topaz	Topaz	Topaz	Topaz	Topaz	Topaz Pearl, Opal	Topaz	Topaz	Topaz Citrine	Golden Sapphire
December	Ruby	Ruby	Ruby	Ruby	Turquoise	Ruby	Ruby Bloodstone	Turquoise	Ruby	Turquoise Lapis Lazuli	Blue Zircon

*Courtesy, Lapidary Journal

Subject Index

Page numbers in **bold** refer to illustrations

Acetone, in dopping opal, 60
Agate
    cabochon of, **27**
    carving of, 144, **145**
    hardness of, 4
    polishing of, 52, 53
    sculpture of, **169**
Almandite, polishing of, 53
Amber
    carving of, 152, 155, **158–160**
    composition of, 3
Amethyst, 3
    hardness of, 4
Apatite, 47
    hardness of, 4
Aquamarine, 47
    asterism in, 44, **44**
Arrowheads
    mosaic of, **176**
    of stone, 1
Asterism, 40
    in stones other than sapphire and ruby, 43, **43,**
        44, **44**
Azurite, polishing of, 49, 50

Banding, 41
Bead mills, 155, **159, 160**
Beilby layer, 117
Beryl, 125
    asterism in, 44, **44**
    green, 47
    star, orienting rays of, 44, **45**
Birthstones, 189
Blades
    diamond, 11, 12, 64
    dishing of, 18, 19
    notched, 11
    sintered, 11
    steel, 11
Bookends, making of, 162–164
Boule sections, star, 45
Brilliant
    cutting of, 103–107
    double-mirror, cutting of, 113–116

Brilliant preform
    dopping of, 95–98
    grinding of, 100, **101**
Bronze Age, 2, 77
Burnite, polishing of, 51

"C" axis of crystal, 41, **42**
Cabochon blanks, nibbling of, 27, **29**
Cabochons
    cutting and polishing of, 25–39
        dopping stone in, 29–31
        grinding in, **34,** 35, **35**
        from jadeite, 69, **70, 71,** 72, 73
        marking slabs in, 26–29
        polishers and polishing agents in, 38
        removing gem from dop in, 38, 39
        sanding in, 35–38
        special techniques for, 49–63
        with trim saw, 20, **20,** 21
        types of grinders used in, 31, **32, 33,** 34
Calcite, 117
    hardness of, 4
Carborundum hone, for cleaning diamond laps,
        88, **89**
Carnelian cabochon, **27**
Carver, point, 139, 140, **140**
Carving(s)
    of gems, 136–161
        amber, jet, and coral in, 152, 155, **158, 159,**
            160, **160,** 161
        continuous chain-link necklace from, 145–150
        equipment needed for, 139, 140, **140**
        history of, 136, 137
        hollowing-out process in, 21, **21,** 143, 144
        internal grinding in, 144
        rough grinding to general shape in, 141, 143
        sawing out blank in, 141
        soft materials used for, 137–139
        tools needed for, 140, 141
        with trim saw, 21, **21**
    made of gem materials, 150–161
Cat's-eye, cutting of, in sapphire, 43
Cat's-eye gems
    cutting of, 40–48

Cat's-eye gems (*Continued*)
    diamond-impregnated wood wheel in, 45–47
  filling pores of, 47, 48
Cement
  acetone, 60
  cyanoacrylate, 72
  Eastman 910, 72
  epoxy, 135
  Peel 'Em Off, 35, 36, 72, 140
Ceramic laps, 120, 121
Cerium oxide, in polishing cabochons, 38
Chrome oxide paste, as polishing agent, 49
Chrysoberyl, 47
Chrysocolla, polishing of, 51, 52
Citrine, 3
  hardness of, 4
Clark standard sizes for rocks, 183
Cold dopping, in faceting, 99, 100
Colony Coral, 61
Coral
  black, polishing of, 50, 51
  composition of, 3
  carving of, 160, 161
  Colony, 61
Cordierite, polishing of, 53
Corundum, 40, 116, 117
  hardness of, 4
  synthetic, 125
Corvus oil, 14, 15, 21
Crocidolite, 47
Crystal, "C" axis of, 41, **42**
Cuneiform writing, 136
Cyanoacrylate cement, 72
Cymophane, 47

"Damascus ruby powder," 116
De Berquem, Louis, 77
Diamond(s)
  "American cut" of, 102
  Duke of Tuscany (Florentine), **76**
  Great Mogul, **76**
  hardness of, 4
  Hope, **77**
  qualities of, 3
  Tavernier Blue, **77**
Diamond abrasives, 185
Diamond-impregnated wood wheels, for polishing
    star gems, 45–47
Diamond laps, 64
  care and cleaning of, 88, 89, **89**
  contamination of, 88–90, **90**
  recharging of, 88, 89
Diamond point, invention of, 137
Diamond powders, 64
  standards for sizing of, 74
Diamond products, 64–74
  advantages of, 65
  cutting and polishing with, 69–73
  in syringes, 73, **73**, 74
  types of, 65–69
  use in cutting jadeite cabochon, 69, **70, 71,**
    72, 73
Diamond saw, 10–12
  suggested speeds for, 184
Diamond saw blades, 11, 12, 64
Diamond wire saw, 174, **174**
Dichroism, 103, 104

Diopside, asterism in, 44
Dop sticks, 31
Dopping
  of brilliant preform in faceting, 95–98
  of cabochons, 29–31
  cold, 99, 100
  of fancy-shaped stones in faceting, 99
  of heat-sensitive and large stones in faceting, 99,
    99
  of step-cut or rectangular preform in faceting,
    98, 99
  "stove" for, 30, **30**
Dopping methods, in faceting, 95
Dopping pot, 30, **30**
Drills, gem, 155, **158**
Drums, sanding and polishing, 35, **36, 37,**
    134, 135
Duke of Tuscany diamond, **76**
Dumortierite, 47
  polishing of, 52

Eastman 910 cement, 72
Emerald, qualities of, 3
Engraving of gems, 136–161
  history of, 136, 137
Enstatite, 47
Epoxy cements, for filling pits in flats, 135

Facet, definition of, 4
Facet cutting. *See* Faceting
Facet head, 81, **82, 83,** 84
  essentials of, 84–86
  vernier or "cheater" adjustment on, 86
Faceter's trim saws, 121, 122, **122**
Faceting, 75–124
  adjusting angles at which facets are cut in, 101,
    102, 186
  care and cleaning of diamond lap used for, 88,
    89, **89**
  cold dopping in, 99, 100
  cutting crown facets in, 107, **107,** 108
  cutting crown girdle facets in, 108, 109, **109**
  cutting crown of step-cut stone in, 113
  cutting double-mirror brilliant in, 113–116
  cutting girdle in, 100, 101, **101**
  cutting and polishing laps for, 88–90, **90,**
    118–121
    scoring of, 90, **91, 92**
  cutting "star" facets in, 110
  cutting step-cut gem in, 111–113
  definition of, 4
  dopping brilliant preform in, 95–98
  dopping of fancy-shaped stones in, 99
  dopping of heat-sensitive and large stones in, 99,
    99
  dopping methods in, 95
  dopping step-cut or rectangular preform in, 98,
    99
  fundamentals of, 81–86
  grinding of preform for round brilliant in, 93,
    94, **94**
  historical background of, 75–78
  indexing in, 86–88
  making preforms for step-cut gems in, 94, 95, **95**
  planning correct proportions for gem in, 102,
    103
  polishing crown facets in, 110, 111

Faceting (*Continued*)
    polishing of faceted stones in, 116–118
    polishing out "tail" on crown mains in, 111
    polishing pavilion facets in, 113
    preparing preform in, 92, 93
    selecting gemstone rough for, 91, 92
    skills required for, 78, **79**
    steps in cutting brilliant in, 103–107
    turning gem in, **97,** 98
Faceting angles, 101, 102, 186
Faceting bench or desk, **80,** 81, **81**
Faceting materials, collection of, 125–129
Faceting units
    indexing gears on, 86–88
    types of, 81, **82, 83**
Feldspar, hardness of, 4
Fibrolite, 47
"Fish-eye" stone, 94
Florentine diamond, **76**
Fluorite, hardness of, 4

Garnet, 125
    asterism in, 43
    polishing of, 53
Gem drills, 155, **158**
Gem faceting material, 126–128
Gem and mineral clubs, 7
Gemological measures, 188
Gems. *See* Gemstone
Gemstone(s)
    bola ties of, **168**
    carvings and sculptures of, 150–161
    cat's-eye. *See* Cat's-eye gems
    classification of, 2, 3
    collection of, 5–9
    comparative sizes of, 188
    composition of, 3
    crystalline structure of, 40–43
    definition of, 3
    engraving and carving of, 136–161
    faceted, cutting of. *See* Faceting
    mosaic and intarsia of, **170–172,** 173–175,
        176–179
    pictures made of, **170–172,** 173–175, **176–179**
    qualities of, 3
    rare, 128
    sources of, 5–7
    star, cutting of, 40–48
    step-cut. *See* Step-cut gem
    synthetic, 129
Gemstone novelties, making of, 162–166, **167–172**
Gemstone rough, selection for faceting, 91, 92
Goldstone, polishing of, 53
Great Mogul diamond, **76**
Grinders, types used in making cabochons, 31, **32,
    33,** 34
Grits, size and kind used in lapping, 131
Grossularite, polishing of, 53
Growth lines, 41
Gypsum, hardness of, 4

Hardness, 3, 4
    Mohs scale of, 4
Hexagonaria, 61
Hollowing-out process, 21, **21,** 143, 144
Hope diamond, **77**

Intarsia, gemstone, **171, 172,** 173–175, **176–179**
Iolite, 47
    polishing of, 53

Jade
    carving continuous-link necklace of, 145–150
    nephrite, 47
        ancient Chinese axe of, **1**
        carving of, **142, 145**
        polishing of, 53–55
        sculpture of, 152, **153, 156, 157**
    polishing of, 53–55
    "Transvaal," polishing of, 53
    Wyoming, 6
Jadeite
    cutting cabochon of, 69, **70, 71,** 72, 73
    polishing of, 53–55
Jasper, brecciated, sculpture of, **167**
Jet
    carving of, 155, 160
    composition of, 3

Kunzite, 47
Kyanite, 117

Labradorite, asterism in, 44
Lap(s)
    ceramic, 120, 121
    cutting and polishing, for faceting, 88–90, **90,**
        118–121
        scoring of, 90, **91, 92**
    diamond. *See* Diamond lap
    hardwood maple, 90, 119
    linoleum, 90, 120
    Lucite, 89, 118, 119
    muslin-faced wax, 90, 119, 120
    tin, 89, 119
    tin-type metal combination, 89, 119
    vibrating, 134, **134,** 135, **135**
    wood, diamond-impregnated, in polishing star
        and cat's-eye gems, 45–47
Lapis lazuli
    composition of, 3
    polishing of, 50, 55
Lapping, 130–135
    alternate methods of, 133, 134, **134, 135**
    equipment needed for, 130, **130,** 131
    filling pits in flats in, 135
    flat, on steel plate, 120
    sanding and polishing drums in, 134, 135
    size and kind of grits used in, 131
    technique of, 131–133
Limonite, 52
Linde A powder, 50, 116, 119
Linde Star stones, 45
Linoleum lap, for faceting, 90, 120
Lucite lap, for faceting, 89, 118, 119

Marble, polishing of, 59
Mineral(s)
    definition of, 3
    quartz family of, 3
Mohs scale of hardness, 4
Morganite, 47
Mosaic, gemstone, 173–175, **176–179**
Mud saw, 10

Nephrite jade. *See* Jade, nephrite

Obsidian
  carving of, **145**
  polishing of, 55, 56
  sculpture of, 152, **154**
Onyx, polishing of, 56, **57, 58,** 59
Opal
  dopping of, 60
  dopping doublet of, 61
  grinding of, 60
  making doublets of, 61
  polishing of, 59–61
"Orange peel" polish, 72
Orthoclase, hardness of, 4
Oxalic acid, in polishing process, 56, 59, 133

Pearl, composition of, 3
Peel 'Em Off cement, 35, 36, 72, 140
Pencils, of aluminum or bronze, for marking slabs, 26, **26**
Petoskey stones, 6
  polishing of, 61
Petrified wood, **14,** 163
Phantoms, 41
Point carver, 139, 140, **140**
Polishing
  of cabochons, 25–39, 49–63
  diamond products used in, 69–73
  on drums, 134, 135
  of faceted gems, 88–90, **90–92,** 110, 111, 113, 116–121
  of star gems, 45–47
Polishing agents, 133
Polishing laps
  for faceting, 89, 90, **90,** 118–121
    scoring of, 90, **91, 92**
Preform(s)
  definition of, 92
  dopping of, in faceting, 95–99
  grinding of, for round brilliant, 93, 94, **94**
  preparation of, for faceting, 92, 93
  for step-cut gems, 94, 95, **95**
Pulley sizes, relation of rpm speeds to, 187

Quartz, 3, 47
  asterism in, 43
  cutting brilliant of, 103–107
  faceting of, 91, 123, **123,** 124
  hardness of, 4
  polishing of, 51, 52

Rhodolite, 125
Rhodonite, polishing of, 50, 61, 62
Ricolite, polishing of, 59
Rock-collecting trips, tools and attire for, 8, 9
Rock hobby, magazines about, 7, 8
Rock shops, 8, 9
Rockhounding, geography and, 5, 6
Rockhounds, definition of, 5
Rocks
  Clark standard sizes for, 183
  definition of, 3
  as first possessions, 2
RPM speeds, in relation to pulley sizes, 187
Ruby

crystal form of, 40, 41
  hardness of, 4
Rutile, 40

Sanding
  of cabochons, 35–38
  on drums, 35, **36, 37,** 134, 135
  wet versus dry, 36, 37
Sapphire, 47
  carving of, 139, 150, 151, **151**
  hardness of, 4
  orienting of asteriated gems in, 41, **42–44**
  orienting cat's-eye in, 43
  star, 43, **43, 44**
    cutting and polishing of, 44, 45, **45**
Saw(s)
  diamond. *See* Diamond saw
  mud, 10
  slabbing, 10, 11, **11,** 12, **12**
    coolant in, 14–16
    description of, 14–16, **15**
    dishing of, 18, 19
    use of, 13–19
  trim
    care of, 24
    carving and hollowing out with, 21, **21**
    coolant in, 21
    in cutting of cabochon blanks, 20, **20,** 21
    faceter's, 121, 122, **122**
    use of, 20–24
  wire, 173, 174, **174**
Saw blades. *See* Blades
Scapolite, 47
Sculptures, of gem materials, 150–161
Seals, early, 136, 137
Serpentine, 6, 47
Sillimanite, 47
Slab grabber, 18, **18**
Slabbing saw. *See* Saw, slabbing
Slabs
  cutting of, 16, **17**
  marking of, for cabochons, 26–29
  thickness of blade and cut in, 16, 18, **18**
Sodium silicate, in filling pores of cat's-eyes, 47
Spar, 47
Spearheads, of stone, 1
Spessarite, 125
Sphere machines, **163,** 164, **164, 165**
Spheres, making of, **163,** 164–166, **167**
Spinel, 117
  asterism in, 44
Spodumene, 47
Star gems, cutting of, 40–48
    diamond-impregnated wood wheel in, 45–47
    in sapphire, 41, **42–44**
Steel blades, 11
Steel plate, flat lapping on, 120
Step-cut gem
  cutting crown of, 113
  cutting girdle on, 100, 101
  cutting of, in faceting, 111–113
  making preforms for, 94, 95, **95**
Stone(s)
  "fish-eye," 94
  precious, 2, 3
Stone Age, 1, 2

Talc, hardness of, 4
Tavernier, Jean Baptiste, 75, **77**, 78
Tavernier Blue diamond, **77**
Templates, 26, **26**, 27, **27–29**
Tigereye, putting "eye" in, 48, **48**
Tin lap, for faceting, 89, 119
Tin oxide, in polishing cabochons, 38
Titanium dioxide, 40
Topaz, 125
    blue, 6
    hardness of, 4
Tourmaline, 47, 125
    asterism in, 44
    cabochon of, **27**
Travertine, polishing of, 56, 59
Trim saw. *See* Saw, trim
Tripoli, 116, 118
Turquoise
    "coloring" of, 62
    polishing of, 50, 62, 63

Unakite, polishing of, 63, 132

Variscite, lapping of, 132, **132**

Wax lap, muslin-faced, for faceting, 90, 119, 120
Weapons, of stone, 1, **1**
Wheels
    silicon carbide "soft bond" (heatless), 151
    wood, diamond-impregnated, in polishing star
        gems, 45–47
Williamsite, 47
Wire saws, 173, 174, **174**
Wood, petrified, **14**, 163
Wood lap
    diamond-impregnated, in polishing star and
        cat's-eye gems, 45–47
    hard maple, for faceting, 90, 119

Zircon, 117

Equipment Index

Page numbers in **bold** refer to illustrations

Allen Lapidary Equipment Mfg. Co., faceting
unit, **83**
American Standard Corp., faceting unit, **82**
Arrow Profile Co.
    Sapphire faceting head, **82**, 84
    Sapphire faceting unit, **80**, 84

Blake gem polisher, 46
Brad's Rock Shop (Division of Lapidary Hobbycrafts), horizontal unit, **32**

Covington Engineering Corp.
    automatic gem drill (silicon carbide abrasives),
        158
    automatic Little Sphere Maker, **165**
    automatic slab polisher, **134**
    automatic sphere machine, **164**
    automatic vibrating lap, 134
    belt sander, **33**
    combination cab unit, **36**
    diamond gem drill, **158**
    faceter's trim saw, **122**
    heavy-duty trim saw, **23**
    horizontal diamond unit, **66**
    horizontal lap kit, 130
    trim saw, **23**
Crown Mfg. Co.
    bead gripper, **159**
    Crown arbor, **32**
    Crown bead mill, **160**
    Crown combination arbor, **32**
    Crown rock clamp, **159**
    diamond cab unit, **67**
    drill for bead mill, 155
    Exacta faceting unit, **83**

faceter's trim saw, **122**
trim saw, 24
vibrating lap, 134
Crystalite Corp.
    Crystalite lap, **65, 70, 71**
    Crystalite pad, **70, 71**
    diamond abrasives and products, **65, 70, 71**
    diamond cab unit, **66, 70, 71**

Diamond Pacific Tool Corp., Diamond cab unit, **67**

Earth Treasures, horizontal cab unit, **32**

Fac-Ette Mfg. Co.
    faceter's trim saw, 121
    faceting unit, **83**

Gem-Tec Diamond Tool. Co., diamond cab
unit, **67**
Henry B. Graves Co.
    Cab-Mate cab unit, **33**
    faceting unit, **82**
Great Western Equipment Co.
    cabochon unit, 31
    slab saw, **12**
Gryphon Corp.
    diamond wire saw, **174**
    Ten-in-One cab unit, **66**

Highland Park Mfg. (Division of Musto Industries)
    belt sander, 31
    cabochon unit, **33, 37**
    faceter's trim saw, **122**
    faceting unit (Imahashi), 81
    round bead mill (Imahashi), **160**

Highland Park Mfg. (*Continued*)
    slab saws, **11, 15, 17**
    sphere machine, **163**
    swing lap, 133
    trim saws, **22**
    ultrasonic drill (Imahashi), **158**
    Vi-Bro-Lap, **134**

Lee Lapidaries
    faceting head, **82**
    faceting unit, **82**

A. D. McBurney
    cab unit, **32**
    dopping pot, **30**
    trim saw, **24**
MDR Mfg. Co.
    cab unit, **33**
    faceting head, **82**
    faceting unit, **82**

Prismatic Instruments, faceting unit, 83

Ran-Co Lapidary Products (Division of Standard Abrasives), diamond cab unit, **66**
Raytech Industries
    diamond and silicon carbide combination unit, **66**
    faceting unit, **83**
    trim saw, **23**
    vibrating lap, **135**
Rose Enterprises, reciprocal lap, **134**

Jack V. Schuller, diamond abrasive products, **73**

Terra Products, diamond cab unit, **67**

Ultra Tec (Stanley Lapidary Products), faceting unit, **83**

(Clairmont Portrait Studio, San Diego)

PANSY D. KRAUS

PANSY D. KRAUS, a charter member of the Gemological Society of San Diego, was instrumental in organizing the society. She served as its secretary, vice-president, and president and is currently serving on its Advisory Board. She is also a member of the San Diego Mineral & Gem Society and the Mineralogical Society of America. In 1960 she received her Fellowship Diploma in Gemology (F.G.A.) from the Gemological Association of Great Britain, and in 1966 her Graduate Diploma (G.G.) from the Gemological Institute of America at Los Angeles, California. Having served as editor of the *Lapidary Journal* since 1970, she has been responsible for the publication of a number of books dealing with gemstones. She also frequently gives lectures to gem and mineral societies and sometimes teaches classes in gem identification. She is listed in *Who's Who of American Women*.